John Walker's Shetland

John Walker's Shetland

Wendy Gear

The Shetland Times Ltd.
Lerwick
2005

John Walker's Shetland

Copyright © Wendy Gear, 2005.

ISBN 1 904746 12 8

First published by The Shetland Times Ltd., 2005.

All rights reserved.
No part of this publication may be reproduced, stored in a retrieval system, or transmitted, in any form, or by any means, electronic, mechanical, photocopying, recording or otherwise, without the prior written permission of the publishers.

British Library Cataloguing-in-Publication Data
A catalogue record for this book is available from the British Library.

Printed and published by
The Shetland Times Ltd.,
Gremista, Lerwick,
Shetland ZE1 0PX, UK.

CONTENTS

	List of Illustrations	vi
	Foreword	ix
	Acknowledgements	xi
Chapter One	Beginnings	1
Chapter Two	To Australia and Back	4
Chapter Three	Early Days in Shetland	17
Chapter Four	New Rules and Blue Slips	30
Chapter Five	Threats and Boasts	51
Chapter Six	Development and Obstruction in Yell	60
Chapter Seven	Kelp and Other Burning Issues	75
Chapter Eight	Government Incentive	88
Chapter Nine	Lean Years	97
Chapter Ten	Steam	111
Chapter Eleven	Politics	120
Chapter Twelve	Walker and the Commissions	126
Chapter Thirteen	Smacks, Blubber and Other Schemes	137
Chapter Fourteen	Crisis in Bressay	144
Chapter Fifteen	Haaf Grunie	156
Chapter Sixteen	Chromate Contrivance	163
Chapter Seventeen	Walker and the School Boards	171
Chapter Eighteen	Sandlodge Copper Mine	180
Chapter Nineteen	Bankrupt	193
Chapter Twenty	South Africa	198
Chapter Twenty-one	Home Again	208
	Appendices	217
	Maps	229
	Index	233

ILLUSTRATIONS

		page
1	Visiting Bigsetter	2
2	William Walker's Shop, Aberdeen	5
3	Old St. Paul's, Melbourne	13
4	Wedding Photo, Mary & John Walker	14
5	The Walkers before leaving Australia	15
6	Sixern *Lady* at Foula	19
7	Catherine Sutherland (née Walker) & Amelia	22
8	Group at Hillswick, early 1880s	23
9	Looking across Bressay Sound, 1890s	27
10	Maryfield	28
11	Planticrubs	32
12	William and Margaret Spence	38
13	Loch of Lumbister	40
14	Signatures from Volister	41
15	Volister	42
16	John and Grace Mann	43
17	The Geo of Vigon	45
18	Croft house of Vigon	47
19	View from Gremster	53
20	Ruins of croft houses at Burraness	54
21	Sheep fank at Kirkabister	55
22	Burraness with Fetlar in background	57
23	Windhouse	61
24	140 year old fencing strainer	62
25	View from Logie	65
26	Looking across Gloup Voe	66
27	Taricrook	76
28	Garth House, Delting	78
29	Letter from John Walker	82
30	Sheep fank at Swinister	94
31	Da end o da daek	107
32	Croft house at Still	109

		page
33	Alexander Sandison and family	114
34	S.S. *Chieftain's Bride*	118
35	Shipping in Bressay Sound 1872	123
36	Peat Carrier	127
37	Looking towards Lerwick in the 1880s	134
38	Smack *Petrel*	141
39	Caain/Pilot Whales	143
40	Annsbrae House	146
41	Anonymous letter to John Walker	146
42	Major Thomas Mouat Cameron	148
43	The Island of Noss	154
44	Haaf Grunie	158
45	Disused quarry at Hagdale	169
46	Ulsta School and Schoolhouse	179
47	Sandlodge Copper Mine 1905	182
48	Sandlodge House and Copper Mine	186
49	Plan of engine house at Sandlodge Mine	190
50	Section of engine house at Sandlodge Mine	191
51	Cartoon of John Walker	204
52	Advertisement for Walker's Tea	209
53	Six sons of William Walker	211
54	Walker family group	218

FOREWORD

SHETLANDERS in mid-Victorian times needed their scattalds, their common land, to survive. For dozens of centuries the scattald had provided people with grazing and peats. John Walker erupted in Shetland in the 1860s. 'I saw that the commons were of no use to the people, and were doing them harm,' he said. 'I at once resolved to take the commons from them.'

Up till then Shetlanders hadn't seen much of mid-Victorian 'improvement'. They didn't enjoy it. Walker made life impossible for the tenants on the estates that he leased. He cleared many of them out of their homes, and sometimes right out of Shetland. In their place he installed sheep.

Some of the victims went quietly; others threatened him with violence. Most of his peers, Shetland's long-established landlords and merchants, didn't like the whirlwind of change that Walker inaugurated: at least not at first. They called him 'The director general of Shetland', and gloated when he went bankrupt.

Wendy Gear has pursued John Walker for ten years. Intrigued by stories of ancestors evicted from Bigsetter in North Yell, she determined to find out about the man who had cleared them. She found his letter books at Gardie House, full of instructions addressed to the hapless tenants. In the Shetland Archives she untied bundles of court processes, where Walker was sometimes pursuer, sometimes defender. Often there were stories about Walker in newspapers, in Shetland and further afield; and there were censuses and valuation rolls to sift.

Wendy sought Walker furth of Shetland too. She followed in his footsteps to Australia, where he had sought his fortune in the 1850s, and she has traced his career in South Africa in the 1880s, after the Shetland episode. He caused havoc there too. Finally, she examines his career as a councillor in Wandsworth in London, and later in Aberdeen, at the end of his life.

John Walker's Shetland is a wonderful book. Wendy Gear keeps her indignation under control, but doesn't conceal her feelings about Walker. At one point she inquires why nobody tried to murder him. She paints a convincing picture of the man himself, and she beautifully portrays Shetland in the third quarter of the nineteenth century: the community that John Walker tormented for twenty years.

Brian Smith
Shetland Archives

ACKNOWLEDGEMENTS

SINCE I began researching the 'notorious' John Walker I have had help and encouragement from near and far. I am especially grateful to Susan Cooper, who gave me the use of her research into the Williamson and Tulloch families of Delting, and who has worked hard at contacting and obtaining information and photos from the extended Walker family. Dull moments were lightened by the laughs with Susan and Jane over the 'John Walker Appreciation Society'. Shetland Archives, has proved to be a rich source of material, and help from Brian Smith and Angus Johnson has been invaluable. I am indebted to John and Wendy Scott for permission to use Gardie papers and for additional information on the Cameron/Mouat family, also to Jan Sandison for use of the Sandison's Archive.

I really appreciate the help from everybody who has read my text and provided positive suggestions, especially Brian Smith, Peter Gear, Jim Sutherland, John Graham, Susan Cooper and Wendy Scott. Many thanks to John Ballantyne for unearthing material in Edinburgh and South Africa; to the late Betty Ambrose in Zimbabwe and Barry, her son in Florida, for permission to use extracts from the diary; to Dave Rhind and Elizabeth West in South Africa; Bishop James Grant and Coleen Jenson in Australia; Hamish Walker in Germany; Dorothy Duncan in East Sussex; Linda Riddell in London; Derek Flinn in Liverpool; Rosemary Baxter and Barney Crockett in Aberdeen; Willie Thomson in Orkney. Nearer home I am grateful to Laurence Tulloch for permission to use his father's stories and for help from George and Helen Bell; Jane Manson; Ann and Allen Fraser; the late May Sutherland; Mairie Anderson; George Jamieson; and Shetland Museum Staff.

My thanks to everyone who contributed photographs especially Andy who also produced the maps, and to him and the other members of my long-suffering family who have, over several years, been subjected to "John Walker's Shetland".

Abbreviations used in footnotes:
    S.A. = Shetland Archives
    L.B. = Letter Book
    N.A.S. = National Archives of Scotland

Chapter One

BEGINNINGS

21st September, 1867
William H. Spence
Bigsetter
   Sir,
   This is to inform you that unless you can discover and inform me of the names of the parties damaging our fences that there will be no chance of your remaining a tenant upon the property after Martinmas 1868.
          Yours etc.,
           John Walker.

**   **   **

JANE Mary Spence died, aged six weeks, on the first day of December, 1868. Her mother always said the baby caught cold on 'the journey'. Jane Mary was the firstborn child of Margaret and William Spence, my great-grandparents, then a young couple who tenanted a croft at Bigsetter in North Yell, Shetland. William was a fisherman. 'The journey' was made in a small open boat from Basta Voe to Reafirth, Mid Yell, on a chilly November day in 1868.

They walked the mile from their croft to the side of Basta Voe over the bleak, peaty hillside. Walking was no hardship to Shetlanders in those days, even when carrying heavy burdens. While the boat was loaded with their few possessions, Margaret's sister Marion, who lived nearby, brought a thoughtful gift for her sister – a stone, heated in the open peat fire and wrapped in cloths, to warm Margaret's feet during what was to be a rough and wet journey. A nursing mother must not catch cold. Jane Mary was cocooned in a leather bucket to protect her from the salt spray.

** ** **

William Walker died, aged sixteen weeks, on the thirteenth day of January, 1869. He died of measles, a dangerous infection in those days. William was the first son born to Mary and John Walker, of Maryfield, Bressay, Shetland. John was a farmer and factor for the Garth and Annsbrae Estate. William's arrival had given cause for celebration as the couple already had eight daughters. Four of the Walker children were very ill that January, but only William succumbed. He was buried in the Bressay churchyard. Maryfield was a fine, three-storey house, recently built and well furnished. Most of the family's provisions came from mainland Scotland. To help with the children and household chores, Mary Walker had a governess and two servants.

The Walker family left their Bressay home in 1872. By then John was deeply involved in business and other concerns in Shetland to which he remained committed during the 1870s, although living in Aberdeen and later in Edinburgh.

Visiting Bigsetter. Looking towards North Sandwick and across Colgrave Sound to Fetlar. © *Andy Gear*

Many people, both rich and poor, who lived in Shetland during the 1860s and 1870s had their lives changed, for better or worse, by John Walker's stratagems and schemes.

A tiny baby's journey in a leather bucket fades into obscurity among all the rest ...

**   **   **

The family story of the baby in the leather bucket, and the hot stone at my great-grandmother's feet, moved me to look further into the circumstances which caused the Spences to leave their home in November 1868. Imagine my excitement when, on my first visit to Gardie House, Bressay, I was lucky enough to find a copy of the above letter addressed to my great-grandfather, William Spence, from the controversial factor John Walker! In the following chapters I have attempted to show how, even though he only lived here for twelve years, John Walker left his mark on Shetland.

Chapter Two

TO AUSTRALIA AND BACK

Sermon was preached down in the tweendecks but I didn't go to it in case the abominable smell which is always there should upset me.
20th February, 1853. Extract from John Walker's diary of his voyage to Australia.

A STORM was brewing in North East Scotland on Tuesday, 30th November, 1852. In Aberdeen harbour the barque *Lord Metcalfe* (501 tons) was set to sail for Australia with Captain William Cargill in command of a crew of eighteen. Eighty passengers were crammed into the unsavoury quarters known as 'tweendecks', which would no doubt have compared somewhat unfavourably with the accommodation bagged by the five ship's cats. In relatively comfortable conditions the twelve cabin passengers were settling in for the long voyage. One of them was a seventeen-year-old Aberdonian, John Walker.

These and other details of the voyage have survived in a diary kept by John during the journey. There we read a fascinating account of travel under sail as experienced by a Victorian teenager setting out on an enormous adventure. We even find a mention of Shetland in the diary. When the *Lord Metcalfe* was approaching Cape Town, John wrote that Saldanha Bay reminded him of the north-east end of the island of Bressay. Years later, in 1871, he would tell the Commissioners investigating the Truck System, that he had been acquainted with Shetland since he was a boy. So we have evidence that he had visited Shetland before the age of seventeen, but I have been unable to find out when or why.

Stowed in the hold of the ship John had a quantity of goods which he intended to sell on arrival down-under. We can guess what these goods might have been as John's father, William, previously a linen weaver, had built up a successful business at 52 Union Street, dealing in spirits, wine and tea. (Next door, at nos. 54 & 56 was a Temperance Hotel[1]). The family home was at 3 Adelphi, in a court with its entrance on Union Street almost opposite the shop. His mother, Amelia, a Duthie before her marriage to William, had carefully packed his trunk which had been covered in canvas by his father. That trunk was also stowed in the hold as the clothes it contained were too fine to wear at sea. No doubt some of John's five brothers and four sisters (see appendix) would have been on the quay to see him off.

William Walker's shop at 52 Union Street, Aberdeen.

No sooner had the *Lord Metcalfe* left the harbour to sail north around Scotland than they ran into a westerly gale and our intrepid emigrant was sick all night. So fierce was the weather that Captain Cargill was forced to seek shelter at Longhope, Orkney, and was storm-bound there for nine days – the first of many delays on the five-month journey to Australia. While they were there, news reached Orkney that Napoleon had been declared Emperor of France, and the cabin passengers responded by giving three hisses for Napoleon!

After they left Orkney the weather deteriorated again. Ten days later they were being blown back the way they had come but John had obviously got his sea-legs as he noted in his diary that he had enjoyed *a jolly good dinner of roast beef and plum duff.*

On the twelfth of December, the minister on board the ship, the Rev. Maxwell, was unable to preach for sea-sickness and it was arranged that John should read a sermon. Unfortunately his choice turned out to be rather long and *the people grew cold and tired and walked. The Captain himself grew some fidchety and even now and then jumpt from his seat and looked on to see when it was to be finished.*

13th – We have at last got the minister and his wife on his legs again but they are looking most miserable. Indeed Mrs M. was so weak that she, tho I think there was a little affectation in it, had to be tied to the mast to keep her up.

22nd – Having had no fun since I left Aberdeen and tired of such a wearisome life I set this morning about getting some – so as Mrs Maxwell has been appearing for the last few days in what I consider rather an unsuited dress – coming to table with half a dozen rings and broches that might serve the whole ship's company – I politely asked her if she would like to see the 'gelly', for which offer she thanked me and said she would require to dress before going – just the very thing I wanted – when she was thus employed I told James Anderson my intentions and also asked the Captain to assist me. Out her ladyship comes, dressed in a fine new merino dress, tartan plaid fastened with a splendid gold broach, when Mr A. gives her one arm and I another and away we go ... Presses her to take a view from the top of the forecastle and up she goes and exclaims, "This is really delightful, I don't wonder how people like to be sailors", when – down goes the vessel's head and in comes a jolly good sea and drenches the minister's wife from the crown of her head downwards ... We had taken the precaution to put on Waterproofs.

25th – Christmas! At Sea! Last night we all drank Sowens till most of us did ourselves harm. All that landsmen could have we had for breakfast – fresh eggs etc. About 12 we had lunch of wine and Helen's cake which was praised by every person, the only fault being that both it and Mama's were finished too soon. At dinner – hens, ducks, ham and all that you might look for in a first class hotel ... A couple of plum puddings ... Wine of all sorts ... At eight we had a jolly bowl of punch to drink a few toasts with, after royalty, the health of all friends in Aberdeen. We are in now what Sailors call the "Roaring Forties" and I think they are well named.

27th – I was forced this afternoon to give Hepburn a good drubbing. I had to break out upon him because he went to the Captain and some of the passengers and fabricated lies upon Mr Taylor and me. I gave him what he won't forget in a hurry ... stupid, insignificant, bombastic ass ... It will show him he's among gentlemen.

30th – A fair wind, the first we have had since we left Longhope – just exactly three weeks this day. I spent a most glorious forenoon in studying the "Successful Merchant" than which I never read a book with more interest and gratification.

31st – At 11 the Cabiners retired to sit in the New Year and Mrs Maxwell made a decoction of eggs, whisky and water called "egg nock" wherewith to drink in the year.

1st January 1853 – Mr Farquhar gave me a piece of advice before beginning viz "If I wished to advance in this world I would need to sacrifice my feelings and sometimes get drunk." To which I replied that I would rather sacrifice my advance in the world than become a beast, to which text I rigidly adhered. By doing so I was enabled to get plenty of fun when the others were in a beastly state ... I did not join them in more than one glassful ... Our dinner went off in grand style, the only thing which I think worth mentioning is that Mrs Maxwell appeared in a new velvet dress and according to my wish she got it destroyed by throwing the whole body of a roasted duck in her lap.

2nd – Yesterday I agreed with Bell Ritchie that she would wash as many clothes as I wish for 10/- during the voyage.

5th – This being old Christmas the Captain indulged them in an <u>extra glass</u>, which upset Farquhar and after the ladies went to bed he commenced dancing naked on top of the table and other such feats.

On the sixth the trunks were taken up for inspection and John was pleased to find that both the trunk and its contents were in good condition. *I find my linen cloths are both too fine and too well made for sea ware; I am entirely at a loss what to do, all day I have been endeavouring to buy some regular slop things.*

12th – This is Old New Years Day so we are having a regular jollyfication. I must away and get a dance, the fiddle is going mad ...

14th – The heat is grown quite intolerable now, am forced to sleep with only one fold of a blanket and during the day wear a pair of trousers, coat, shirt and flannel shirt. Nothing more, neither stockings, neckerchief nor braces, nor vest and even for all that I am too hot.

16th – Sabbath – In the morning I was seized with a most violent pain in my stomach and bowels which continued most excruciatingly all day.

Five days later he was thinking positively – an attribute which would later serve him well in face of business failure. *I have come to the conclusion that it is flatulency which has troubled me of late, caused by so inactive a life as this is ... The whole day I have just run about the decks like a sailor in every respect except going aloft and tarring ropes.*

21st – James Anderson not being very well today I had to act as schoolmaster to the Apprentices on board but what a set of thick skulls I never saw. They beat mine and I thought it was thick enough.

John had left the Grammar School when he was fifteen, declaring that he had got more than enough of Latin and Greek and wanted to be a merchant[2]. At least three of his brothers had gone on to University and all his brothers became prominent in their chosen professions. Did John suffer from an inferiority complex because of this? In his business ventures in Shetland and elsewhere, was he trying to prove himself as successful as his brothers?

22nd – A rather warm discussion passed between Mr Farquhar and me after the evening's grog (or rather during) a conversation arose about honesty – I said that I held every man honest until I found him out otherwise, upon which Mr Farquhar gave a long speech about how I would do when I got to Australia with this principle – becoming as I thought rather personal ... I was forced to tell him to hold his tongue with regard to me ... He threatened to bring his hand in close proximity with my face etc concluding his remarks by saying that as he was in possession of facts how I was here I would better take care as he would do me as much injury as he could and that would not be little. All of which I cared as little for as if it had been said by a cat.

So Farquhar is claiming to have inside information which could be damaging, and, in spite of John's declaration of nonchalance, he was upset. Had he got into trouble back home, and hence the trip to Australia? We don't know.

23rd – On the Equatorial line.

24th – Able to steer the vessel without any person being near me. I some nights have more than an hour at it alone.

25th – I have commenced to "Uncle Tom's Cabin" which I do believe will serve me for nearly a month. My face, hands and feet are becoming like negroes for darkness.

Uncle Tom's Cabin, newly published in 1852, became an anti-slavery best-seller. Its American author, Harriet Beecher Stowe, was a friend of the Duchess of Sutherland, and visited her, in the Highlands of Scotland, during a European tour in 1856. By that time thousands of tenants had been driven from their homes on the Sutherland Estate, to make way for sheep farms.

Harriet Beecher Stowe was sent pamphlets, written by Donald MacLeod on the pitiless clearances, in the hope that they would help her to understand that not all Uncle Toms had black skins. She also received a gift from the Duchess, *An Account of the Improvements on the Estate of Sutherland* by James Loch, Commissioner to the estate. This publication was devoted to justification of the policy of clearances. In it Loch claimed that the 'Improvements' were carried out *to emancipate the lower orders from slavery.* And that this had been *the unceasing object of the Highland Proprietors for the last twenty years.*

Harriet Beecher Stowe made no acknowledgement of MacLeod's pamphlets, but in her subsequent publication *Sunny Memories of Foreign Lands* she defended the 'improvements' and dismissed as slander stories of cruelty towards the thousands of tenants whom the Sutherlands' factor had inhumanely cleared from the Straths[3]. No doubt John Walker would later have become familiar with Loch's publication and approved his arguments that the production of wool justified the removal of people to make money from sheep. But meanwhile, back to the voyage.

28th – I have given Miss McKenzie my watch to wear till we get to Australia as she expressed a wish to have one to wear, I have however to give it its supper every night.

30th – Mrs Maxwell was not able to be at Sermon today having been seized last night with a slight stroke of paralysis. A few days later John had sorted out the cause of her ailment:- *Mrs Maxwell has never recovered yet but ... whatever the Doctor says she must always have her mouth full of something, and it is that which makes and keeps her so often ill.* Here we see a self-assured young man who is inclined to see other people's misfortunes as weaknesses which they ought to be able to overcome by strength of character. In the late 1860s he was to look on the poverty caused by the disastrous failure of crops in the North Isles of Shetland as:- *an apt illustration of the fable of the Boy and the Wolf*[4]. But that's another story.

1st February – We have now been exactly nine weeks out of Aberdeen and really the time seems very short. We enjoy ourselves best in the evenings squatted on the poop hearing some fine songs from Miss McKenzie.

The tropical heat was causing John worry as well as discomfort. He had with him sealed testimonials from leading gentlemen of Aberdeen city, including the Lord Provost himself. *2nd February – I yesterday afternoon noticed that the intense heat of this climate had obliterated a little of the seals attached to some of my certificates, but as I intend to examine them every day after this, I don't think they will get worse.*

12th – I have been making some more bargains today having sold half a doz. Coloured shirts (some of them used) for 4/- each and an old satin vest (aged about 6 years) for 4/6. The shirts are those bot from "Gall & Bird" @ 3/3 ea. So that I have got 9d upon each and the use of some to the bargain. I sold them to our Stewart.

John Walker's Shetland

18th – All this forenoon I have been thinking of all the good folks in 3 Adelphi this being Mamma, George & Robert's birthday.

20th – Sermon was preached down in the tweendecks but I didn't go to it in case the abominable smell which is always there should upset me. We are often reminded of the class segregation on board ship. As one of the twelve cabin passengers, John did not consider it necessary to express sympathy for the eighty or so tweendeckers who would have been travelling in unspeakably cramped, unhygienic conditions. As a 19th century youth from a fairly well-to-do background, he would have found it as natural a divide in society as he saw the difference between lairds and Shetland crofters among whom he would work in the 1860s.

24th – We had two sets of quadrilles in its [moon] *light and it was glorious fun to see all of us every now and then giving some splendid revolutions by way of variety to the movements. Our quorum consists of Miss Jack and Miss McKenzie, Mr Taylor and I. Happy four!!!*

28th – It is most comical to speak to some of the tweendecks about how far we are from Australia. None of them will believe us that we are 700 miles yet from, almost getting angry when we speak of such a thing, but they'll see.

On the 8th March they were *safely anchored in Table Bay. We agreed with a boatman to attend upon the ship and Cabin passengers. We soon had plenty fruit on board which was a most glorious treat to us – it was with difficulty that some of us were restrained from eating too many ... Upon landing the first thing that struck us was the number of Blacks and men of every nation that we found on the streets which are not causewayed with anything but are one mass of dust and no pavements at the side. The houses however are rather neat and only two storey high and at the front of mostly every one are grapes growing in abundance.*

What a pleasure it must have been to set foot on dry land after such a tedious voyage! Perhaps that feeling of excitement and relief on landing stayed with him and influenced his choice of escape route after his bankruptcy in 1881, when he and his family moved to South Africa. After three days, stocked with the necessary provisions for the last leg of the journey, the *Lord Metcalfe* set sail for Australia.

1st April – The tweendeck passengers began again to be very anxious to know where they are but it has been resolved not to let them know for many reasons. This day being "All fools day" there have been a good few set down as belonging to that class ... As yet tho tried more than once I have not been fooled.

6th – It was our Captain's intention to have sighted St Pauls had the wind been favourable but now there is no chance of our seeing it which will put the "Indignant emigrants" (tweendeckers) fairly off the scent where we are. I believe most of them expect to be landed early next week. I wish they may be!!!

26th – A woman in the tweendecks was this morning delivered of a child which only lived four hours and was buried this afternoon at 5pm.

27th – I rose this morning at 4am and was not up an hour when I was more than gratified at seeing Cape Ottoway light right ahead. By 8am we were abreast of it.

Saturday, 30th April, 1853 – This day landed in Queens Wharf, Melbourne.

** ** **

Unfortunately, not a great deal is known about John Walker's years in Australia. No doubt the goods he brought with him would have proved profitable. The sealed testimonials from the gentlemen of Aberdeen city surely stood him in good stead, as he was soon offered employment. In his obituaries we read that his first job was managing a gold-buying business which had been established by the chemist who had assayed the first gold specimen in Victoria; that before his eighteenth birthday he had secured another appointment as manager of a firm of importers at £500 per annum; that within twelve months he had begun an extensive export business[5].

A slightly different picture emerges from reading Walker's written answers to questions put to him prior to his appearance at the bankruptcy court at Edinburgh, in 1880/81.

Question: *When did you go to Australia and in what business were you engaged there?*

Reply: *Left Aberdeen 30th November, 1852 – Manager Gold buying business 6 mos: Manager Bean and Henn 6 mos: Walter Hood & Co. 3 years General Inspector.*

Walter Hood & Co. was a ship-building company in Aberdeen. From 1839 until it merged with Alexander Hall & Co. in 1881, about forty clippers were built in their yard including the *Thermopylae*, one of the fastest sailing ships ever built. We know that some of these vessels, including the *Thermopylae*, carried wool from Australia[6].

Again in the obituaries we read – *He* [Walker] *saw much of the wild life associated with the gold rush at Ballarat, and was foreman of the jury at one of the trials there of a leader of a gang of desperadoes*[7]. It would have been impossible for anyone living in the newly independent colony of Victoria in the 1850s, not to witness 'the wild life'. When gold was discovered in the Ballarat area in August 1851, thousands rushed there to the diggings. *They came in drays, in carts, on foot, in wheelbarrows. Bank*

11

clerks, captains of ships, aldermen, councillors, lawyers and doctors, every grade of human being down to the man who humped his swag, poured into Ballarat[8].

Diggers who had struck lucky were caught up in a mad frenzy of spending. Manning Clark tells of one digger who *bought up the entire stock of champagne in a hotel, poured it into a horse trough, and asked the passers-by to take a swill.* Crime and lawlessness abounded, and social status crumbled. The latter was epitomized in the story of a *true blue gentleman* who offered a digger a shilling to lift a bag of sugar off a dray. The digger looked at him for a moment and then, putting his foot on a stump, said, *There, tie my shoe and I'll give you five shillings.* As one observer put it – *Your father might have been my Lord-of-England-all-over, it goes for nothing in this equalising colony of gold and beef and mutton*[9].

With his sealed testimonials and merchandise, John Walker sailed into this 'equalising colony'. How would this youth, who considered himself to be a gentleman, have fitted into the rough, tough life in Victoria of the 1850s? He would have had to overcome his disgust at the grimy, drunken condition of the diggers, in order to take their money for his goods. And how would he have viewed the despicable treatment meted out to the Australian aborigines by the colonists? Did their brutality towards native people later influence his attitude towards the Shetland crofters? If only we could eavesdrop on his comments on life in Australia!

There was rumbling unrest over the licence fee imposed on the diggers, and their lack of franchise. Perhaps John watched the procession of two thousand miners who marched to an anti-licence meeting, on 28th August, 1853, carrying banners and accompanied by musicians. He would have seen miners wearing red ribbons in their hats. The aim of the 'Red Ribbon Movement' was to offer to pay only ten shillings of the licence tax and allow themselves to be arrested, thus clogging up the prisons and administrative process[10].

By late 1854 it was obvious that only a minority of diggers were paying their licence fee. This blatant insubordination was considered insufferable, and furthermore, the revenue from the licence money was needed to meet government overspending. In the eyes of the diggers this was overspending by an administration which did not keep its promises. Corruption was rife among the officials. Most diggers didn't find enough gold to pay their fees, and anyone caught without a licence was harshly punished, sometimes being chained to a tree for a whole day, in the blazing sun.

On the 30th November about a thousand angry diggers marched to the Eureka diggings at Ballarat, with a hastily designed flag, depicting the Southern Cross, flying before them. They then set to work constructing a stockade from disused pit-props. On Sunday, 3rd December, it was decided to send three hundred troops and police to attack the stockade. Believing nothing would happen on the Sabbath, most of the diggers had retired to their tents, leaving about a hundred defenders who fought a brief battle with the military before the stockade was over-run. Four soldiers and about thirty diggers and bystanders were killed, and many more injured. After the shooting and bayoneting had subsided, over a hundred prisoners were marched off at bayonet point[11].

The inhabitants of Melbourne were divided as to where their allegiance lay. The law-and-order men deplored the behaviour of the diggers; others dubbed the government *a set of wholesale butchers*[12]. We don't know what John Walker's views were, but we can be sure he would have followed events and kept a strict eye on what would best benefit his business interests.

Old St Paul's, Melbourne.   *Courtesy Bishop James Grant*

On 6th December, about six thousand Melbourne residents congregated in the vacant ground north of St Paul's Church[13] to protest against the treatment of the diggers by the authorities. Ten days later a crowd probably gathered again to watch a bride and groom leave the same recently built church. John Walker and Mary Ball Plummer married there on 16th December, 1854. From the marriage certificate we learn that the young couple were both nineteen and that their witnesses were Sarah Dixon and Alex Bruce. The occupation of the bridegroom was given as

Wedding photograph, Mary and John. *Courtesy D. M. Rhind*

general merchant, and that of the bride's father, Charles Plummer, as carpenter. The bride's mother, Mary Ball, had died in 1836 when her daughter was only eighteen months old. Charles had afterwards immigrated to Australia from Brixton[14].

Women in the colonies survived in conditions of varying degrees of severity. On the goldfields they weltered through muddy winters and choked through dusty summers; rocked the baby's cradle and rocked the gold cradle; pushed barrows, pulled carts and carried children; faced fire, flood, fever and childbirth in their tents.

No doubt in more comfortable surroundings than most, Mary Walker gave birth to the first of her fifteen babies on 8th November, 1855. It was a girl; Amelia Mary. On 29th April, 1857 a second daughter was born; Mary. From the birth certificates we learn that the Walkers were resident at Auckland Street in St Kilda, a suburb of Melbourne, and that father John was still a merchant.

Later in 1857 John, Mary and their two daughters returned to Scotland. We can only speculate as to why he left Australia when apparently doing well in business there. Perhaps they felt that a penal colony was no place to bring up a family. Or had his impulsive nature proven dangerous in that rough, raw country? Had he made enemies there

TO AUSTRALIA AND BACK

The Walkers, shortly before they left Australia.   *Courtesy D. M. Rhind*

as he tended to do elsewhere? Perhaps his persuasive tongue, which was to prove so useful in later life, was no asset among the tough, unsophisticated colonists.

I have been unable to find anything about the next two years, other than that the family were living in the Aberdeen area where two more daughters, Isobel (26/9/1858) and Catherine (15/4/1860) were christened.

Five years later, on Monday, 17th July, 1865, thirty-two young women left Lerwick, Shetland, for Queensland, Australia. Their emigration had been organised and paid for by Arthur Anderson[15], who was there in person to assure the girls that everything had been arranged for their comfort and convenience. John Walker was one of the farewell party on board the *Prince Consort*, and his words of comfort to the young emigrants included the reassurance that he had lived near Queensland [he was in Victoria!] and he believed that *they were doing the very best thing for themselves that could be done in endeavouring to obtain a settlement there*[16].

So why did he leave Australia?

When bankrupt in Edinburgh in 1880, and questioned in court about events leading up to his bankruptcy, Walker said, *I returned* [from Australia] *to this Country in 1857. I had about £600 when I returned, money made in Australia. I was not engaged in any business for the first two years after my return. I then took two farms in Shetland ...*[17]

15

JOHN WALKER'S SHETLAND

1. 1902-03 Aberdeen Street Directory
2. John Walker's obituary, *Aberdeen Daily Journal*, 1st January, 1917
3. John Prebble, *The Highland Clearances*, London 1963, pp.309-311
4. *Daily Review*, 7th February, 1870
5. *Aberdeen Daily Journal*, 1st January, 1917
6. *Aberdeen 1800-2000*, edited by W. Hamish Fraser & Clive H. Lee, Tuckwell Press 2000, p.85
7. *Aberdeen Daily Journal*, 1st January, 1917
8. Manning Clark, *History of Australia*, London 1993, p.231
9. Manning Clark, *History of Australia*, London 1993, p.232
10. Ian MacFarlane, *Eureka, from the Official Records*, Public Record Office of Victoria 1995, pp.188 & 189
11. Ian MacFarlane, *Eureka, from the Official Records*, Public Record Office of Victoria 1995, p.197
12. Manning Clark, *History of Australia*, London 1993, p.264
13. Bishop James Grant, *Old St Paul's*, Melbourne 2000, p.4
14. Information from the Walker family bible
15. Shetland benefactor and founder of P&O
16. *Times* (London), 8th August, 1865, copied from *Northern Ensign*, Wick.
17. N.A.S. CS 318/37/321

Chapter Three

EARLY DAYS IN SHETLAND

*An abject dependence is the conseqence that
ensues from the state of tenures in Shetland.*
Samuel Hibbert, on visiting Shetland about 1820.

T HE rough, dusty, fortune-seeking Australian life of the mid 19th century could hardly have been further removed from the cool, well-watered isles of Shetland. However, oppression was to be found in both places. In Australia the persecution was cold-bloodedly sadistic while in Shetland it had advanced insidiously over many years.

Rich fishing grounds surrounding the isles have sustained generations of Shetlanders, helping to compensate for the low summer temperatures and acid soil which make for poor cultivation. During the 16th and 17th centuries the Hanseatic fish merchants traded in Shetland, dealing directly with the fishermen. About the same time the Dutch herring fishery in Shetland waters gradually increased. However, a succession of European wars led to the depletion of the Dutch fishing fleet, culminating in 1703 when the French descended on the harbour and torched over a hundred busses[1]. What a terrifying sight that must have been for the Shetlanders who had traded with the Dutch for over half a century, and who had themselves suffered at the hands of plundering French privateers during the previous decade.

The Germans also withdrew in the early 18th century, and some of the more enterprising Shetland lairds moved in to fill the gap in the export trade. In the 1740s a succession of failed harvests left the tenants heavily in debt to the lairds who had provided them with meal to avert starvation. The lairds needed to recoup their losses and an expansion of the fishing followed, with the fishermen becoming enmeshed in fishing tenures – an arrangement which compelled them to sell their fish to the laird who usually didn't set a price for the catch until the end of the season.

The 'Old' Statistical Account, compiled in the 1790s from the answers to questionnaires sent to every parish minister in Scotland, gives an opportunity to glimpse life in Shetland at that time, albeit as seen through the eyes of the clergy. Although they criticise excesses of tea-drinking and other so-called extravagances, the ministers, on the whole, sympathised with the lot of the fishermen. The Rev. John Menzies, from the united parishes of Bressay, Burra and Quarff wrote:[2] *they must fish for their masters, who either give them a fee entirely inadequate to their labour and their dangers, or take their fish at a lower price than others would give.*

The vessels used for fishing at the 'Far Haaf' (deep sea, as opposed to coastal fishing) were known as sixerns – open, six-oared boats in which the men rowed or sailed as far as forty miles to set their lines for ling and cod from mid-May till 12th August. As the boats were often at sea for days (and nights) at a time, they could take advantage of the prolonged daylight enjoyed in the north at the height of summer. Many a time the boat and its crew, often from one family, were caught in a sudden storm and never returned.

Samuel Hibbert, who visited Shetland about 1820, tells of his encounter with a sixern crew who had lost their fishing lines in bad weather.[3] Although the £20 loss would have been shared among the crew, to each of them it was adding a substantial sum to the debt which would be deducted from any payment they might receive at the end of the season.

The lairds needed as many men as possible to row their fishing boats so, over the years, they had encouraged men on their estates to marry young and raise families (more hands on oars), allowing the crofts to be subdivided into less and less viable units to accommodate the growing population. The subsequent lack of self-sufficiency forced the tenants to become increasingly dependent on the lairds for credit in hard years. The control of previously ravaging smallpox was another factor which led to the sharp increase in the population of Shetland, reaching a peak in 1861 of 31,670 as compared to 22,379 in 1801.

The population explosion was nationwide. In Britain as a whole the population more than trebled in the century and a half before 1900.

Sixern *Lady* at Foula. *Courtesy Eric Isbister*

During that time new farming methods had significantly reduced the number of agricultural labourers, and muscle power was being replaced by steam power in the textile industry and elsewhere. So families were forced to move from country to town where, in order to eat, even the youngest children had to work for a pittance in nightmare conditions. For incredibly long hours they toiled in factories operating dangerous machines or in mines carrying coal to produce the steam to drive the machines – a vicious circle of inhumanity and pollution. This is what one of the pit children told a government inspector in 1842:[4] *I been down almost three years* [that is since he was four and a half]. *When I first went down I couldn't keep my eyes open; I don't fall asleep now; I smokes my pipe.* Compared to that even the poorest Shetland children were living in paradise.

One means of easing the pressure on the arable land in Shetland was to portion off a part of the scattald and let it to a tenant who then had to build a house and toil to break out the rough ground for cultivation. This was known as an 'ootset'. Such a tenant might find himself obliged to accept the sort of agreement Andrew Grierson offered to Magnus Georgeson in 1806 in Aithsting,[5] a classic example of a fishing tenure contract ... *to set you said outset ... upon the following conditions: for your encouragement you are to have it for seven years, from Martinmas first, free of all rent; but upon the expiry of said seven years ... you are to pay to me and my heirs the sum of twelve pounds Scots, four poultry fowls or two geese, all at Lerwick, besides rowing to the ling fishery in a six oar'd boat to me from this date and during the currency of your tack (if able and in health), for such sum of fee as I may yearly give to any other of my tenants; and failing of your rowing to the sea to me you are in that case hereby taken bound to pay me or my heirs yearly the sum of eighteen pounds Scots, with the poultry fowls or geese above mentioned.*

He goes on to point out that if Georgeson sells fish or oil to anyone other than Grierson, or falls into arrears of three months with his rent, his tack will be declared null and void. Ironically the document ends: *Heartily wishing you every success I am, Magnus, your well wisher.*

(signed) Andrew Grierson

Meanwhile a third class was emerging in Shetland's social and economic scene – landless merchants. They made a living in a variety of ways including smuggling (most were ship owners); acting as agents for the Greenland whaling; importing goods e.g. salt, meal, spirits and timber; acting as export agents (dried fish and other produce) for the lairds, and as tacksmen on some estates. In the latter two functions they became central to the truck system (chapter 12). During and after the Napoleonic wars this merchant-driven economy continued to diversify – the Greenland whaling prospered; the herring fishing boomed; sloops were introduced to fish for cod; docks were built at Lerwick; ship and boat building flourished; kelp prices improved; chromate was quarried in Unst. When the sailors who survived the wars came home (3,000 had been pressed or volunteered into the Royal Navy), still more men were available to fish at the Far Haaf. And in 1821, two of the most enterprising merchant-traders, William Hay and Charles Ogilvy, took the daring step of forming a Shetland Bank.

But sadly this prosperity was not to last. In the 1830s fishing disasters and failed harvests took their toll. Difficulties arose in marketing dried fish and salt herring, and, in 1842, the Shetland Bank crashed. Hundreds of men and women were out of work.

The 1840s were hard years for the Shetlanders. Yet again they suffered poor harvests and mediocre fishing. But the enterprising spirit was not dead. The sloop owners turned their attention to Faroe where there was cod aplenty, the1850s saw a revival in the herring fishing and, of course, the Haaf fishermen were still at their oars struggling to stay out of debt.

Meanwhile, the landowners were finding 'public burdens' increasingly onerous. Land tax, prison money, school repairs, teachers' salaries, poor rates and tithes were some of the assessments they had to pay. Out of an estimated rental of £14,000 for the whole of Shetland in 1851 these assessments amounted to £7,500.[6] It was felt that from a purely economic point of view something had to be done to make landowning a more attractive proposition.

One effect the industrial revolution had on Shetland was through the increased financial importance of sheep. Improved communications with mainland Britain opened up new markets – wool was needed to feed busy looms and mutton to feed hungry mouths. Wool was also in demand for military clothing – increased by the outbreak of the Crimean War in 1854. The small native sheep could not compete financially with the bigger, new breeds now introduced, which sold for four or five times the price. The development of commercial sheep farms was underway.

Division of land (legally sorting out ownership with mutually beneficial exchanges) associated with the formation of sheep farms, did not in itself deprive the crofters of the scattald (common grazing), but it was a necessary precursor. As Lord Napier said in 1883, if a division took place and a proprietor *got his own share ... and left it to the occupation of his own crofters, they would not say that he had taken away their land, would they?* [7]

Eviction of tenants in order to enclose sheep farms started in Shetland about ten years before John Walker was born. Between the 1820s and 1850s, Arthur Nicolson evicted over three hundred people from his estate in Fetlar;[8] David Dakers Black cleared the upper Weisdale area about 1850; Veensgarth and Dale, on the Hayfield estate, was made into a 4,000 acre sheep farm in the 1850s-60s.[9]

** ** **

The etiquette I have been hitherto accustomed to (which however may be unsuitable in Shetland) prevents me, a stranger in a strange land, intruding myself upon anyone.
John Walker to Joseph Leisk, Inspector and Clerk to Lerwick Parochial Board.

I really don't know why John Walker decided to move to Shetland. Ever the entrepreneur, he undoubtedly was full of plans. In October 1859, his name appears as a witness at the wedding of Jonathan Ratter and Agnes Williamson, both from Ollaberry. His brother-in-law, Rev. James Rose Sutherland, was officiating at the ceremony.[10] It seems likely he was visiting his sister Catherine at the Hillswick Manse on that occasion.

John Walker's Shetland

Perhaps he had come to Shetland to view the Keldabister Farm in Bressay, which, in the spring of 1860 he leased from the Cameron Mouat family (see appendix).

John Walker's sister Catherine, wife of Rev. James Rose Sutherland, with her daughter Amelia Duthie Rose Sutherland. Taken about 1860, they were at that time living in the Hillswick Manse, Shetland.
Courtesy Dorothy Duncan who is Amelia's grand-daughter

Amelia, with her husband Rev. John Low Brown standing behind her, is on the left of the middle row. Her sister Margaret (Peggy) is seated far right. Their father, Rev. James Sutherland, is next to Amelia in the middle row wearing a 'lum' hat. At front are Herbert and William Walker, John's nephews. Photo probably taken in Hillswick in the early 1880s.

Courtesy Dorothy Duncan

A letter dated 28th May from Anne Cameron Mouat to John Phin, solicitor, told of the change of tenancy from Thomas Pennie to John Walker who, she said, was a great friend of Mr Hamilton.[11] Zachary Macaulay Hamilton was then the parish minister of Bressay and could have been the 'Mr Hamilton' referred to in the letter, or perhaps it was his son Robert, who had been a student at Aberdeen University, and might have known John's brothers.

The new tenant immediately began to assert himself. On 18th August, 1860, the *Orcadian* printed the following notice: *Noss – Intimation has been given to the inhabitants of Lerwick by the present proprietor* [he was lessee] *of the Island of Noss, Mr John Walker, that on and after the 19th inst, no person will be allowed, without having an order from him, to land on the island, and he has also intimated that for the future no one, unless on business, is to be permitted on Keldabister farm.*

So John Walker was firmly established in Bressay before Major Thomas Mouat Cameron retired from the army. In the summer of 1861 the Major and his family moved to Shetland. This occasion was marked by a celebration.[12]

Major Cameron, of Bressay, accompanied by his lady and children, arrived here [Lerwick] *per steamer on Saturday. At Bressay, great preparations are being made for his reception. The inhabitants of the Island, to show their respect and appreciation of the gallant Major, are to meet in the evening between 7 and 9 o'clock, at Gardie House, and are to go in procession, to be headed by a band of various musicians to the top of the Wart Hill – where a large bonfire is to be lighted, the stuff for which will be supplied by the Rev. Mr Hamilton and Mr Walker, of Maryfield; and Mr Walker has kindly agreed to cart it up the hill as far as a cart can go, when the willing inhabitants will take it to the top of the hill.*

Almost immediately (June 1861), Major Thomas Mouat Cameron wrote to Charles Duncan who had previously been factor for the Garth and Annsbrae estate:[13]

Having returned to Shetland I wish to take the Management of my Property into my own hands and to recall for the future the Factory and Commission granted you in 1852.

In the 1861 census the Walker family are resident at 65 Commercial Street, Lerwick, a house with seven rooms. John, aged twenty-five, is described as a farmer of 220 acres arable and 1200 acres pasture, employing eleven labourers. His daughters, aged five, three, two and eleven months have a nurse, Mary Forbes from Ross-shire, and wife Mary also has sixteen-year-old Margaret Pennie from Bressay to help in the house.

From the Sheriff Court records we know that, on 25th November, 1860, another Bressay girl, Christina Yorston, had quit her job as a servant to the Walkers. John was so annoyed that he took her to court, demanding £2 compensation for the inconvenience she had caused the family by leaving. We don't know the outcome of the case nor is there any indication as to why Christina walked out, or what John's motive was for making such a fuss about it. Perhaps he was seeking publicity, or thought it would bring other servants to heel.

The three thousand or so inhabitants of Lerwick were no doubt alerted to the Walker presence in their midst by another incident – a drawn-out case over his non-payment of sixteen shillings and four pence halfpenny due for poor rates. The Walkers had occupied the house on Commercial Street from Martinmas 1860 till Whitsunday 1861, before moving to their new home, Maryfield, in Bressay (see appendix). The rates for the six months stay in Lerwick had not been paid. When the notice of this debt was handed to him on the street by a policeman, Walker was miffed. When he read the intimation on the notice that after three

Saturdays the most rigorous measures would be taken to receive payment, he was incensed, declaring that, until this threat was withdrawn and a suitable explanation offered, he would refuse to do anything about it. All this he expounded in no uncertain manner in writing to Joseph Leisk, Inspector and Clerk to the Parochial Board, adding, *a matter which, if there be a mistake in, you yourselves are wholly to blame.*

Joseph Leisk wrote a politely worded reply explaining that he would have to do his duty and take Walker to court if he did not pay. He also pointed out that he had no authority from the board to write such an explanation. I suspect, from subsequent events, that Leisk would later regret writing this private letter to Walker. The replies he received were anything but polite. For example: *I have seen a little of the world, and until coming to Shetland always considered the saying that "civility was dirt cheap" an axiom; yet, though in Lerwick dirt is certainly cheap and abundant, civility seems immensely dear and scarce, at least with the Parochial Board of that Parish.*[14]

Early in 1863 the case came before the Sheriff and, conducting his own defence, Walker pointed out that the Board had their Assessment Rolls made up into two books while an Act of Parliament directed that it should be made up in one roll. Also, columns had not been titled according to the Act. Furthermore, notes in the Board's minutes had been written in pencil, which, Walker alleged, was illegal. The *Shetland Advertiser* reported that the defendant *expatiated at great length on the law on the subject, and added that his object was not to keep the money, but to teach those who live in glass houses not to throw stones.* Although the Sheriff considered that Walker had acted wrongly in not admitting having lived in Lerwick, he sustained the defence.

In a letter by 'Vox'[15] we read a cartoon-like description of Walker's appearance in court: *We all saw him march into, and, to speak metaphorically, prance about the court on a defiant, snorting, kicking, biting horse; with rare legal acumen, singular conciseness in statement and debate, with an infinitesimally minute and thoroughly absurd mastery of Dunlop and the poor Law Act, support his cause. In plain words he has barely succeeded in avoiding payment of a debt admitted by him to be 'in justice due' because our Sheriff Substitute has been pleased to give effect to certain technical objections – quibbles in reality – with very doubtful propriety in point of law.*

In other published correspondence a smug Walker delights in his own ingenuity:[16] *I am pleased at being the means of giving one lesson to the Parochial Board of Lerwick, and glad that today's decision proves that I can at least read an Act of Parliament.* He urged the rate payers to *bestir themselves and with a united push place at the Board those who can at least read an Act of Parliament.*[17]

He then decided to donate his 16s. 4½d to the Dorcas Society, a charity run by Lerwick ladies, who returned his donation, apparently on the advice of Mr Sievwright, a lawyer. Sievwright was a shareholder in the Subscription Rooms, in which the Dorcas Society used a room free of charge. He pointed out that if the Dorcas Society held money which rightly belonged to others, they would no longer be a charitable association. Again letters appeared in the *Shetland Advertiser*. Walker wrote: *Mr Sievwright, who I presume is the same individual who thinks nothing of giving the 'lie direct' tells you, as a lawyer that my donation was 'justly due and owing by me to the Parochial Board of Lerwick'.*

So he offered the money again, and declared that either himself or his friends would finance the Dorcas Society to pay for the use of the accommodation in the Subscription Rooms until they could get better quarters or *until Mr Sievwright's superiors decide on his conduct ... in the interests of the poor I beg of your accepting of same, and thus at once shake off the venomous thraldom of a would-be tyrant.*[18]

If he had not already done so, it seems safe to assume that by the end of this case he would have successfully drawn attention to himself, and, at the same time antagonised at least a few Lerwegians, especially William Sievwright. In the many court cases Walker was involved in during his time in Shetland, Sievwright was frequently the lawyer defending those whom Walker was prosecuting. With hindsight it also seems obvious that any future employers or business partners should have heard warning bells ringing about this brash, over-confident young man. But perhaps they admired his assertiveness and were impressed by his knowledge of Acts of Parliament.

In 1862 Walker was elected to the Parochial Board for Bressay, Burra and Quarff, and in December that year sundry Acts of Parliament arrived for the board which had been *ordered to be purchased*. Walker frequently chaired the meetings of the board in the absence of Major Cameron who had been elected chairman. He apparently made an impression in his work with the board as, in the late 1860s, a verbose tribute was paid to him for his work in the 'Williamson Case'. Minuted on 7th May, 1869, it speaks of *unremitting care and attention bestowed by him,* and his *masterly manner in expiscating facts and dates from persons the most adverse and in circumstances most difficult.*[19]

Meanwhile another daughter had been added to the Walker nursery. Helen was born in July 1861, shortly after the family moved to Bressay. As they were to have a governess, none of the Walker girls would have attended the Bressay school, but their father was seen to take an interest in education on the island. After examinations were held in the Bressay school in March 1866, *a number of valuable prizes were presented to those pupils who had proved the most deserving. The prizes were the gift of John Walker who was present at the examination, and who is well known for his numerous acts of liberality.*[20]

We hear again of his reputation for generosity when the *Shetland Advertiser* describes a 'Harvest Home' held at Keldabister Farm, Bressay, in November 1862. The host of the evening is described as *the present liberal occupant, Mr John Walker ... upwards of two hundred people – some of them from the most distant parishes of the Mainland – assembled at the farm-house and barn, where the good things prepared for the occasion were in readiness. After the usual loyal and patriotic toasts were drunk and responded to, dancing commenced – Mr and Mrs Walker being among the first to take the floor – and was kept up with great spirit till an advanced hour the following morning.*

Poor Mary must have had to wear a brave face that evening as she had suffered the still birth of a baby girl as recently as October.[21]

It would be interesting to read the guest list for that party. Since it was a gathering from all over Shetland we can be sure that Walker would have selected those whom he considered were worth trying to impress. Would the conversation at the tables have touched on international affairs? Did they argue about the wisdom of the British government's determination to remain neutral in the American Civil War? Toasts would likely have included health to Queen Victoria who was in a state of nervous collapse following the death of her beloved Albert.

Looking across Bressay Sound at Maryfield with gunboat H.M.S. *Firm* and drifter LK512 *Jane Anderson*. Photo taken in 1890s by J. Irvine.
© *Shetland Museum*

So he continued to farm in Bressay, and successfully too, as seen at the first Lerwick cattle show held in August 1864: *In the improved cattle and sheep classes the prizes were awarded almost entirely to Walker of Maryfield, Bruce of Vinsgarth and Umphray of Reawick.*[22] R. Scott-Skirving, writing in 1874,[23] had also been impressed with Walker's ability as a farmer, claiming that the farm in Bressay was producing four times as much as it did before Walker took over, and that he was the only farmer in Shetland growing swedes. At Maryfield, Skirving saw the only steam powered threshing mill in Shetland. Water power or the flail was used for threshing elsewhere. This glowing report on Walker's achievements is followed by an account of the 'insuperable difficulties' the proprietor and factor of Bressay were experiencing with their tenants who were determined to 'cling to ancient customs' rather than co-operate by accepting 'favourable leases' and improve the husbandry of the island. While it can be argued that country folk – not only in Shetland – are reluctant to accept change, we must also remember that poverty breeds inertia and drains morale. During the destitution years, in the second half of the 1860s, poverty was rife among the Shetland crofters. Furthermore, the terms of the lease offered to the tenants were not really 'favourable' to them, and, from all I can gather of Walker's plans, were never intended to be so. The terms of that lease are detailed in the next chapter.

Meanwhile plans were being drawn up for 'Improvements' to the Garth and Annsbrae Estate which, besides Bressay, included land in Unst, North Yell and Delting. Having served in the army in India and survived the Indian Mutiny, Major Cameron, in spite of what he wrote to Charles Duncan about wanting to manage his own estate, seemed happy to leave the management to a newly appointed factor. So we can safely assume that most of the planning was done by the opportunistic John Walker. As soon as he became factor for the estate in 1866, everything happened at once.

Maryfield, now a hotel, is little changed since Walker's time. © *Andy Gear*

1   Hance D. Smith, *The Making of Modern Shetland,* Lerwick 1977, p.7
2   The Statistical Account of Scotland Vol. XIX
3   Samuel Hibbert, *Shetland Islands,* Edinburgh 1822, p.515
4   Peter Moss, *History Alive 1789-1914,* London 1978, p.17
5   Brian Smith, *Toons and Tenants,* Lerwick 2000, p.95
6   Hance D. Smith, *The Making of Modern Shetland,* Lerwick 1977, p.47
7   Brian Smith, *Toons and Tenants,* Lerwick 2000, p.47
8   Robert Johnson, 'The Deserted Homesteads of Fetlar', *Shetland Life,* No.13
9   Brian Smith, *Toons and Tenants,* Lerwick 2000, p.50
10   Information from Tony Gott
11   Gardie House, Bressay. Gardie Papers 1860/1
12   *Orcadian,* 29th June, 1861
13   Gardie Papers 1861/6
14   S.A. Letter Book, Lerwick Parochial Board
15   *Shetland Advertiser,* 16th February, 1863
16   *Shetland Advertiser,* 5th February, 1863
17   *Shetland Advertiser,* 9th February, 1863
18   *Shetland Advertiser,* 9th March, 1863
19   S.A. CO 6/3/1
20   *The Orkney Herald,* 13th March, 1866
21   Information from the Walker Family Bible
22   H.H. Dixon, *Field and Fern (North),* 1865
23   S.A. 2/307, R Scott-Skirving, *On the Agriculture of the Islands of Shetland,* p.256

Chapter Four

NEW RULES AND BLUE SLIPS

I saw that the commons were of no use to the people, and were doing them harm. I at once resolved to take the commons from them, but offered every tenant on the property a lease.
John Walker addressing the Commission on the Truck System 23/1/1871

IN THE early months of 1866 there could have been little warning of the hardships which lay ahead. The next three successive summers of unseasonable weather brought failed crops and unsuccessful fishing to every district in Shetland, but the crofters on the Garth and Annsbrae estate also had to face the programme of change drawn up by the super-energetic factor recently taken on by their laird.

John Walker must have dipped and drained a few bottles of ink during the first months of his appointment. His mind and his pen would have been in overdrive. Plans for sheep farms had to be drawn up; fencing material had to be ordered; contracts to be arranged for erecting fences, fanks and houses for shepherds. And in order to make the sheep farms possible, he was busy writing new rules for the tenants. The rules were then printed in a neat, but imposing, fifteen page booklet:[1]

ARTICLES, REGULATIONS
AND
CONDITIONS OF LEASE,

Which are to have the same effect as if engrossed at length in the Leases
AGREED BETWIXT
The Proprietor of the Estates of Garth & Annsbrae,
ON THE ONE PART,
And the Tenants of said Lands,
ON THE OTHER PART.

The booklet included an introductory letter from the Major declaring that he approved of, and concurred with, the system to be adopted by Mr Walker in the management of his property which was now to be entirely in his factor's hands. After the nineteen clauses of the terms of lease came a lengthy explanation of the new rules, written by Walker himself, and described by the Major as 'remarks' to which he gave his full approval.

The books of new rules were then sent out to the tenants with a letter from the factor informing them of his appointment. Typical of these letters was the one addressed to Peter Simpson Blance of Scatsta:[2]

Sir,   *3rd August, 1866*
Annexed you have Major Cameron's intimation of my appointment as his Factor and I have now to inform you that from and after Martinmas next no Tenant upon his Scatsta Property will enjoy any of the privileges of the Scattald – The agreement concerning your Farm does not expire till Martinmas 1867 but should you wish to take a lease of your House and such portion of land as may be agreed upon, you will have to make up your mind before September next – I send you a copy of the Rules that are laid down for this Property and will be glad to arrange with you upon the conditions stated therein.
Yours truly,
John Walker

So what were these new rules and how workable were they for the tenants?

Rule 1 – *The lease shall be for ten years from Martinmas* (11th November). *The rent shall be due and payable at the term of Martinmas every year.*

That's fair enough, provided the fishermen had been paid for their catch by then. The settling-up didn't always happen before Martinmas.

The houses were to be let along with some arable land cultivated under a proper system of cropping laid out in Rule 6. They were to be let at such a rent *as would be the present <u>agricultural</u> value, irrespective of the additional value which every house possesses of being situated in the midst of wealth to be easily obtained from the sea.* This claim of the ease with which wealth from the sea could be obtained must have stuck in the throats of the Haaf men. These fishermen, of all ages, had to set out in the early hours of the morning to row, or sail, all day till they arrived at the fishing ground where they 'shot' miles of line armed with thousands of baited hooks. They then had a well-earned break for food. Next came the *hauling* [of] *six miles of line laden with live kicking fish from depths ranging from thirty to ninety fathoms ... a supreme test of muscle power.*[3] Depending on weather and other circumstances, they would either shoot the lines again or set off for base. 'Wealth' for whom? 'Easily obtained' by whom?

Surely the most devastating of the new regulations must have been the loss of the use of the scattald – common grazing on the hills and shores neighbouring the crofts. Rule 13 states: *All privileges of grazing upon scattalds, removing 'truck', etc is reserved by the proprietor. No tenant is allowed any privilege outside the boundary of his farm, with the single exception of the boats 'nousts'*[4] *as presently enjoyed.*

For hundreds of years the scattald had been used by Shetlanders, not only for common grazing of the hardy native sheep, pigs and cattle, but also for other essentials including cutting peat for fuel, poans for use in thatching, and planticrubs for nurturing young cabbage plants. In his 'remarks' Walker excused the loss of the scattald by declaring that it had only been of use to a few and then *in so small a degree as to fail to be apparent.* What is apparent is that Walker wanted the scattald for sheep farming and that he knew that most of the crofters could not survive without it.

Planticrubs. *Courtesy Eric Isbister*

Rule 9 – *No tenant is allowed to keep any bull, stallion, ram or boar, except such as has been approved of and permitted in writing by the proprietor or his factor.*

When questioned on this clause at the Truck Commission, five years later, in 1871, Walker declared: *I found that the lame, the halt and the blind were being kept for breeding purposes.* This may well have been the case when the tenants, in dire straits for money to pay rent or debt, were forced to sell their best animals or had the best beasts taken in lieu. It's unlikely that Walker would have been content to appropriate the lame, halt or blind for settlement of a tenant's debt. Average rent for a croft on the Garth Estate in North Yell in 1866-67 was £4.10s. with some paying £7 or more.[5] An account from James Williamson's papers[6] in 1867 shows fat cows selling for £4 and two-year-old oxen for £1.15s. But without the use of the scattald for grazing, few would be able to keep their animals.

And until such time as results of such a policy could provide some good breeding stock, would debt be overlooked? Rule 15 answered that question: *It is expressly stipulated that when any act of bankruptcy upon the part of the tenant takes place, that his lease shall terminate.* Rule 17 pointed out that any tenant not complying with the new regulations would immediately lose their 'farm' (the term 'croft' was not then in common use) and forfeit all the benefits of the lease. Walker devoted a lengthy paragraph to explaining away Rule 17. He started by admitting that it may seem hard that forfeiture should follow a breach of the minor regulations but then pointed out, in typical manner, that *a bargain is a bargain all the world over,* and ended by emphasising that every tenant should ascertain exactly the meaning of every condition as there would be no acceptance of excuses like: *not understanding this, that, or any other part of the agreement.* Given that the rules were quite complicated and couched in grandiose language, it would not have been surprising if the crofters, many of whom had never attended school, found the document somewhat daunting.

They were not to be allowed to keep a dog, nor to sell any straw, turnips, hay or dung. No longer was there free access to peat which, of course was the only fuel available, or to seaweed and sand. Seaweed was used as fertiliser. Sand (shell sand especially) improved drainage, provided lime for the peaty soil and was needed for poultry to strengthen egg shells. All these had to be allotted to the tenant by someone appointed by the proprietor.

To enable the proprietor to establish fishing villages, etc., should such become necessary or desirable, Rule16 granted the proprietor *the right to grant feus[7] off any farm*. So, if the laird wanted to use a section of the croft for some other purpose, or lease it to another party, he could take it at any time – presumably with a suitable reduction in rent to the crofter. Even if the tenant could follow all the rules to the letter, he still did not have any security of the land which he might hold under the new regulations.

And what about repairs to the houses? Rule 4 – *The tenants are bound to maintain, keep, and leave at the end of their lease, in good tenantable condition, the houses, and all permanent improvements handed over ...*

Now let's look at the complex instructions for permanent improvements and related percentage alterations to rent expounded in Rule 5: *In consequence of the land being unenclosed, and in need of draining and other permanent improvements, the tenants are bound to annually expend upon their farms, in such manner as may be pointed out by the proprietor or his factor, improvements equal in value to the amount of the annual rent. During the first five years of the lease the proprietor will allow annually an amount equal to one half of such permanent improvements as may have been executed in a satisfactory manner (said amount in no case to exceed one half of the amount of rent). During the last five years of the lease, the tenants are bound to pay in addition to the annual rent a further rent charge, at the rate of seven per cent. per annum upon the total sum or sums allowed for improvements during the first five years of the lease.*

This clause seems to be tailor made to give Walker an opportunity to expound on one of his favourite themes – laziness of Shetlanders, but more of that later. Because the amount of 'permanent improvements' to be carried out is entirely at the factor's, or the proprietor's, discretion, it would enable him to get rid of any undesirable tenants who may have had the nerve to accept his terms, by simply declaring that the work had not been 'executed in a satisfactory manner'.

The tenant did not ultimately reap the benefit of his labours, because Rule 19 stated that, on expiry of the ten year lease: *Every tenant shall be bound to remove from the houses and lands without notice of removal and shall be liable to double the previous year's rent for every year that he or she may remain in possession after the termination of the tack.* However, tenants could claim an extended lease at any time, upon stamped paper, at their own expense.

The explanation of the new rules was followed by two pages of what might be called 'encouragement' (depending on your point of view), with phrases like: *care and industry will soon show you the benefits ... be industrious six days in every week ... I shall at all times be ready and willing to assist you ... do not hesitate to come and ask my advice ... mutual confidence will enable us to easily overcome the many small difficulties ... it is necessary for your welfare as a body ... those who do not wish to try this new system may prepare to suit themselves elsewhere ... prepare yourselves for one change or another ... you will in every way be "Freemen".*

The book of rules was sent out in August 1866 and meetings were held in September to learn what decisions the tenants had made. Those who were leaving had to be out by Martinmas.

It seems he met the Delting tenants first. Writing to the Major on 10th September he sounded pretty confident:[8] *If the Yell people settle down as quietly as the Delting folks, I think of taking a week or two in Aberdeen from 20th inst. before commencing to lay off the lots to Tenants.*

Alexander Sandison (see appendix), merchant in Uyeasound, Unst, wrote to Walker on the 29th August,[9] hoping that he would be met *in peace* in North Yell and advising him to *be as kind and merciful to them as you can*. Again on 12th September urging him to *do good and not evil all the days you are there.*[10]

Whether or not as a result of Sandison's admonitions, Walker did concede that to prevent hardship, some tenants, under certain conditions, would be allowed to remain on their property for a further twelve months. If only we knew more about these September meetings! Were they well attended? Was he heckled? The only information we have comes from the pen of the man himself – hardly an unbiased view.

On the 18th he wrote to William Duncan with just a hint of relief that the Yell visit was over:[11] *I returned safe and sound from North Yell yesterday having found the Tenants quite peaceable – true they had not all to come under the New Rules this year but I believe those that have to will be contented and happy by and by.*

And on the same day to George Henderson:[12] *I consider I succeeded with our North Yell Tenants better than I expected – some three or four have left us but we required this as we lay out Burraness and some of West-a-Firth in town lands.* As both these areas were to become sheep farms, presumably he meant they were to be enclosed. 'Some three or four have left us' was a gross understatement. Taking Burraness as just one example, all eight families had left by February 1867.

In the booklet the final statement read: *Unless you adopt one of the courses suggested, you will receive legal warning to quit, and your farm will be otherwise disposed of.*

** ** **

North Yell people are not in a good humour
– the false reports have unhinged them.
John Walker writing to Alexander Sandison, 11th February, 1867

Imagine the heart searching that must have followed the arrival of the books of rules. There would have been argument, indecision, discussion, gossip, threats, and above all, anxiety. The September meetings were held, but we have no idea what was said, promised or threatened at these meetings. Decisions were made, and agreements, set out in the factor's distinctive handwriting, still survive on slips of blue paper, like bookmarks, among the Gardie papers. Signatures and marks (X), some firm, some shaky, conform to Walker's wishes. The blue slips give us the stark facts but not the persuasion used to obtain these signatures, and certainly none of the emotion which must have prevailed.

The following examples, all dated 12th September, 1866, concern tenants from Burraness and Kirkabister in North Yell and were witnessed by Peter Mouat Sandison who was a merchant in Cullivoe and had the Garth tenants on his accounts.

I hereby give up the Farm as occupied by me in Burraness, from and after Martinmas next and agree to hold the house alone for half a year to Whitsunday 1867 at 15s rent.

signed Thomas Scollay

An identical agreement was signed by Barbara Williamson for the farm held by her husband in Burraness.

Robert Nisbet agreed *to rent from Major Cameron the Farm as at present occupied by me in Uncadale for the rising year till Martinmas 1867 at the rent of £4.10s including 25s for a share in the Undivided Scattald – Peats to be cut under Rule 12.* Jeremiah Moar and William Irvine, both in Kirkabister, signed similar slips with rent £3.5s and £3 respectively and 5s and 2s 6d for their share in the scattald.

Thomas Nisbet put his mark against an agreement *to give up the Farm as occupied by me in Kirkabister from and after Martinmas 1867 and agree to hold the farm as at present during the rising year until Martinmas 1867 at the rent of £7 including 27s for a share in the Undivided Scattald. Peats to be cut under Rule 12.*

Andrew A. Anderson signed away his farm under the same agreement, rent £6, share in scattald, five shillings. Laurence Williamson's agreement was slightly different in that his ended with: *I am to get an offer of a Lease of a Farm under the new rules.* But surely they had all been offered a lease? William Williamson was to leave Burraness and go to J. D. Fraser's at Cullivoe. He was a stone-mason and presumably considered useful.

I have found agreements signed by nine families in the Burraness and Kirkabister area. Perhaps the 'blue slips' relevant to the other eight families living there did not survive, or the tenants were obliged to leave under some other pretext. For example, in the following year, some of the tenants received letters ordering them to find out and tell who was responsible for what Walker called 'mischief' to the fences he was erecting around the scattald. If they didn't co-operate, they had to go.

The townships of Burraness and Kirkabister and the nearby crofts of Uncadal and Bigsetter lie on a peninsula on the east side of Basta Voe. In 1861[13] this peninsula supported seventeen families, one hundred and two people with an average age of forty-five for the head of the household. Eight of the 'heads' were described as fishermen/farmers; one a knitter (of ladies stockings); one mason/grocer/farmer (the William Williamson who was to move to Cullivoe). Seven were farmers including two married women whose husbands were absent – probably merchant seamen. Twenty-eight of the children who lived there would be primary school age in the present day. It was a youthful community, surrounded by good fishing grounds, with gently sloping rigs, handy boats' noosts and fine sandy beaches. Even 'da craigsaets'[14] at Burraness are better than average – providing fish for a month longer than others in the neighbourhood.[15] Ironically, the houses on the outer point of Burraness look across the sea towards the north west side of Fetlar which had been cleared for sheep farming by Arthur Nicolson during the previous half-century.

But by 1867 Burraness was empty, and the following year all the tenants had to leave Kirkabister, Bigsetter and Uncadal, except seventy-year-old Magnus Nisbet who was still paying 10s rent for his house.[16] My great-grandparents, William and Margaret Spence from Bigsetter, with infant Jane Mary, went to Mid Yell. William's mother, also Margaret, a widow, went to a little house in Sellafirth. The knitter went to Lerwick. Seven families flit elsewhere in North Yell – but all to property other than Cameron's. It appears that no effort was made to re-house any except Williamson the stone mason. By that time the Major and Walker had a flock of 450 Cheviot ewes with Leicester rams[17] grazing where the Kirkabister crofts used to be.

On 20th June, 1867 Thomas M. C. Pole of Greenbank [North Yell], wrote to Walker on behalf of one of the families:[18] *James Clark who lately left Burraness wishes me to ask you if you would be kind enough to give him a farm. Poor fellow he is in much need of one. I suppose he would not much care where it was or whether good or bad. Hoping you will kindly think of the above.*

It's amazing how quickly mail could be delivered in those days. Walker, in Bressay, was penning his reply to Pole on 22nd:[19] *Yours of 20th anent James Clark duly to hand – You must be unaware that Clark left this Property indebted to the extent of £3:9:11 which until settled prevents me considering any application for a farm on his behalf.*

37

William and Margaret Spence in their later years.
Courtesy Sandison family, Altona, Mid Yell

Nine months earlier, on 18th September, 1866, Walker had written to James Clark:[20] *Unless the enclosed be duly signed by you before Witnesses and reach my hands before noon of Monday next a Summons of Removal will issue against you.*

The 'enclosed' to be 'duly signed' was as follows:-

    Burraness   September 1866
I hereby give up and agree to remove from the Farm as occupied by me in Burraness, at Martinmas first.

Next day, 19th September, Walker was writing to the Major:[21] *From what I now learn the tenants are anxious to try the new system whilst I am every day more convinced of its desirability and greater success than I even anticipated.*

So Walker, the factor, could tell Major Cameron, the laird, that the tenants were 'anxious to try the new system', when in reality, Walker was, by one means or another, coercing them into signing away their homes and moving elsewhere. Was the Major so completely out of touch with what was happening on his estate that Walker could tell him anything and get away with it? Or did the Major prefer to remain in ignorance?

There were blue slips from tenants on the other side of the voe at Basta. One of these was witnessed by Walker himself, as well as Peter Sandison. It would be interesting to know why that one had special status. It was signed by Robert Ramsay – rent £5 : 5s including 5s for a share in the Scattald and a chance of a lease under the new rules. But Ramsay didn't stay on, as there's a letter from Daniel Moar in Colvister asking for Ramsay's croft. His letter of 23rd April, 1867 is spattered with 'Dear Sers' and a desire to please:[22] *Dear Ser within three weks thy all will be cutting ther peats so I would be good to know if I was to get it – or not if you plas. Dear Ser ther is another thing that I have to say to you that Arthur Mor your tannat in Basta is pold down all the office houes and bront the feals that was on the gavels of the offices howes*
Ser I do not know his intisuan for dong so
Dear Ser you would ned some parson from you to see to that,
Dear Ser you nead not fear the rent of Basta for I have allwies payed my Rent but it is the ling that the Nort yell lords laukes for Yours Trouly Daniel Mor
A strange mixture of managing to spell tricky words correctly e.g. 'would' and 'know' and at the same time getting simpler words wrong. It is as if he had a list of 'words difficult to spell'.

In December of the same year William Sievwright represented Ramsay in demanding 10s from Daniel Moar for having had some occupation of Ramsay's croft during 66/67. To this Walker replied that, if any money was claimed from Moar, he would impose a charge for damages on Ramsay for leaving his farm 'waste'. It is not altogether clear what was going on there. But we do know that Walker was always on the lookout for informers, and Daniel Moar was successful in his attempt to curry favour by telling tales about Arthur Moar burning the 'feals'[23] from the gavels of the out-houses. In Walker's reply, telling Daniel that he would get Ramsay's farm, he added: *I am obliged for the information about the house.*[24] At the very time when the crofters would have needed to present a united front, this sort of clyping, boot-licking behaviour must have significantly aggravated feelings of anxiety and distrust.

Other blue slips included one combining signatures from more outlying areas in North Yell, witnessed by P. M. Sandison at Cullivoe, on 14th September, 1866:[25] *We the undersigned Tenants of the respective Farms named and designated opposite our respective signatures, hereby give up the said Farms as occupied by us from and after Martinmas next, and we hereby agree to take a tack of such land as may be laid off to* accompany the respective Houses of said Farms, for the term and on the conditions specified in the New Rules and Regulations to be enforced upon the Estate from the date of Martinmas next – provided that the rent of said Land be fixed and mutually agreed to before entering upon the occupation of said Land.

In the event of the said rent <u>not</u> being so agreed upon then we the undersigned Hereby agree to hold the <u>Dwelling Houses only</u> as now occupied by us, for one year from Martinmas first at a rent of 30s per annum payable half yearly at Whitsunday and Martinmas and without any of the privileges attaching to the Land.

Farm	West o Firth	C. C. Williamson (X his mark)
"	Graven	Laurence Tulloch (X)
"	Volester	John Mann
"	"	Ann Anderson (X) for Jerome Anderson
"	Setter, West o Firth	Samuel Johnson (X)
"	Volester	Alexander Williamson (X)
"	Graven	John Tulloch and Andrew Smith
"	Vigon	John Omand

Volister, on the east side of Whalefirth, and Lumbister north over the hill, had been cleared to make a sheep farm by John Mouat of Annsbrae in 1834, but this venture did not prove successful.[26] Fifteen years later houses were re-built there, and, by 1861 there were four families living in Volister – Scollays, Jamiesons and two Anderson families, twenty-four people altogether, while in Lumbister there were three families, thirty-one people – Urquaharts, Moars and Henrys. For a Shetland settlement, Lumbister is unusual, being about a mile from the sea. The houses and rigs (cultivated strips) were situated beside a fair sized loch.

Loch of Lumbister. © *Andy Gear*

NEW RULES AND BLUE SLIPS

I wonder if the unsuccessful 1834 attempt at sheep farming in Yell, and the subsequent rebuilding of the tenants' houses by John Mouat, was what was in the Major's mind when, in November 1867, he instructed his factor to:[27] *take out doors and build up voids in empty houses to keep roofs from blowing off (should it be found advisable to re-tenant in a few years).*

In April 1867 the Volister and Lumbister tenants must have realised that they wouldn't hold their crofts for another season when William Pennie (Walker's man in Yell, more formally known as grieve for the estate) came to sow grass seed among their corn. Walker sent the following instructions to Pennie:[28] *You will receive per 'Alice' sacks grass and clover seeds for Volister and Lumbister – to be sown amongst Tenants corn.*

By September 1867 the writing is truly on the wall:[29] *I enclose letters for the Volister & Lumbister tenants to sign where marked in pencil. Try to return them to me by Monday's post.*

In October he's being accommodating, but with a sting in the tail:[30] *You can let the Volister and Lumbister tenants know that I wont be very exact for even a few weeks if things move quietly in their neighbourhood, but that if the least annoyance takes place they must move.*

And in December:[31] *Andrew Williamson should have told you of the destruction by pigs before the Volister Tenants left.* From these three letters to Pennie we can deduce that the 'toons' of Volister and Lumbister were empty by Martinmas 1867.

My great-grandfather John Mann, with his Anderson in-laws, was cleared out of Volister at that time. He had a wife and three young sons. According to the story passed down in the family they had until 11am on a certain date to empty the house. Any belongings left after that time

41

Da toonship o Volister, still green after nearly 140 years. © *Andy Gear*

must be abandoned. William Pennie came to nail up the door at the appointed time but was apparently intimidated by John Mann's threats, and allowed extra time to clear the house. Grace, John's wife, had been anxious to get away before Pennie arrived as she was sure John would murder him!

I wonder if John Mann's ire arose from him feeling that the agreement, as laid out by Walker, was not as straightforward as it should have been. It seems unlikely, from what we know of my great-grandfather, that he would have signed a document unless he felt satisfied with the terms. If only we knew more about the methods of persuasion used on the tenants. The Manns and Andersons moved into a barn at Bouster on the other side of Whalefirth, and eventually got a house there.

John Mann went to the gold-diggings in Australia not long after they were cleared from Volister. He also sailed quarter-master on the *Great Britain* and was away from home for a number of years. On his return, he span many a yarn to an impressionable audience of young boys. Few of the stories survive, but his nephew (one of the boys) used to recount how John Mann and John Walker met, on horseback, at a watering hole in Australia. No doubt the boys were hoping for action.

"An what happened Uncle?"
"Walker turned his horse an rade awa."
"What wid you a don if he'd bidden, Uncle?"
"My boy, wan o wis widna a left dat watterin-hol alive."
I would love to be able to say that the two Johns were in Australia at the same time, but the dates I have, so far, don't seem to match up. However, the story does serve to illustrate the crofter's dislike of Walker. In their eyes he was the guilty party.

John and Grace Mann taken outside their home at Lusetter, Mid Yell, shortly before she died in 1904, aged 66.

JOHN WALKER'S SHETLAND

** ** **

Another area, further north in Yell, and appearing in blue slips, is West o Firth. In September 1867 Walker wrote to Major Cameron:[32] *I would now attempt briefly to post you up in matters connected with your property ... the tenants' enclosure at W. of Firth I've divided into three – and John Oman is allowed another year in Vigon – the enclosures at W. of Firth are substantial and suitable – no draining will be done this year.*

In 1867 there were sixteen families in West o Firth.[33] By 1871 the census shows only four tenants – two crofters (who had taken leases), a pauper and a shepherd. The 'substantial and suitable' enclosures mentioned in the letter would have included scattald and arable land cultivated by generations of crofters. In the valuation roll 1869/70 it is listed as a 'farm' occupied by Major Cameron and John Walker – occupied by their sheep, of course.

Tom Tulloch, Gutcher, a fine Shetland story teller, spoke of the time of these clearances:[34] *An da most o dis property ida nort end o da Mainland an in Yell belonged ta Major Cameron and evidently he wis a fairly humane man, he wis not caused much disturbance til his tenants at all until he got dis factor fae Scotland, a John Walker. An it wis Walker at induced Cameron til evict tenants. An needless ta say, Walker wis a very hated man . . . In Wast-a Firt dey wir something in da region o thirteen families evicted wi a population approachin 120. An dat wis all evicted aless wan hoosehold. An dat wis me great-great-graundfaider an his dowter an da dowter's husband. Dey wir keepit on ta look efter da shepherds an da fencers an da drainers.*

In North Yell the blame for the evictions was laid firmly at Walker's feet.

Tom again: *An da last, as I sill caa it, civilian, ta come oot o Wast-a-Firt, wis a graundaunt o mine, a Charlotte Scolla. An sho wis da very last person ta be shifted oot o Wast-a-Firt, an dey took her an her bits o belongings wi a sixtreen an launded in at da beach o Whallerie. An hit wis an uncle o hers at volunteered ta kyerry her oot o da sixtreen on upo da shore because sho still hed on her smucks. Sho wis nivir hed ony idder thing upo her feet bit her smucks, dis wida been hom-made smucks, certainly no bowt smucks. Bit dis uncle wis gettin ta be a kind o an elderly man an he trippit an fell ida process o takkin her oot o da sixtreen an sho wis pretty nimble upo her feet an sho clappit her smucks atween his shooders an sho jimpit ashore an nivir wet her feet.*

Of the crofters who had to leave West o Firth Tom said:[35] *Dey wir some a dem it guid is faar awa is Canada – severals a dem guid ta Canada. An dey wir some a dem it shiftit across ta Gloup, an some a de ta*

Midbrake. It wis very aften a case a maybe twa faemilies goin intil a hoose whaur dey wir onnly been wan faemily afore. Dey got despersed an guid onyway it dey could git a röf ower dir heed at all, fur da laird an da factor wisna carin whaat cam a dem, is lang is dey got dem oot a da hooses an got da laund led doon ta da sheep.

Incidentally, a clause in Rule 3 of the 'Articles of Lease' states: *only one family shall occupy the subject let.* Walker's enlargement of this rule explains: *as the houses are not constructed to accommodate more than one family in each, and as the health and morality demand, it is decided as stated in this rule.* As Tom said, at the time of the clearance, two or more families were often crowded into one house. We're speaking about big families and little houses. What else could they do? Kindly neighbours and relatives would take them in until they found a roof of their own, in Shetland or much further afield. It would seem that the risks to health and morals caused by overcrowding did not bother Walker as long as it didn't take place on the estate for which he was factor.

The most remote croft in West o Firth was Vigon. Tom Tulloch described it as:[36] *da best croft it wis in Wast-a-Firt, bit it wis ootside da hill daeks, it raelly wis jöst a peerie settlement on its own, an it wis a famous place fur driftwid. Dey wir clos ta da banks broo. An da geo a Vigon wis considered ta be a graet place fur drift of all descriptions – in fact it wis said da Vigon fok more or less lived oot a da geo a Vigon.*

Da Geo o Vigon. © *Andy Gear*

The last family to live in Vigon were the Omands. There is an intriguing series of letters from Walker to John Omand, an interesting character who had been at the gold diggings in Australia and had sailed steward on the *Great Britain*. Reputedly handsome, he was admired by rich lady passengers, and one romantic story was of a proposal in the form of a note dropped at his feet in the dining saloon. But he never married. In 1834 John Omand's father, James, had been moved from Holsigarth, at the head of Whalefirth, to make room for sheep, and the family moved to Bouster, in the Herra. When John came home from some of his travels he found he could not comply with the conditions imposed by the Fetlar minister, Rev. David Webster who was then proprietor of Bouster. So the family flit to Vigon.[37]

What makes Walker's letters to Omand especially intriguing is the fact that they were polite – at least to begin with. Letters to ordinary tenants normally opened with a stark 'Sir', and ended with 'Yours etc', the message in between usually peremptory to the point of rudeness. Remember, 'strikin tek/theck'[38] was against the rules, and furthermore we find that Omand has dared to keep a dog and used it to hound off the estate's sheep![39]

Mr John Omand   18th Oct. 1867
    Dear Sir,
        I am duly in receipt of yours of 17th asking leave to strick 'Theck' at Vigon and informing me that our sheep have been on your farm – This latter I warned you must yourself prevent ... as to the 'Theck' I don't know what to say –

Walker lost for words? There's an unusual situation.

It is quite against our Rules and system to allow anything of the kind and I have already fined Tenants for so doing – In your case as you say that you are so hard up for Fodder I would rather give you some indulgence for your Cattle in the Hill and allow them to strick 'Theck' rather than you – But as to this matter I expect to be North about the 15th November when I will arrange with you if I can at all help you in your difficulty.
                    Yours truly,   John Walker

If this were the only letter in existence written by Walker to a tenant he would have gone down in history as a considerate, almost kindly, factor. Omand had the temerity to write again on 8th April, 1868 complaining about the Garth sheep and the reply is still graced with 'Dear Sir' and 'Yours truly' and retains a degree of restraint:[40] *As to our sheep being on Vigon I am sorry we cant help it as you know how we let the Farm – After the liberal offer I once made to you and the positive manner in which you declined to remain under our Rules I am surprised that you could still write an offer of Vigon and as I had resolved that it should not*

be set to anyone I dont see how it would now do letting you remain –
however I am to be North next week you should then see me when I'll be
able to say whether or not I can again give you a chance.

In the third letter, dated 20th June, it's plain that Omand has gone too far:[41]

I have again to warn you that you are incurring a serious liability on yourself by Keeping a Dog and hounding off our Sheep – I am told that [?] Lambs have been found eaten by a Dog. Should you not put away your Dog or Dogs within one week I must apply to the Sheriff for an Interdict against which will be an addition to damages for keeping a Dog until now.
Yours etc,   John Walker

Over a hundred years after the Omand family left Vigon, the remains of the croft house stills stands. Note the marked step in the well-built gable to accommodate the thick thatching for the roof.   © *David Gear*

Walker took people to court at the drop of a hat and certainly for offences much less serious than sheep-worrying. But there is no evidence of his threat to Omand being carried out. Perhaps Walker could empathise with Omand's obstinacy or was he, like many a bully, a coward at heart, and buckled under when someone stood up to him? It has been suggested that he was afraid of Omand for another reason. James Omand, John's father, was still living in Vigon at that time, and was said to be able *tae dö mair as maet himsel*, in other words – was reputed to be a warlock!

JOHN WALKER'S SHETLAND

** ** **

John Murdoch, in an article in the *People's Journal*, September 1866, wrote of the changes taking place in the Garth and Annsbrae Estate:[42] *We are not going to call the right of the landlord or his factor in question – although we may, in passing, say that the best foundation on which a landlord or a factor can rest his claims is that supplied by a prosperous and contented tenantry working in love and understanding with those above them ... As the matter appears at present, most persons will conclude that the whole plan is a plausible project for getting the tenants to eject themselves. And indeed so much is it the fashion now to prefer land without people, it is not unreasonable to suppose that this uncharitable supposition is, after all, the truth of the matter.*

Murdoch had been resident in Shetland since March 1864 and his articles in the *People's Journal* reflect a lively interest in local affairs and a generous measure of common sense. Among other things he advocated extending the telegraph to Shetland, building a proper pier at Lerwick and bringing water into the town from the Sandy Loch. He was a champion of the fine Shetland wool, and suggested the need for a factory in Shetland for weaving woollen cloth. In January 1866, he wrote:[43] *If the fine wool bearing sheep are allowed to be extirpated, the finer sorts of Shetland Hosiery will be knocked on the head.*

He also had practical suggestions for raising the morale of the crofters – much needed at that time:[44] *The Shetland [Agricultural] Society should institute prizes for the best managed farms and the tidiest cottages. And while doing this and other things to improve the skill and habits of the Shetland farmers, something would require to be done to remove the impression among tenants that good produce is a snare – that he who improves his land merely offers his landlord an excuse for raising his rent.*

Murdoch was not the only critic of the changes in the administration of the Garth and Annsbrae Estate. Writing to Dr Basil Spence, Thomas Edmondston of Buness had this to say:[45] *You will have heard something of the "Cameronian" and "Walkerian" plans for the improvement of Shetland and the Shetlanders. I have a copy of the printed "Rules and Regulations", and although I have no fault to find with the theory of them, they have this ruinous drawback – they are unworkable and therefore impracticable. I rather think they will either withdraw them or allow them to die a natural death.*

When the Books of Rules appeared in August 1866, Major Cameron was out of Shetland. Aware of dissent among the tenants he wrote a warning to his factor:[46]

New Rules and Blue Slips

My sister writes the Mid & South Yell men have met & agreed to stand firm to each other & bound themselves to get hold of you when you come to Cullivoe next month & either get what they want or kill you – the latter I doubt but you had better be on your guard. Were I at home I have a small revolver that might have been of use ...

1. S.A. Midbrake Papers 392/86
2. Gardie Papers L.B.1 p.7
3. A. Halcrow, *The Sail Fishermen of Shetland,* Lerwick 1994, p.70
4. Hollowed out and/or built up shelters at the edge of the beach where boats are drawn up
5. Valuation Roll
6. Robert L. Johnson, *A Shetland Country Merchant,* Lerwick 1979, p.37
7. Perpetual lease at a fixed rent
8. Gardie Papers L.B.1 p.40
9. Gardie Papers 1866/72
10. Gardie Papers 1866/91
11. Gardie Papers L.B.1 p.42
12. Gardie Papers L.B.1 p.43
13. 1861 census for North Yell
14. Places good for rock fishing for home use.
15. Oral Tradition – J. Ramsay
16. Valuation Roll
17. S.A. 2/307 R. Scott-Skirving, *On the Agriculture of the Islands of Shetland,* 1874
18. Gardie Papers 1867/286
19. Gardie Papers L.B.2 p.64
20. Gardie Papers L.B.1 p.44
21. Gardie Papers L.B.1 p.48
22. Gardie Papers 1867/187
23. Peaty turfs often used to build the peaks of the gables of outhouses and sometimes used for building dwelling houses
24. Gardie Papers L.B.2 p.7
25. Gardie Papers 1867/187
26. Robert L. Johnson, 'Lonely, Lovely, Lumbister', *Shetland Life,* No.75.
27. Gardie Papers 1867/549
28. Gardie Papers L.B.1 p.203
29. Gardie Papers L.B.2 p.112
30. Gardie Papers L.B.2 p.146
31. Gardie Papers L.B.2 p.263
32. Gardie Papers L.B.2 p.106
33. Robert L. Johnson, *New Shetlander,* No.149
34. S.A.1978/63
35. Auld Haa, Burravoe
36. Ibid
37. Robert L. Johnson, *New Shetlander,* No.149
38. Cutting heather and/or rough grass from the scattald for animal fodder, animal bedding and thatching
39. Gardie Papers L.B.2 p.171
40. Gardie Papers L.B.2 p.358

41 Gardie Papers L.B.2 p.423
42 Ed. James Hunter, *For the People's Cause, From the Writings of John Murdoch,* Edinburgh 1986, p.132
43 Ibid p.130
44 Ibid p.131
45 S.A. D 12/116/6/14
46 Gardie Papers 1866/68

Chapter Five

THREATS AND BOASTS

I did carry a revolver for a month but I had no occasion to use it.
John Walker giving evidence before Mr Sellar, Commissioner
of Inquiry into Truck System. Edinburgh, 23/1/1871

PEOPLE sometimes ask why unpopular characters like John Walker were not quietly 'bumped off'. "Surely there were plenty of chances on a winter's night in a place like Yell?" they say. So why was that dark deed never done? On this we can only speculate. Most people in those days were deeply religious and believed in the dire fate of sinners. The consequences of discovery in this world would also have been an effective deterrent. There was always the risk of being spied on by someone willing to tell tales in order to curry favour with the laird or factor, or even the minister, in order to better their own position.

Our far-seeing journalist, John Murdoch, having offered advice to those in charge of estates, also had a word for the tenants:[1] *We have been told that threats of violence have been scattered far and wide through Shetland against the new factor – that his life is not safe among the people and that Shetland will soon be another Ireland.* He went on to warn the Shetlanders against using physical force, pointing out that, although the Irish cause was as good as that of any nation, the Irish who took the law into their own hands *while thinking they were serving their country and their race, were in reality putting a powerful weapon into the hands of their enemies ... So let the Shetland Peasantry take warning ... In taking vengeance out of His* [God's] *hand, they are also placing themselves beyond His protection and laying themselves open to the legal power which their enemies may be only too anxious to bring against them.*

There was some unease in the Cameron Mouat family for Walker's safety. As we heard at the end of the previous chapter, Miss Mouat had heard rumours, but Walker was determined to bluster through. To the Major, 23rd August, 1866:[2] *I note what Miss Mouat has been informed about the Yell men – neither their threats nor their flattery will induce me to depart from what I believe right for them and you – I certainly will keep a sharp look out upon them and intend taking a Revolver with me but I hope and believe it is all* bosh.

Walker was never physically attacked, but there were attempts to intimidate him. In August 1866, with two friends from Aberdeenshire, he went to Delting to view the scattalds with an eye to sheep-farming. After landing at Calbackness they took care to keep away from the houses, obviously expecting hostility. This is how he described the scene to the Major:[3] *We were soon discovered and surrounded by about 30 of the inhabitants – every one fiercer than the other – their talk at first was outrageous but they soon cooled down without attempting to carry their threats as to murdering me into execution and I believe the explanation I gave them should do much, not only to convince that we are in earnest, but that the change is meant for their good ... they did not like the idea of a lease nor the loss of the hill but said they would pay double their rent to be allowed to remain as at present ... The sum total of my Delting visit is that I have succeeded* too *well as I fear everyone will stay.*[4] And that would never do!

Early in the following year Walker was again threatened, this time in Yell. He must have felt more intimidated on that occasion as he took his supposed assailants to the Sheriff Court, thus providing us with more details.

It happened on the 13th February, 1867. Walker was out surveying his forthcoming sheep farm in Burraness, North Yell. His companion, David Henderson, was then resident in Gremster, a toonship[5] roughly half way between Cullivoe and Gutcher. Five months earlier David Henderson had signed an agreement giving him the lease of Gremster, but some of the rules of the lease had been excluded, e.g. the rule covering the ten years of land improvement and, strangely, the one banning dogs. Walker's motives for bending the rules in this case would become apparent within the year.

One of the houses in Gremster had previously been occupied by Basil and Helen Tulloch and their family of four sons and two daughters. Their son, William, later wrote an account of why they had to leave:[6] *A most*

Looking across Bluemull Sound to Unst and Fetlar from Gremster.
© Andy Gear

remarkable event occurred in summer 1866, Major Cameron ... gave over his lands into the hands of a man named John Walker. This man is said to have caught the Major on his weak side ... Walker was hated by the North Yell people. I have no hesitation in saying as much as the evil one himself. The people were so enraged that Walker's life was threatened. William Tulloch went on to explain how the new regulations for working the crofts and the lack of hill pastures had been the cause of a number of families leaving their holdings. This seems to have been why the Tulloch family flit to Fetlar.

If you walk to Burraness today you will see the ruins of a cluster of five croft houses near the broch. In 1866 about thirty adults and bairns were living there. But the following year, 1867, Walker and Henderson were walking among the empty shells of a deserted toonship. Moving on past the recently occupied crofts, perhaps they discussed the line of the fence planned to enclose the sheep farm which had already been advertised for let, or the use of the empty houses to make sheep shelters. As they approached the still tenanted, neighbouring toonship of Kirkabister, two young men ran up to meet them. Subsequent events are, of course, open to question, but we can read the evidence given later in Court and play at being judge and jury.

In a precognition[7] against the young men given on 20th February, John Walker stated: *I have lately entered into an arrangement with Major*

Ruins of a cluster of five croft houses at Burraness. Backs and some gables have been retained to form part of a large walled enclosure. © Andy Gear

Cameron, Proprietor of certain lands in North Yell, for effecting certain changes in the mode of occupancy of his property in that quarter. These changes in so far as seemed necessary were some time ago intimated to the tenantry but gave so much dissatisfaction that I have repeatedly both directly and indirectly been threatened with violence if I presumed to attempt to carry the proposed changes into effect.

On Wednesday the thirteenth of this month when I was in the vacant and unoccupied room of Burraness in North Yell in company with David Henderson, two young men came up to me and asked where I was going. I replied that I was going to the adjoining room of Kirkabister.

Although a reason for the visit to Kirkabister was not given in court, if we read an extract from a letter written by Thomas Edmondston of Buness to Dr Basil Spence, we find a possible explanation:[8] *Walker was in North Yell last week intending to measure a 'Town' there, but was met on the outskirts of the 'Town' by two young men, but lately returned from the south, and apparently imbued with liberal principles. These lads informed Mr W. that they did not intend to have their farms measured just then, and hinted very unmistakeably that if Mr Walker dared to enter their premises he would require to be carried thence.* Edmondston added, *we have managed to keep Walker at arms length.*

Back to Walker's evidence: *They said I would better take some other road and not go any farther because if I dared come inside the dykes (meaning the dykes of Kirkabister) they would knock me down and knock my brains out.*

The two young men were John Anderson, whose parents stayed in Kirkabister, and Andrew Gray from a neighbouring estate. According to Walker they were trying to prevent him and his companion from entering the toonship of Kirkabister. The houses and arable land of a toon or

There is little sign of the croft houses of Kirkabister as the stones were used to build this sheep fank which was completed by December 1869. The ruin in the foreground must have served some other purpose to have survived. © *Andy Gear*

toonship were separated from the common grazing of the scattald by 'hill dykes' which kept animals out of the crops during the growing season.

Undaunted, Henderson and Walker carried on, and by the time they arrived at the houses of Kirkabister, Henderson had apprised Walker as to the identity of their troublesome escorts. Continuing Walker's evidence: *Gray and Anderson went into the first house we came to and while the Tenant, whose name I forget, was outside speaking to me they came out repeating their threats of violence and passed on to the next house occupied by Andrew Anderson, father of the said John Anderson, which they entered. After remaining there a few minutes they came out accompanied by another young man said to be William Gilbert Nisbet ... The three men came up to me and I cautioned Nisbet to have nothing to do with his companions. He told me to go to hell, and challenged me to fight. I believe they continued their annoyance and threatening language for nearly an hour.*

So Andrew Gray, age 21, John Anderson, age 22 and William Gilbert Nisbet, age 23, charged with Breach of Peace and Assault, were taken to court on 22nd March. There, Andrew Gray told his side of the story. His father's croft was not on Cameron's property, but the worry was that Hoseason, their laird, and Cameron shared ownership of the scattald used by the Grays. He had heard of change in the mode of management of the estate, and Walker was to be the instrument of that change. Then he came on to the events of the thirteenth: *I saw Mr Walker at Burraness in North Yell in company with David Henderson ... Mr Walker first of all said he would shoot us and I thought that too strong language and called him a Cowherd. Then we asked him in to Kirkabister to have Tea and joked with him to give us one of his daughters for entertaining him as we were young men.*

I did not threaten to knock David Henderson down. I merely said to him why would he assist Mr Walker to shove poor people out. He said if he could, by that, get a days work why should he not do it, and I replied that I would rather beg than do it. That was all that passed between David Henderson and me. We left Mr Walker at Kirkabister and went home.

Fifty-year-old David Henderson was also in court. He told how Walker had called a meeting at Cullivoe the previous hairst[9] to tell the tenantry of the change of management and that the scattald was to be taken from them. This had caused great dissatisfaction, not only among Major Cameron's tenants, but among those of adjoining proprietors who shared the scattald. Henderson continued: *One day in the month of February last, I accompanied Mr Walker to Burraness and Kirkabister, two places belonging to Major Cameron. Burraness is vacant but Kirkabister is still occupied by Tenants. As we approached the Dykes of Burraness Mr Walker stopped to speak to a woman and the day being rough I took shelter under a peat stack. At this time I observed two men coming running towards us from Kirkabister ... They first came up to me and asked where I was going and I replied, "To Kirkabister in company with Mr Walker." They said I had better turn back. They then went up to Mr Walker and demanded to know where he was going and he replied that he was going to Kirkabister. They told him he had better not and on his repeating his determination to go through John Anderson swore that if he entered within the town dykes of Kirkabister he would knock him down. Both of the men then broke out into abuse of Mr Walker and did all they could to intimidate him from going to Kirkabister. Andrew Gray did not threaten to knock Mr Walker down nor make use of any threatening language in particular that I can call to mind, but he was conjunct with John Anderson, both of them appearing as one in their attempt to intimidate Mr Walker and both were equally abusive.*

While we were in Kirkabister they all abused me for being in company with Mr Walker, and Andrew Gray said he had a good mind to knock me down. None of them challenged me to fight and I did not see any of them attempt to throw off his jacket nor hear any of them challenge Mr Walker to fight.

THREATS AND BOASTS

I cannot say what the real intention of the men was as I could not read their minds but they were very fierce and violent in their manner and did appear to be serious in their threats.

Robert Nisbet, father of William Gilbert, also gave evidence. On the day of the rumpus Walker had told Robert that he would send William Gilbert to jail for his behaviour. Robert had apologised for his son, saying he must have been influenced by others, but the words were not out of his mouth when up came young Willie Gibbie himself, and when Walker repeated his threat to send him to jail, Willie Gibbie said he was welcome do so! His father emphatically denied any knowledge of a conspiracy to intimidate Walker and averred that no threats or abuse were made in his presence.

The three young men were fined £1:1s each for *wickedly and feloniously attacking and assaulting John Walker.*[10]

Burraness with Fetlar in the background. The remains of the Broch still stands on the point with a cluster of croft houses to the right.
© *Andy Gear*

We can't tell whether Andrew Gray knew that this was one of the farms advertised for let as early as January 1867, but he was right that the people were to be 'shoved out'. The actions of the 'young men' couldn't prevent it happening, but their protest was courageous and would at least have drawn attention to what was going on.

Within a year of this incident David Henderson was employed, by Walker,[11] *to look after the enclosure to be found South of Cullivoe* [Gremster] *with the stock thereon and any orders I may from time to time give.* His wage was – £10 per annum in cash, six bolls of meal, ten cwt. potatoes or ground for same, grazing for one cow in summer and permission to go for five or six weeks to the herring fishing provided his family did the work during his absence.

So that was why Henderson had got a lease under special terms and why he was allowed to keep a dog.

JOHN WALKER'S SHETLAND

** ** **

I have visited your property about twelve times – had the whole tenants meeting me four times in Yell and Delting and once in Unst and visited every farm twice many places oftener.
From John Walker's report to Major Cameron at the end of his first year as factor

The previous September Walker had written to Peter Sandison, Cullivoe:[12] *I hope all the nonsense that I am told is in your neighbours heads has disappeared as I desire to meet the tenants as their friend.*
The crofters never saw Walker as a friend. Could he really have deluded himself or others into thinking they would? However, he is confident that he has Major Cameron's approval when writing on 23rd September, 1867:[13] *I am proud to find that my exertions so far in managing your Properties has your approval – you cannot however be convinced that our exertions are for the best until I realise my expectation with regard to the Improvements – I feel confident of success altho. I have and will have to struggle through difficulties which were not to be expected – still with your kind confidence and support I can do anything.*
So he did admit to having difficulties. We can only presume that his employer didn't question what these difficulties were, or was content to leave it to his factor to sort out.
At the end of 1867 Walker gave the Major a lengthy statement on his management of the estate up to Martinmas.[14] He also presented his account books requesting that the Major examine them carefully. The report started with a detailed list of his activities, mainly negotiations for exchanges and leases of property from other proprietors, most of which he had drawn up himself. These included a twenty-five year lease of 300 acres at West-o-Firth from Thomas Irvine, *thus making a very desirable sheep run of above 2,000 acres within a small volume*; a nineteen year lease of Windhouse, *rendered necessary to save fencing and to avoid the erection of a house etc*; a twelve year lease with John Spence & Co of the most of the Garth and Annsbrae lands in Unst; and the legal division of the Brough and Sandwick scattalds in North Yell which was, at that time, still running its course through the Court of Session.
After listing several lesser leases, and the arrangements about kelp shores, he arrived at number 22, and here there is a discernible change of tone. He began by stating that *putting the small tenants under suitable leases has occupied much time*. He claimed that in Delting the change was complete, but in Yell *I believe many tenants who have left the property desire to return*. We know of one – James Clark mentioned in the last chapter. *But I consider this undesirable, as there have quite enough*

remained and taking them back now would injure my prestige in management. Those who left were frightened away by designing would-be-friends, who now leave them to their fate ...

By the would-be-friends he meant the merchants, who were to crop up again in 1871 when Walker was presenting evidence for the need for investigation into 'Truck' in Shetland (Chapter 12). At that time he declared that the merchants were solely responsible for the tenants not accepting his lease policy. Well, he had to blame somebody!

During his first year of management he had written over six hundred letters and received a similar number. There had also been law suits: *In consequence of the conduct of a few of the Tenants leaving the Property I have been necessitated to enforce your rights by appeal to the Sheriff Court in some five cases, but in all have been successful.*

In the last paragraph of the report he invited the Major to commend or censure his management, *hoping that you will seek information upon any point you may not understand. I desire your frank approval or otherwise of my actings.* I think the latter request was a shrewd move on Walker's part. If things went wrong, he had it in writing that Cameron had been asked at the start and finish of the document to examine the books, voice an opinion, and take part in decisions on what was to happen on his estate. The report ends: *I do not wish to claim more than a conscientious discharge of my duty – if I have fulfilled that to your satisfaction I am indifferent to the invidious abuse of others.*

It's a great pity the Major didn't stop to wonder why his factor was receiving 'invidious abuse' from anybody.

1   Ed. James Hunter, *For the People's Cause, From the Writings of John Murdoch*, Edinburgh 1986, p.132
2   Gardie Papers L.B.1 p.20
3   Gardie Papers L.B.1 p.15
4   Gardie Papers L.B.1 p.39
5   A group of houses with arable land and associated common grazing in the scattald
6   S.A. 2/104
7   S.A. SC 12/6/1867/1
8   S.A. D 12/116/6/14
9   Harvest time
10   S.A. SC 12/6/1867/12
11   Gardie Papers L.B.2 p.603
12   Gardie Papers L.B.1 p.35
13   Gardie Papers L.B.2 p.128
14   Gardie Papers 1867/655

Chapter Six

DEVELOPMENT AND OBSTRUCTION IN YELL

I'm sorry that the innocent must suffer but I am resolved to clear out every tenant in North Yell if the mischief continues.
John Walker writing to William Pennie, October 1867

WILLIAM Pennie has already been mentioned briefly as working in Yell as grieve for Garth and Annsbrae, and before investigating any more of the problems he had to deal with, it seems appropriate to look at how he was employed.

Early in 1864 John William Spence had let Windhouse, in Yell, to William Pennie. The mansion house and estate of Windhouse, including Volister and Lumbister, lie to the east side of Whalefirth. Today the ruins of the house (heightened and extended in the 1880s) can still be seen on the ridge of the hill, famous now because it is said to be haunted, for dark deeds associated with the Neven lairds, and the mystery of a human skeleton found by workmen in 1887.[1]

Spence wrote[2] to his uncle expressing relief that he had *got it off our hands. It has been nothing but a dead loss.* He is sure that Pennie, who had previously been grieve to Mr Mill at Lund, will make a good tenant: *He is a very steady, hard working man. He gets the sheep in steel bow*[3] *and the house and farm (exclusive of Thomas Johnson's farm which is £4 :10s) at a yearly rent of £40.*

On 21st December, 1866 John Walker wrote to John William Spence:[4] *I now beg on behalf of Major Cameron to offer for a lease of*

Windhouse. © *Andy Gear*

Windhouse and Scattald as occupied by William S. Pennie and Thomas Johnston for 25 years from Martinmas next, the Lease however to be in two periods of 5 & 20 years respectively – upon the understanding that, as your part, you give the power to sublet. And a week later:[5] *That we get possession of Windhouse and the right to carry on the proposed Improvements.*

So in February 1867, William Shand Pennie and Windhouse (including Volister and Lumbister), came under John Walker's jurisdiction. Walker clarified Pennie's conditions of service:[6] *I now put in writing what I offered you to engage with me from one year from Whitsunday first, as general worker on the Yell properties I may have in my own hands. The Principal thing to do will be the taking charge of the grounds – looking after the Fencing – keeping other stock from trespassing – and probably looking after a few sheep which I may put on the ground – Any time I may be at Windhouse your wife would have to wait upon me.* Pennie's wife, Elizabeth Jaffray, had been a servant at Belmont at the time of their marriage at Watly, Unst, in 1861.[7] *The wages I offer is £22* <u>Twenty Two</u> *pounds in money, Eight Bolls Oatmeal, Two Bolls Potatoes and keep of a cow for seven months – you of course have accommodation in Windhouse but would have to secure fuel for yourself and sufficient to fire the House.*

The fencing material ordered by Walker was top quality and strands of three ply wire and strainers can still be found in North Yell almost a hundred and forty years later. J. D. Scott of Brechin, writing to negotiate a contract for erecting the Garth estate fences, strongly recommended that a 'Darlington Rugester' cast-iron, self-fixing and winding straining pillar, be placed every 350 yards, at six shillings per 100 yards extra cost. J. D. Scott would no doubt be pleased to know that some of these strainers still stand. The one in this photo was taken at Moss Houll in North Yell.
© *John Ballantyne*

On the face of it, a fair deal. At that time £22, plus the perks, would have been a reasonable wage for jobs that don't seem too onerous. But had Walker given a fair description of the job? It's not clear what he had in mind for 'Yell Properties I may have in my own hands'. However Walker's air of ownership did not escape the eyes of others.

25th November, 1867, from John William Spence to Thomas Irvine, Midbrake, North Yell:[8] *I have let Windhouse to Major Cameron, and Mr Walker, in negotiating with you for a lease of part of your Scattald, will be doing so on behalf of the Major and not on his own account.*

So what exactly did Pennie have to do for his wages? One job was *looking after the fencing*. A great deal of fencing material had to be imported, not only for Windhouse, but for miles of enclosure over extensive areas of scattald in North Yell. Cargo[9] landed at Mid Yell on 25th May, 1867 included, 2,000 larch posts; 2 barrels coal tar; 30 bundles wire; 6 x 3ft. gates; 6 x 4ft. gates; 2 x 8ft. gates. On the same day at Kirkabister, Basta Voe, 700 larch and 800 red wood posts, and 2 barrels tar were landed.

Pennie had to deal with the fencing material when it arrived, and often the women in the district were employed to carry and stack the posts. They also carried wire as we are told by Nina Charleson, Camb, Yell:[10] *Dey* [women] *kerried everything, never spaek aboot whit dey didna kerry. You ken whin Walker began ta rail aa da hills da women, weel, da men hed ta wirk, I tink, sae muckle an kerry stakes an stuff, an da women kerried da wires. Fur Elizabeth Robertson kerried wire till sho took da skin aff o her back.*

And then there was 'the mischief'. Naturally, the tenants didn't want their scattald fenced off, so Pennie had to cope with various acts of vandalism carried out on the fences in protest at the enclosures. Pennie to Walker, 30th May, 1867:[11] *I have been at Kirkabister and am sorry to say that the whole larch stabs below the East House is all burned, about 350. The red wood ones was quite close to them but are not touched. Middle Houses one cask tar burned, no stabs hurt. Westmost Houses a fire had been kindled but only about 20 destroyed. The tenants observed the fire yesterday morning between 5 & 6 when the whole was destroyed they appear all to be vexed about it. Andrew Anderson's people did not go to bed till 12 o'clock all was safe then.*

And again on 6th June:[12] *I was at Kirkabister on Tuesday. The rest of the stabs is safe but the scamps had kicked in the bung of the other Tar Barrel and the most of it is lost. A barrel of tar had also been burned, with nothing left but the iron hoops.*

A doubtless irate Walker wrote to C. G. Duncan the Procurator Fiscal in Lerwick:[13] *William Pennie knows from hearsay that two women* were the parties engaged and he has written me that it is understood the light or burning peat was taken out of William Irvine, Kirkabister's, house for the purpose. The officer you send can take Pennie along with him if required.

So a case of malicious mischief was brought against some persons unknown, of burning stakes at Kirkabister, North Yell.[14] Giving evidence on 29th August Pennie declared: *I have not the most distant suspicion of who may have done the mischief – I was told by a girl of the name of Coghile or Russell residing in the Southmost house of Southerhouse of Basta – daughter or step-daughter of John Russell – and also by Daniel More in Colvister* (Daniel from chapter 4) *that a daughter of William Irvine's in Kirkabister had said that if she got a pound she would tell the house from which the fire was got that had consumed the posts.*

Osla Barbara Irvine, aged about fourteen, daughter of William Irvine of Kirkabister, gave evidence: *I mind the day when a stack of wood which was built close to my father's house was set on fire. The wood was intended for putting up fences and was built on the ground by William Pennie. The first I knew about it was from my mother who called me when in my bed about 7 o'clock in the morning that some one had set Mr Walker's wood on fire. I got out of bed and clad me and ran down to the place where I found one of the stacks reduced to ashes. The bottom of it was still burning. I do not know how or by whom the wood was set on fire. I never said to anyone that I would tell for a Pound where the fire came from. I had some conversation with Ann & Peggy Brown who reside in Burraness as to the affair – I had gone to their house for some blaand to my mother a few days after the burning. They were speaking about it and one of them remarked that it would be as bad a job for anyone who gave the fire as for the body that burned the wood. To this I remarked that I would for Mr Walker's £20 that it was found out, meaning by that that the punishment would be so heavy that I would not on any account wish to see anyone subjected to it. I know that there was a public report that I said I would tell if I got a pound, but it was a downright lie. My father and all the men of the neighbourhood except Andrew Anderson were at the fishing at the Gloup Station the night of the fire.*

I cannot write never having been at school.

Ann and Peggy Brown were two elderly, unmarried sisters who lived at Braewick, described as an outset. It is not difficult to imagine the fourteen-year-old excitedly gossiping about the burning and possibly pretending to know more about it than she really did. Or maybe the fire was carried from her father's house and she knew it all.

Walker was incensed at the damage done to the fencing materials. In an attempt to quash the resistance it was decided to make an example of two boys, although no firm evidence was found to prove their guilt. On 23rd September, 1867 he again wrote to C. G. Duncan:[15] *I have no doubt that you are resolved to bring the Anderson boys to justice, but might I urge your doing so as soon as possible for the mischief they did is only part of a system which still continues – in fact only last week we had a considerable quantity of fencing torn down at Kirkabister (where they burned the wood) and a warning in their case might operate in that of others.*

What crime had the Anderson boys committed to justify Walker urging the law to hold them up as an example?

On the morning of 30th July, 1867 the two brothers, Edward and James Anderson, walked from their home at Logie, Sellafirth, North Yell, to Gloup Voe to collect fish heads from a boat lying there. This is a walk through the hills of approximately four miles as the bonxie flies. At Gloup

Looking towards Bayanne and across Basta Voe to Colvister, from the gable of the old house at Logie. © *Andy Gear*

Voe that morning a barrel with some tar in it was overturned and lay on its side with the contents spilling over the beach.

The Old Parish Records allow us to calculate that James Anderson was then twelve and Edward, his brother, twenty. In court[16] they both declared they didn't know what age they were. We learn from the Prison Records that they were both very small, no doubt suffering from malnutrition. Edward – at 4ft 11ins weighed 84lbs; James, 4ft 7ins, 63lbs. They would have needed to be strong to topple a barrel two thirds full of tar. Edward's toes curled underneath his feet so he was never able to wear shoes, only sukkalegs (stockings without feet).[17]

Asked at the Sheriff Court about the barrel, James declared: *It had been tumbled over before we saw it ... William Pennie came after us. We had come a piece past when he came after us ... There was a little tar on my hand before I left home. My brother had got the tar for a little ship he was making.*

William Pennie, in a statement given at Uyeasound on 29th August said: *I am Superintendant of Works on Major Cameron's property in North Yell. For some weeks past I have been employed superintending the erection of fencing on the property adjoining Gloup Voe. On the 30th July last, when employed in that neighbourhood, I had a barrel containing about two thirds of the fill of Coaltar standing on the seabeach above highwater mark. I left the place to fetch some stakes accompanied by Charlotte Scollay, Robina Robertson, Elizabeth Smith, Willa Smith and Mary Smith. We were absent about an hour and three quarters and on our return I found the barrel with tar capsized and the contents poured out on the ground. The only persons to be seen near the place were two boys who were going South from the Voe.*

Looking across Gloup Voe towards Wast-a-Firth. Memorial for fishermen lost in the 1881 fishing disaster in foreground.   © *Andy Gear*

DEVELOPMENT AND OBSTRUCTION IN YELL

As we know, Pennie caught up with the boys who denied overturning the barrel. However, when asked their names they claimed to be sons of Thomas Irvine of East Sandwick. Pennie was not deluded by this as he happened to know that Thomas Irvine had no sons. They then alleged their father's name was Ramsay and they were Thomas Ramsay and James Irvine Ramsay. In his statement Pennie also said he had seen tar on the younger boy's hand and a patch of soft tar on his 'frock'.

Charlotte Scollay or Williamson, from West o Firth, was one of the women employed by Pennie to carry wood for fencing from the West Side of Gloup Voe to Vigon. She gave evidence at Bayan [Sellafirth] on 31st August: *The only persons to be seen near the spot were two boys who came up to us from a boat lying about a bughts length* [forty fathoms] *off. They had been taking fish heads from the boat. I hailed them and asked if they had spilled Mr Walker's tar and they replied no – that they had passed higher up the brae than where the tar cask was standing ... It was the youngest one who spoke to me ... the oldest boy is somewhat silly. I did not observe any tar on their persons or hands – I did not think of looking.*

Robina Robertson corroborated Charlotte's evidence but added: *I think it possible that a party might have turned over the cask and escaped before we discovered it, but it must have been thrown down immediately before as the tar was still summing slowly.*

David Anderson, the boys' father, went to Pennie the day after the incident to say that his boys denied having meddled with the cask, but whether innocent or guilty he was willing to pay the value of the tar rather than be put to farther trouble about it. His offer was turned down and the boys were found guilty and imprisoned in the jail at Fort Charlotte, Lerwick, for six days. When released they were shipped to Burravoe where they were met by their father who carried Edward home on his back.[18]

Although once more in Boyndlie, Major Cameron knew about this incident even before Walker wrote to the Procurator Fiscal requesting that an example be made of the Anderson boys. On 26th August, the Major wrote:[19] *I hope the Procurator Fiscal will blacken the faces of the youths who emptied our tar into Gloup Voe.*

**   **   **

Now to return to William Pennie's duties. He had to deliver letters and messages – mostly unpleasant, some threatening.
Dear William,   *21st September, 1867*[20]
I hear the Basta Voe folk are doing mischief again – I enclose letters to the tenants there and to their proprietors – those you will deliver at once

67

personally and you will let the other folk's tenants read the notice I have written. You may tell them that come what may they will suffer one way or another – See that you get the names of any trespassers within the Fence and send me them. Scott[21] *writes that he is stuck again for material at Windhouse. How is this? The lambs and cattle are down but I have not seen them. Do you know of a good young calver cow to calve at the end of November?*

I hope you are managing to push through with the bustle of work.

Yours sincerely, John Walker

We don't know how Pennie managed to 'let the other folk's tenants read the notice', but a copy survived so we can read it:[22]

TO THE TENANTS AND OTHERS NEAR KIRKABISTER

This is to point out that any destruction to the fencing at Kirkabister or elsewhere can only hurt those living in the locality since the fence will have to be repaired at the expense of others than Major Cameron and until the fence be repaired all animals found trespassing will be strictly poinded. Mr Walker therefore wishes to show those who think they are injuring him that the loss must fall upon themselves.   Maryfield, 21st September, 1867

Pennie was ordered to personally deliver letters to William Spence, Bigsetter; Thomas Moar, Cunningster; and in Sellafirth to Robert Anderson and Meran Donaldson. All these letters were identical and read:[23] *This is to inform you that unless you can discover and inform me of the names of the parties damaging our fences that there will be no chance of your remaining a tenant upon the property after Martinmas 1868.*

Robert Nisbet, his wife and family lived at Uncadale which lies between Kirkabister and Cunnister. His letter was in a slightly different vein:[24] *This is to inform you that unless you can inform me of the names of the parties destroying our fences or <u>trespassing</u> within the same – there will be no chance of you remaining on this property and that the rent of your house till Whitsunday next will not be less than <u>Five Pounds</u>. Of course if the destruction to our Property ceases I may not charge any rent.* Notes to the tenants above all began with a stark 'Sir', and ended 'Yours etc'.

However, Mr Hoseason Jr., of Mossbank, proprietor in Basta Voe area, merits a 'Dear Sir':[25] *I am just informed that your <u>peculiar people</u> in Sandwick, North Yell are commencing to destroy our fencing – May I ask you to send them such a notice as would deter them from doing further mischief as should more damage be done we must get the County to bear the loss and keep a few extra policemen to check matters. I would be glad that you sent a notice by their mail.*

Yours sincerely, John Walker

DEVELOPMENT AND OBSTRUCTION IN YELL

But smaller proprietors like William Nisbet of Cunnister, fell into the 'Sir' and 'Yours etc' category:[26] *I am informed that some evil disposed persons are injuring the newly erected fence at Kirkabister: this is to point out to you as a proprietor that you will be bound to pay your share of repairing all damage done and also must have to fear the expense of a special policeman should the mischief be continued. I hope therefore that you will use your endeavour to find out the offenders and save further taxes being brought upon the lands.*

Another small landowner, and thorn in Walker's flesh, was James Brown of Cunnister. He is described in the 1871 census as 'Proprietor of 4½ merks Land & Fisherman'. Walker wrote to him on 18th September, 1867:[27] *William Pennie writes me that you object to the line of Fence between Cunningster and Uncadale at which I am surprised as Major Cameron was entitled to insist upon the Scattald up to the Cunningster dykes for Burraness and Kirkabister and may do so yet – To accommodate you for this season only I have sent north Step Styles so that you may get your peats and we will allow you to keep for this winter at least your quarter share in the Mill – If the people in the neighbourhood stop abusing our Property certain privileges may still be allowed but any annoyances must entail our taking effectual means to prevent it.* In a letter to Pennie on the same day he comments – *James Brown may whistle about the fence.* I wish we had a record of James Brown's reaction to the step-styles.

Five months later James Brown received another epistle from the Garth Factor. William John, James' oldest son, had not only been seen trespassing on Kirkabister on 23rd January, 1868 (tenants were still living in Kirkabister at that time), but he was also said to have threatened Robert Mouat, who was employed by Walker. With what, or why he threatened Mouat we don't know, but as he was shortly afterwards to marry one of the Spence lasses from Bigsetter, perhaps he was just trespassing in order to court his sweetheart. This time Walker wrote:[28] *If your son is aware of the wrong he has done and chooses to write to me saying he is sorry for his conduct and promises not to repeat it, I may forgive him this once, but should I not hear satisfactorily from him within the next ten days I will put the matter into the hands of the Sheriff.* William surely decided to toe the line as he apologised for having 'ignorantly trespassed' in the park at Kirkabister and that he would not do it again – ever.[29]

Back on 1st October, 1867, Walker was still issuing dire threats to the North Yell tenants, with a bit of blackmail thrown in. I wonder how Pennie reacted to this irrational epistle:[30] *I'm vexed to hear about the damage done at Kirkabister, I think you had better offer to the people in the neighbourhood that if they pay the expense of repairing the fence I may so far overlook the matter – if they do not they must put up with the consequences – I'm sorry that the innocent must suffer but I am resolved to clear out every tenant in North Yell if the mischief continues – you may tell James Brown of Cunningster that if he does not find out the offenders we will take care to secure the most of the Scattald lying round Cunningster which was intended at one time to have not insisted upon to oblige them ... You may tell the Basta tenants and Thomas Nisbet who goes to Stenesetter that it must be their turn to be warned should any more damage be done and not found out.*

Another of Pennie's problems was *keeping other stock from trespassing.* The small Shetland sheep could bore through fencing that would defy the larger Cheviots and Blackfaces. Spence still had sheep in Windhouse, in the care of his shepherd, Thomas Johnson, and they were constantly straying onto the ground Pennie was trying to cultivate. *Thomas will not look after them,* he complained.

Straying animals were to be poinded, that is, confined until redeemed by their owners. To keep Pennie right on the 'Poinding Charges' he was to make, Walker sent the following list:[31]

Damage – sheep 1/-; cattle 2/-; horses 2/-
Expenses of catching @ 5/- a day
Keep – sheep 4d per day; cattle 1/- per day; horses 1/6 per day, besides the wages of any person who notices them.

Hefty charges for crofters who could expect to get £3 to £4 for a cow at a sale. Later Pennie was urged by his boss:[32] *I hope you are making your wages at poinding.*

Another responsibility for Pennie, *probably looking after a few sheep which I may put on the ground.* When R. Scott Skirving wrote his report on *The Agriculture of the Isles of Shetland* in 1874, he claimed that Major Cameron and Mr Walker had 3000 blackfaced sheep in Windhouse. Pennie left Windhouse in 1869 and even then the flock was more than just 'a few'.

Instructions poured in steadily by mail to William:[33] *I enclose particulars of Cullivoe Sale which you can let people know about ... I'll send you a notebook to keep account of your daily work etc and a small one to keep jottings when from home ... I also hope all of you are watching that no scab gets into the skin of any of your sheep or lambs ... By next mail I'll send you particulars as to such Tenants as have to send Cattle to the sale ... The 'Prince Consort' was lost on Saturday morning, lost totally. If you see Mr Keith tell him his Turnip seed went with her ... I will send full particulars as to the landing of posts at the different points ... You will require to get the sawn Timber and Gates to Windhouse at once in case of mischief ... The posts will have to be tarred before carting ... You will see that somebody at each place stacks the stabs nicely up so soon as landed – women will do this best I think ... I will of course first be at Cullivoe when you will meet me ... I hope you have got all the pastures burnt black with this fine weather ... I would like the calf cow bought from John Oman sent to Ulsta and boated over to Mossbank ... continue your utmost to secure trespassing stock ... I presume you got Nicol Moar's cow ... What have you set Robbie Mouat to do? ... Get a few good farrow cows as cheaply as you can ... You will require to push on with the West-o-Firth Fencing ... It is likely some of the sheep may have sore feet with the steamer but paring should soon cure them ... You'll require to spend a day measuring the drains finished by George Fraser ... I'll send you a padlock for the West-o-Firth gate ... I may be up any day with Mr Umphray ... You'll not forget about Nicol Moar's cow or the money ... Try to pick up some stock ... I'll see to send Robbie a barrow meantime he can be purling on other work when the fence is finished.* And so on.

On 2nd November, 1867 he started a string of orders to Pennie with:[34] *I suppose after your long holiday that you are pushing on with the odds and ends to do.* As there seems to be no break in the flow of letters of instruction that hairst, it is difficult to imagine when Pennie had a day off, never mind a long holiday! Maybe it was considered to be a holiday one day in the summer of '68 when he was told[35] to meet Walker's brother at Westsandwick, take him to Graveland, row him across Whalefirth, walk up the Daal o Lumbister to the road, and on to Cullivoe where he would get a boat and dispatch the brother to Unst. The instructions ended with – *Now try and not be half a mile from Westsandwick at the right time.*

That hairst it became obvious that all was not well with the flock. The price of lambs had gone down. Walker wrote: *The account of the sheep is very melancholy.*[36] There were other problems. October 1868, to Pennie:[37] *I am more than vexed at the information yours of 21st contains. As it takes no time or trouble worth speaking of to keep stock clean but much time, trouble and expense to make clean animals allowed by carelessness to get dirty – I cannot agree with you that you have had so much to do this season as to prevent you seeing to the stock, especially when I more than once wrote to you to keep a sharp look out. The wedders, after what you say cannot be sold but must be bathed at once and heavily. I send by steamer a 50 gallon cask ... See that the bathing is at once set to and done effectually – The sheep must be permanently cleansed in three weeks else I shall be far from satisfied ... unless written to otherwise you will arrange to ship the 70 H.B. lambs reared in Windhouse. Have the white boat and a sixareen filled with them on the lea side of Burraness about 11.30 am on Monday where the steamer should pick them up.*

JOHN WALKER'S SHETLAND

By December Pennie was on his way out:[38] *Dear William, Seeing that I must get one or two thorough shepherds I fear it would be impossible for me to give you either more wages or more allowances – indeed as the wages are very much lower in the South I must take all the shepherds wages down from Whitsunday. Mr Jaffrey told me that he could make room for you at Uyea and if Elizabeth and you thought you would be better there it would be wrong of me to object. Think the matter over and let me know at once.*

Pennie replied that Walker should be at liberty to engage another in his place as he *could not stop for the same, far less to be taken down.*[39]

Elizabeth and William Pennie left Yell in the summer of 1869, and George Murray, a shepherd from Caithness took over at Windhouse.[40] The Pennies went to Uyea where William died in 1891. One of his last duties for Walker appears in a note dated April 1869. *Have sent 210 oysters to Mrs Walker.*[41]

** ** **

I am utterly unaware of any possible right you have to order me in any manner.
James Irvine writing to John Walker, 14/3/1867

Resistance to Walker's plans came from as far away as Bath, though still with a Yell connection. Thomas Irvine of Midbrake, North Yell, had a nephew James Irvine, an architect, who lived at Coome Down near Bath and was acknowledged for his work in the restoration of many ancient buildings including the Abbey at Bath.[42] On 1st March, 1867, Walker wrote to James Irvine about the division of the Brough and Sandwick scattalds in North Yell, enclosing a Deed of Submission for which he required a signature. James Irvine took umbrage at Walker's request and wrote to Major Cameron telling him so. Cameron replied, explaining that by signing the document Irvine would save them all unnecessary expense, adding, *I saw the letter before it was dispatched and had I supposed it could have given any one offence I certainly would not have allowed it to go. I therefore consider your reply as discourteous to myself.*

Meanwhile, Thomas Irvine was also writing to his nephew pointing out that opposition to the division would involve heavy expense by a Court of Session division: *No one can repudiate a certain scheme now about being introduced here the more strongly than I do – but still I must submit to skathold divisions.* Extra expense would have been worrying to Thomas as he was already suffering financial difficulties.

But James was not to be swayed. His reply to Major Cameron was adamant, ending: *You have my reply and you will see it is final.* He felt so strongly about the whole issue that he composed what he titled a 'Memorandum to Posterity': *I was perfectly aware of the desirableness of doing all that could be done to improve agriculture in Shetland. I would have readily agreed to it had it been for that end. But as it was merely to get rid of the common rights, to exterminate Human life and make all barren sheep walks and cattle pastures, and as I had heard enough of the curses not loud but deep that were uttered in distress by poor old creatures turned out of a miserable home in their old age to knock holes in the banks or wander forth and die in foreign lands I declined to assent to it. I had neither the power or wealth to resist successfully but I could retard for a year the fortunes of the day and did so and refused all assent of mine.*

Walker, writing later to Thomas Irvine, declared: *Your nephew is like fleas, annoying but powerless.*[43]

1 Robert L. Johnson, 'The Windhouse Skeleton', *Shetland Life* No.79
2 S.A. D 12/142/32
3 A contract whereby stock was received from the owner with obligation to return the same amount or value when the lease expired. Meanwhile the lessee could make a profit from the sale of lambs etc.
4 Gardie Papers L.B.1 p.75
5 Gardie Papers L.B.1 p.80
6 Gardie Papers L.B.1 p.126
7 O.P.R. Unst
8 S.A. Midbrake Papers 392/2/16
9 Gardie Papers L.B.1 p.214
10 S.A. 3/1/37/1
11 Gardie Papers 1867/249
12 Gardie Papers 1867/263
13 Gardie Papers L.B.2 p.73
14 S.A. AD 22/2/9/038
15 Gardie Papers L.B.2 p.127
16 S.A. AD 22/2/9/52
17 Information from Ann Fraser who can remember 'Auld Ned' as he was then known, when she was a bairn in Sellafirth
18 Oral Tradition – Ann Fraser
19 Gardie Papers 1867/386
20 Gardie Papers L.B.2 p.124
21 J.D. Scott & Co., from Brechin, had a contract to supply and erect sheep fencing
22 Gardie Papers L.B.2 p.125
23 Gardie Papers L.B.2 pp.121-123
24 Gardie Papers L.B.2 p.121
25 Gardie Papers L.B.2 p.123
26 Gardie Papers L.B.2 p.126
27 Gardie Papers L.B.2 p.111
28 Gardie Papers L.B.2 p.292
29 Gardie Papers 1868/101
30 Gardie Papers L.B.2 p.146

JOHN WALKER'S SHETLAND

31 Gardie Papers L.B.2 p.143
32 Gardie Papers L.B.2 p.159
33 Gardie Papers L.B.2 extracts from various letters
34 Gardie Papers L.B.2 p.184
35 Gardie Papers L.B.2 p.458
36 Gardie Papers L.B.2 p.458
37 Gardie Papers L.B.2 p.557
38 Gardie Papers L.B.2 p.604
39 Gardie Papers 1869/6
40 Gardie Papers L.B.2 p.770
41 Gardie Papers 1869/207
42 S.A. 4/1080
43 Gardie Papers L.B.2 p.238

Chapter Seven

KELP AND OTHER BURNING ISSUES

By refusing to pay as the other buyers do you compel us to prosecute the burners when they will suffer as much as the Little Roe tenant.
John Walker writing to Arthur Nicolson, Gutcher 12/12/1867

THE collecting and burning of kelp in the 19th century was carried out in the western and northern isles of Scotland by crofters, often by the womenfolk. When questioned at the Truck Commission about the number of people he employed to gather seaweed, Peter Sandison of Cullivoe replied: *It is women who do that. They form themselves into companies of two or three or four. They gather the seaweed and make the kelp, and then bring it to a merchant to sell ... If they ask cash they get it.* However they usually got 6d more per cwt. if they took goods instead of cash.

To obtain one ton of kelp, twenty-two tons of wet seaweed had to be gathered.[1] Using a taricrook (an instrument with two prongs at right angles to the shaft) the wet weed was dragged up the beach, spread out to dry then burnt in a stone-lined pit. The residue was left to cool and harden before being broken up and sent away for processing. In Shetland, kelp shores and the labour thereon were rented or leased out by landowners to merchants who then sold the burnt kelp on to the manufacturers of various products, including iodine, glass, soap, gunpowder and manure.

Undoubtedly the work involved in collecting and drying so much to produce so little must have been back-breaking, and the tending of the fire unpleasantly acrid. Crops to the lee of burning kelp were turned yellow by

75

Taricrook, courtesy T. Thomson. © *Andy Gear*

the smoke, and the foul smell could be detected miles away.[2] A tragic story involving the reek from a kelp fire was recorded by Nina Charleson of Camb, Yell.[3] A young couple who lived at Swarister, East Yell had their first babies, twins. The father was away at the whaling: *They were burning kelp doon at the banks you ken. And it was a calm day and the wind laid upo da hoose and filled da hoose wi kelp reek and da bairns of course was. You keen it wis afil poisonus reek. And da auld wife was so stiff* [stubborn] *at she widdna hae the bairns tane furt because they wirna been baptised. This silly notions you keen. And they both started tae vomit and they vomited till they died. And it nearly pat Janet Williamson* [the mother] *oot o her mind you keen.*

According to the Shetland merchants who quoted prices to the Truck Commissioners in 1872, prices paid for kelp to the burners ranged from 3/- to 4/6d a hundredweight. At that time 8lbs of meal cost 1/5d. Little wonder then, that the crofters would sometimes sell their kelp to the buyer offering the best price – but this could lead to trouble!

As factor for the estate, John Walker became responsible for the lease of the Garth and Annsbrae kelp shores. In Delting, James Hoseason & Co. of Mossbank got a lease for three years @ 20/- per ton royalty, and in North Yell, Peter Sandison got similar terms for a twelve year lease.[4] William Duncan at Garth and Robert Murray at Swinister, both merchants, acted as agents for Hoseason. In March 1867, Walker warned them[5] to see that *no Kelp made from the produce of these shores go into wrong hands.*

Earlier that year Walker had alerted Mr Pole, the other partner in the Mossbank business:[6] *You will also have to keep a sharp lookout on the Kelp made at Little Roe as I understand it has generally been given to Mr Morgan Laurenson.* This is the first indication we have of trouble at Little Roe, a small island in Yell Sound which, at the time of the 1861 census, supported a population of sixteen, ages ranging from one to eighty-four.

KELP AND OTHER BURNING ISSUES

There were other covert dealings going on. The Tronaster people had sold kelp to Thomas Hughson, Firth. James Hoseason reported this to Walker and added:[7] *This is the first attempt at smuggling of the kind we have had to do with your shores. We hope you will look sharply after it as a warning for the future – causing the kelp to be restored to us – the parties if possible punished. No kelp from Little Roe yet and no word of any coming.*

On 12th December, 1867 Walker was cautioning Arthur Nicolson, a merchant in Gutcher, North Yell, about the sale of kelp, adding a touch of moral blackmail:[8] *Sir, I wrote you from Cullivoe as to sending me a note of kelp bought by you from the shores of these estates. Of course I cannot hold you responsible legally for a royalty but I would point out that by refusing to pay as the other buyers do that you compel us to prosecute the burners when they will suffer as much as the Little Roe tenant.*

So, what had happened to the Little Roe tenant? David Tulloch and his son John had moved there, with their families, from Firth, where they had been living at the time of the 1851 census. I haven't found the details, but the Tullochs left Little Roe to settle in West Yell sometime before the 4th November, 1867. We know this because of a postscript in a letter of that date to Walker from Hoseason:[9] *We do not know David Tulloch's <u>exact</u> address in West Yell – West Yell <u>proper</u> however is comparatively a small place.*

It would appear that the family left Little Roe hurriedly as it is said they spent their first night in West Yell huddled under a sail in a crö.[10] It would also appear from the snippets of information in the letters that their exit had something to do with Walker and trouble about kelp.

In 1874 Robert Scott-Skirving wrote: *One island, Little Roe, was uninhabited in 1871, whilst in 1861 it contained 16 persons. A misunderstanding with the proprietor led to its evacuation, and it is now kept as a special pasture for rams.*[11]

** ** **

The township of Coldback/Calback, Delting, was vod (empty) for many years before oil came to Shetland – so only the ruins of the old houses were swallowed up in the building of Sullom Voe's massive oil terminal. Garth House and the nearby fank were built by Walker – at the estate's expense of course – for the sheep farm at Garth. Garth House still stands, overlooking the entrance to the oil terminal. I'm sure Walker would approve. He would also applaud the disappearance of the houses at Calback because the tenants there gave him considerable annoyance.

Garth House stands near the entrance to Sullom Voe Oil Terminal. The house is little changed, but signs of the 21st century are seen in the satellite dish and the blazing flare stack which is almost a mile away.
© *Andy Gear*

To have some idea of the size of the community at Calback – the 1851 census records 66 people living in 10 houses. No change in 1861 – 67 inhabitants listed. In 1871, although the population had dropped to 36, nine out of the ten families still there in '71 had been in Calback in '61. These ten families somehow managed to survive the Walker era.

We have already heard how he had been threatened on arriving there, in 1866, with his two Aberdeenshire friends. On that occasion he assured the Major that he had convinced the angry tenants that all the changes were meant for their own good. Maybe they took him at his word – he could be very persuasive – maybe the tenants decided to call his bluff, but by February 1868 he was incensed by their attitude and penned a long address to 'the Tenants of Coldback':[12] (He always called it Coldback.)

I have learned with much surprise and regret that none of you have seen fit to carry out the terms upon which you hold your farms – I fixed the rents of your holdings at little more than one half of their actual value ... I have indulged you by allowing you free pasture for your cattle in the hills. I did not insist last year upon your affecting the improvements you undertook to do as I thought your then neighbours might have annoyed you. To every one of you I have freely granted every liberty you asked – and in return for all this what have you done?

Then he gets on to his favourite theme – laziness. He averred that, since January, the weather had been suitable for any kind of outdoor work, but nothing had been done. He had given them work at draining which they had given up, he claimed, after two days, then declared that this had been to his advantage as he got the work done cheaper and better by workmen from Caithness. However he didn't actually quote any wages for comparison. The epistle ends with a lecture on the consequences of idleness: *You all profess to be Christian – Is a true Christian 'slothful in business'? The meanest creature in God's creation should make you ashamed – read about the Ant and compare your conduct with its but I will not waste more time or trouble with you – Henceforth and until you prove yourselves men I shall not relax in the slightest the conditions upon which you remain as Tenants – I seem to have done too much for you but doing for you is at an end. If you wont work you deserve to starve and believe me idleness is punished both in this world and the next.* John Walker

A few months later we find another bizarre composition from the Walker pen. Simply marked 'Private', it is a list of instructions, to someone unnamed, who is to be employed to spy on the Delting tenants. Unbelievably, it begins:[13] *You will require to be at some of the neighbourhoods every morning at six and ascertain what are the Tenants habits as to early rising.* He continues, in slightly more reasonable vein, briefing his special agent about reporting on the state of the peat banks, examining fencing, measuring drains etc. Great emphasis is laid on secrecy: *All orders sent, unless otherwise directed, are to be kept strictly Private – you are warned that the least thing said will find its way to me.* Then back to the laziness theme: *As these people are naturally indolent and delating, you are expected by your example to show them differently, and advise to enter into as little conversation with them as possible.*

Next, a list of qualifications for Walker's amateur sleuth: *Punctuality, regularity, exactness and neatness is possible, and is a 'sine qua non'* [an indispensable condition] *with these executing my orders. At present I do not require you to interfere in any matter happening – but expect you to report for my information and guidance all that may be going on with Tenant or Servant. Further instructions will from time to time be sent you.* It's no wonder he had a problem retaining staff!

The lean years in the second half of the 1860s left many crofting families in Shetland impoverished. Walker didn't realise or refused to accept that undernourished folk have little energy to work – but more of that in a later chapter.

According to story-teller Brucie Henderson of Arisdale (whose mother was a Blance from Calback) there were still seven strong men in Calback in Walker's time. Jimmy Blance had came home from sea in the midst of Walker's 'improvements' and threatened to *grip da bugger* [Walker] *an twist his heed aff*. He lay in wait for Walker and jumped on him. Brucie averred that it took seven strong men to haul Jimmy off and that Walker never showed his face there again while Jimmy Blance was home.[14]

** ** **

Another family which might be said to have had a *misunderstanding with the proprietor* (or his factor) was the Williamsons of Quoys of Garth in Delting. Hay Williamson and his wife Helen had moved there from Stapness in Walls in 1862 when Major Cameron had given Hay a tack of the Quoys for fourteen years, rent £4:2s. Of course that was before Walker became factor, and before the decision had been made to remove the tenants from certain areas on the estate in order to enclose sheep farms. As early as July 1866 the tenants of Tronaster and Crooksetter were sent letters of 'Notice to Remove'.[15] By September, a long list of heads of households (see appendix) had signed acceptance of eviction from the land they rented, with varying conditions for renting or leasing the dwelling houses only.

The 1861 census shows ten occupied houses at Garth. In 1871 there were only three – Robert McIntosh, a shepherd from Caithness; Gilbert Murray, a merchant grocer; and the Williamson family at the Quoys.

We can imagine Walker's frustration over that fourteen year lease which the Major had given to Hay Williamson. All the more so because Walker's policy was to offer leases (albeit unacceptable ones) to the crofters, insisting that was the only successful way forward for them. So he had to find another way to get rid of Hay and his family. In December 1866 Hay was sent letters alleging that he was breaking the terms of his lease by not working his peat banks properly and allowing his pigs to trespass on other people's property.[16] In May 1867, during a visit to Delting, Walker made some kind of verbal agreement with Hay that he would get additional land in the town of Quoys to make up for his loss of scattald. But no papers were signed.

Walker, meanwhile, had been sending out instructions for sowing grass seed: *on the ground to be vacated at Martinmas*. And he declared in one such: *Donald can explain*.[17] Donald McBeth was his shepherd in Delting at that time, and it is questionable how much Donald would have been able to explain, judging by this letter to his 'Dear Master' whom he seems to have held in considerable awe:[18] *I expect you will have seen Captain Bruce about the boat before this time he left Garth this day Dear Master let me know if you are going to sow grass seed in John Jerom land* at Swinister or in Hay Williamson land at Garth as I heard his liss [lease] was Broken that is all but write soon and let me no if what I have done Pleases you.

Before we leave Donald, a brief look at his demise as Walker's shepherd. He was accused of neglecting and allowing scab into the flock, was dismissed then re-engaged and offered a job in Yell. His reply suggests that he felt he had been unfairly treated:[19] *You no that no man cood agree to the offer you made me in your letter for no man wood agree to make up the loss that might com among your stock ... All my ill wishes came to me through serving you so faithfully.*

Donald got into debt and was told by Walker:[20] *A single man with his mind solely in his work should have saved a lot of money every year ... I was much disgusted to hear of your conduct in Lerwick – such doings can never advance you with anybody ...*

Finally, Walker writing to John Caverhill on 8th December, 1869:[21]

I learn that Dan Orr and Donald McBeth have both <u>bolted</u> by the last steamer.

However, back to Hay Williamson's story and to 26th September, 1867 when William Duncan, the general merchant at Garth,[22] was penning a letter to Walker:[23] *Yesterday morning Hay Williamson went away with a boat of kelp. I sent to Mossbank but he had not been there & he says he has been with it where it pleased himself to go and you can find it out and do your worst that had you given the same price as the other people you would have got his kelp but as you do not the difference of price is as well in his pocket as yours.*

P.S. I wonder if Hay has paid for his dog.

On the same day James Hoseason also reported Hay's selling of his kelp,[24] pointing out that it had not been delivered to any of their stations, adding: *This would need to be looked at.*

So Walker wrote back to Duncan, who lived near the Williamson family:[25] *By him [Pole] I sent a <u>warning</u> to your neighbour which he would do well to profit by and speedily arrange so to his misdeeds – In fact if he does not settle the matter with Mr Pole before Saturday night he'll be turned out yet from the Quoys at Martinmas.*

Perhaps Walker had been hoping that Duncan would sort out the problem for him, but on 30th September he wrote, from Bressay, to Hay Williamson himself:[26] *Sir, You not having seen Messrs Hoseason & Co on Saturday and arranged as to your unlawfully removing Kelp compels me to send you the accompanying <u>Summons</u>. If however you choose to see me here before <u>6pm</u> tomorrow I am yet open to arrange matters – but should you fail to do so I can indulge you no longer.*

Garth and Annsbrae.

Wm Sievwright J. Esqr Maryfield, Bressay,
Shetland, 12th October 1867

Removing
Garriock & Williamson

Dear Sir
Yours of 10th with me late last night —
In accordance with arrangement I have sent to Williamson for execution the Lease we proposed giving him — If he carries out his expressed intention and returns the documents signed — the action will be withdrawn — if he is so ill advised as to act otherwise — I will reply definitely to yours before me on Wednesday — I hardly think you can have a Proprietor's autograph copy Lease of any of the Garth lands

Yours truly
John Walker

Lerwick

KELP AND OTHER BURNING ISSUES

Now the question arises, was it possible for Hay to reach Bressay before 6pm the next day? Would Hay have even received the letter by that time? And when the letter did arrive he had to make his way to Bressay from Delting on foot, by sea, or on horseback. It seems like rather a tall order!

But 1860s communications could cope with Walker's demands. Hay did arrive at Bressay next day to visit the factor, who then wrote to James Hoseason:[27] *This afternoon he* [Hay Williamson] *made his appearance – pleading that he thought my first letter upon the subject was a <u>forgery</u> & hence not seeing you, that he never got a Special Notice not even a copy of our bills as to selling the kelp to you – that he was on his way to Mossbank and could not manage for the weather which took him to <u>leeward</u> and that the Kelp sold was not made from our shores all that his family made from these having been duly sold to Mr Duncan ... Taking his statement '<u>cum grano</u>*' [short for 'cum grano salis' – with a pinch of salt] *and getting his promise to sell all to you in the future I have let him off with paying the expense of the summons – besides if his statement was true that it was made from ware not belonging to us we could have done little ... However I hope he'll be convinced that we wont stand nonsense – Have the Little Roe people brot their Kelp yet?*

By October, William Sievwright is on the case, for Hay Williamson, of course. Walker to Sievwright:[28] *Yours of 10th with me late last night. In accordance with arrangement I had sent to Williamson for execution the Lease we proposed giving him.* (We must bear in mind that Hay Williamson already had a lease from the Major which should last until 1876.) *If he carries out his expressed intention and returns the documents signed – the action will be withdrawn. If he is so ill advised as to act otherwise ...* This half-threat is left hanging in mid-air before aggression towards Sievwright takes over ... *I will reply definitely to yours before me on Wednesday – I hardly think you can have a Proprietrix' <u>holograph</u> copy Lease of any of the <u>Garth</u> lands.* For emphasis Walker had Garth underlined by three heavy black lines.

At the same time Walker was writing to William Duncan with details of the correct procedure he was to carry out when witnessing Hay sign the new lease. He ends with:[29] *I fear Hay would kick even yet – I should hardly give him this chance but it will be the last one. Excuse my troubling you in the matter.*

On the 23rd he again wrote to Duncan:[30] *As matters went Hay Williamson's Lease not being returned was of no moment – we have got matters with him settled at last satisfactorily. It is likely I may see you on 29th if not I'll be on 11th ...*

JOHN WALKER'S SHETLAND

Thanks to the litigation which followed in 1868, a letter written by Hay Williamson to William Sievwright has survived. Dated 22nd October, 1867, he first conveys gratitude to the lawyer for his *kind attention* then continues:[31] *I am satisfied with my lot of land as a full equivalent to what I had before. I also have access now just as formerly to Public Road and the neighbouring towns but if the wire fence was joined to the sea by a Dyke end (which it is not at present) both myself and the public would require a gate at the shore. I would resign the right of keeping sheep in the scattold but I really cannot hold the Farm without the liberty of putting to the hill occasionally the few <u>cows</u> that the Farm can fodder and also of pasturing three or four young cattle on the hill in summer – but neither horses nor sheep ...*

We see here that Hay could write an excellent letter. He was prepared to co-operate with Walker's plans up to a point, but was also aware of the strength of his position as a lease holder. He enclosed a receipt for last year's rent, wrote about the portion of dykes that were his responsibility, and, as regards kelp: *Kelp shores may be reserved to the Landlord but I would require to take a little for manure, loose sea drift or sea weeds brought from off the Voe with my boat ... I do not enclose the draft lease at present but I will be in Town within a fortnight and take it with me, when I will call on you and see and have the matter settled.*

But Hay never got to town to see Sievwright. On 28th October he was found dead on the beach, his body lying below the high water mark. He was only forty-two, and had seven children, the youngest, Barbara, only two months old. We don't know how Walker got word of the sudden death, but it must have reached him fairly quickly as he was the one to convey the news to Sievwright.[32] He also informed the Major in a letter dated 4th November:[33] *Your troublesome Tenant Hay Williamson is dead – He must have been seized with a fit whilst at the <u>ebb</u> and drowned by the tide.*

But the story doesn't quite end there. In November Helen Williamson requested grazing for a few sheep in the Garth Hill for a season. Just as it would be interesting to be in a position to assess Walker's attitude when he brought the news of Hay's death to Sievwright, so I wonder why he didn't reply to Helen, who was by then head of the house, but chose to address his answer to John, the seventeen year old son:[34] *I've been thinking over your mother's request to allow a few sheep in the Garth Hill this season although you should pay for them – but I find it will be impossible to do so after two weeks hence – but I will allow six sheep free from scab to be grazed in Little Roe for a season upon the condition that you help Donald in the boat anytime he has to use it – I mean the small boat.*
P.S. If this suits you show this to Donald

By the first of April Donald McBeth had poinded sheep which the Williamson family had on the Hill of Garth. On 4th April, in a letter to Donald,[35] Walker tells him he has done the right thing but *if he is to take them off the scattald you can let him off at 6d per head*. Remember the going rate for poinded sheep was more than twice that – but there's a sting in the tail. *You will call and offer him this chance and say that if the new agreement is not in force then the old one is broken and that he will lose his place all together.*

Confident that he could get the better of young John, other forms of harassment were used. For example, when the Williamsons' peats were cut that spring, Garth Estate servants threw down the peats and *trampled and destroyed them.*[36]

Sievwright was still involved. He wrote to the Major himself on 6th April:[37] *The lease granted by you being quite good this poor boy is entitled to require that its conditions shall be observed, and with all respect for, it will be a shame if you allow acts of oppression to be done by Mr Walker upon People who are unable to contend with you.*

This approach to the Major surely didn't bear fruit, as, later in the month, on John Williamson's behalf, Sievwright lodged an interdict at the Sheriff Court against Major Cameron for poinding the sheep.[38] Sievwright argued that according to the fourteen year lease granted by the Major to the Williamsons in 1862 they were entitled to pasture their sheep and other animals on the undivided commonty. No new agreement had been signed, and John Williamson, as Hay's *eldest son and heir at law, succeeded him in the Lease of the Farm and Lands and others in Quoys of Garth*.

In the court papers it states that the Williamsons were offered either of two other crofts on the estate if they would move from the Quoys, but they were both *so poor and so inconveniently situated that the Petitioner* [John Williamson] *would not and could not have been expected to accept either in lieu of his present farm. The Petitioner was offered £10 if he would renounce his lease; but as his Lease is of greatly more value to him than such a sum he declined to accept the offer*. Walker had previously proposed a reduction of 12/- from Hay's rent if he would give up his scattald right and restrict himself to the land between the hill dyke and the new wire fence, but Hay's right to the use of the scattald was worth more than that.

As is the case with so much of the litigation prior to the publication of the *Shetland Times* we do not know the exact outcome of 'Williamson v Cameron'. But we do know that Helen Williamson and six of her family were still living in the Quoys in 1871. Garth, the largest of the Cameron/Walker sheep farms, supported 2,500 Cheviot ewes.[39] The Williamson's lease alone couldn't foil that scheme, and, unfortunately other crofters had no such legal backing to help fight their corner. They simply had to move elsewhere, many to unknown hardships in unfamiliar surroundings all over the globe.

As William Sievwright presented such a strong case for the Williamsons, it seems only right to give him the last words on the matter. The occasion was when John Williamson went to pay his rent shortly after the untimely death of his father:[40]

Mr Walker on this occasion attempted to get the better of the Petitioner who is a minor, was very much afraid of Mr Walker, and was ignorant of his rights; but the Petitioner disregarded Mr Walker's threats.

** ** **

The Sheriff Court case being 'Williamson v Cameron' not 'Williamson v Walker' again raises the question of how much, or little, the Major was involved in the affairs of his estate. After all, Walker was only the factor, but his position was clearly set out in the 'Articles, Regulations and Conditions of Lease' sent out to the tenants in 1866. On the first page of the booklet, which came to be known as *Walker's Catechism*, Major Cameron wrote: *The management of the Property upon which you are a Tenant is entirely in his* [Walker's] *hands.*

Another example of the Major's withdrawal from responsibility is seen in a letter he wrote to Walker in October 1866. Robert Jaromson in Laxobigging was willing to take one third of Upper Scatsta for one year under the old regulations. Cameron wrote[41] that he had *told him to see yourself* [Walker] *as I do not wish to interfere with your plans and not knowing what your arrangements may be ...*

Not many years later Major Cameron would rue his lack of 'interference' in the 'arrangements'.

1 *The Orkney Herald,* 9th February, 1864
2 W.P.L. Thomson, *History of Orkney,* Edinburgh 1987, p.210
3 S.A. 3/1/37/8
4 Gardie Papers 23/12/1867
5 Gardie Papers L.B.1 p.109
6 Gardie Papers L.B.1 p.91
7 Gardie Papers 1867/358
8 Gardie Papers L.B.2 p.229
9 Gardie Papers 1867/522
10 Oral Tradition – Mary Ellen Odie
11 R. Scott Skirving, *On the Agriculture of the Islands of Shetland,* p.239
12 Gardie Papers L.B.2 p.295
13 Gardie Papers L.B.2 pp.432 & 433
14 Jonathan Wills, *The Lands of Garth,* Lerwick 1978

15 Gardie Papers L.B.1 pp.13 & 38
16 Gardie Papers L.B.1 p.70
17 Gardie Papers L.B.1 p.200
18 Gardie Papers 1867/194
19 Gardie Papers 1869/206
20 Gardie Papers L.B.2 p.695
21 Gardie Papers L.B.2 p.833
22 1861 Census for Delting
23 Gardie Papers 1867/450
24 Gardie Papers 1867/449
25 Gardie Papers L.B.1 p.141
26 S.A. SC 12/6/1868/29/13
27 Gardie Papers L.B.2 p.149
28 S.A. SC 12/6/1868/29/17
29 Gardie Papers L.B.2 p.167
30 Gardie Papers L.B.2 p.178
31 S.A. SC 12/6/1868/29/14
32 S.A. SC 12/6/1868/29
33 Gardie Papers L.B.2 p.191
34 Gardie Papers L.B.2 p.210
35 Gardie Papers L.B.2 p.342
36 S.A. SC 12/6/1868/29/10
37 Gardie Papers 1868/169
38 S.A. SC 12/6/1868/29/10
39 S.A. 2/307, R Scott-Skirving, *On the Agriculture of the Islands of Shetland 1874*, p.259
40 S.A. SC 12/6/1868/29/10
41 Gardie Papers 1866/154

Chapter Eight

GOVERNMENT INCENTIVE

It is far from pleasant having to do business with Mr Umphray.
John Walker writing to Charles Ritchie, January 1869

HOW WAS the setting up of the new sheep farms to be financed? Could the estate afford miles of fencing and draining, new shepherds' cottages, sheep fanks etc? Unlikely, but the Government had been giving financial help with enclosures for several years.

To facilitate the inclosure and improvement of commons and other lands was one of the aims of the Act of 1845 which set up the Inclosure Commission. The commissioners had to be satisfied that every application for enclosure, in addition to being of advantage to the landowner, was *having regard as well to the health, comfort and convenience of the inhabitants of any cities, towns, villages, or populous places in or near any parish.*[1]

The following year Sir Robert Peel introduced a scheme of Government loans to Landowners who wished to improve their property by drainage. Administration of the scheme was the responsibility of the Inclosure Commissioners, who had to examine and approve all applications for loan. Low interest rates (3½ per cent.) and long term repayment (22 years) ensured that the scheme was an attractive one. It proved popular, and several public companies were formed to lend money.[2] One such was the Scottish Drainage and Improvement Company of which Charles Ritchie was secretary. With its headquarters in Edinburgh, the Company

GOVERNMENT INCENTIVE

was *incorporated in the year 1856, by private Act of Parliament, for the purpose of facilitating the Improvement of Lands and Estates in Scotland.*[3]

In 1860, by an amendment Act, the Company was granted special privileges which meant that their loans for improvements could include, for example, the building of farm roads, farm houses, engine houses, mills, kilns, bridges and even jetties for the transport of stock and produce.[4]

The first hurdle for the applicant was to gain the Commissioners' approval. Their sanction enabled the borrower to set the cost of improvement against tax, further reducing the cost of the loan. Then the Commissioners nominated an Inspector. Neither the company nor the applicants had any say in this nomination, but the Inspector's expenses had to be paid by the applicant and that cost depended on the distance the Inspector had to travel and the number of visits he had to make. For drainage or fencing loans the Inspector had to make two visits. For building loans, three. However, for large transactions, several visits were necessary.[5]

Seven years after the amendment Act, John Walker was finding that the application for loan was testing his ingenuity:[6]

To C. Ritchie, (of Scottish Drainage & Improvements Co.), Edinburgh. 1st July, 1867. Yours of 27th duly to hand – You have given me a huge work to perform and which at best can be but imperfectly accomplished seeing that few, if any, of the places have been measured. (Land here is computed per merk) I will do my best in the matter and send you an application for Garth as required ...

Yours sincerely,   John Walker

Large sums of money were involved in these schemes as we see in the following letter[7] from Walker to F. G. Bruce of the Union Bank of Scotland in Lerwick, March 1867: *I beg to hand Promissory Note by Major Cameron and myself for £1500 which we beg to lodge in security of advances to be made under a special account to be operated by me as 'Factor' for the purpose of carrying out Improvements upon the Garth and Annsbrae Estate under a loan for £10,000 opened with the Scottish Drainage and Improvement Company for that purpose.*

Nowadays £10,000 is not considered a huge sum. So let's look at a few examples to illustrate monetary value in the 1860s. A dry-stone dyke builder was paid at the rate of 8d (old pennies) per fathom (6ft). He would have to build 180ft to earn £1. A widow with two children, living on a poor, outset croft, received an annual allowance of £2 from the Parochial Board. Four lasses got 6d each for a day of cutting corn, and food for the four of them cost 4d.[8] A comparison with present day equivalents gives some idea of the value of £10,000 at that time – we're talking about a multi-million-pound business.

JOHN WALKER'S SHETLAND

Andrew Umphray was the Inspector who had to deal with the loans for Garth and Annsbrae. Umphray was a landowner and partner in the Reawick firm of Garriock & Co., merchants and fishcurers. All through the transaction he exasperated Walker by not turning up to inspect the work when Walker wanted him to. However, Umphray sounded hopeful on 28th March, 1867:[9] *I know of nothing to prevent me going over the plan as proposed to be improved as soon as the weather can be depended upon – I got all the documents and plans on Monday and have been looking over them – I shall send you herewith the Commissioners* remarks *about the Cottages which will be easily got explained. I shall also send you a look of one of their minutes sent for my guidance from which you will see that I have to report as to the number of existing cottages now occupied. Major Cameron and you will be so kind as consider this so as to enable me to do it.*

Dear Mr Umphray,   30th March, 1867[10]
I've no doubt we can get over the scruples of the Inclosure Commissioners as to the Cottages and hope you'll be able to recommend iron roofing to the sheep sheds – Slate is difficult to get put up and worse to get kept up ... As to number of cottages etc. – you puzzle me to answer – for there will be no Cottages *upon the proposed Grazing Farms and the other buildings upon the Estate are the Farm Houses of each holding and therefore I think not* Cottages *in the sense used by Commissioners ...*
                                Yours sincerely,   John Walker

The 'proposed grazing farms' in early 1867 were still tenanted by crofter/fishermen and their families. Were theirs the 'cottages' that should have been reported to the commissioners? Walker evaded Umphray's question by changing the tense to the future – 'there will be no cottages'.

As early as January of the same year John Walker had issued the following advertisement, making it clear that he had no expectation that the crofters on Burraness and Kirkabister, the Windhouse estate and West o Firth in Yell, or Garth in Delting would accept his 'favourable' leases:[11]

SHEEP FARMS TO LET
A few superior and sound Grazings, having arable land included, of 2000, 3000, 4000, & 8000 acres to Let in Shetland. The farms are now being enclosed, drained and otherwise improved and every encouragement will be given to suitable Tenants.
Apply to John Walker, Maryfield House, Bressay, Shetland.

A Captain C. Leith Hay, from Kincardine O'Neill, Deeside, was interested in more detail. Walker replied,[12] painting a rosy picture of sheep farming in Shetland, 25th February, 1867: *I am today favoured with yours of 19th inquiring about the Sheep Farms advertised to Let – it is impossible*

GOVERNMENT INCENTIVE

to give you all particulars as to the Farms in a letter. I have therefore to say generally that Sheep Farming is proven in Shetland to be the most suitable use the ground can be put to and highly profitable for the Tenant – the grounds now to Let have upon some of them tolerable Houses but I may say none of them have steadings – but we are prepared to meet any suitable Tenant in the most liberal manner and give him any reasonable accommodation in the way of Houses and Sheep Sheds – indeed as we are equally disposed to Farm as to Let, we are at present enclosing every Farm, draining it and erecting Sheep Sheds of the best description – all improvements we are prepared to hand over upon Deed [?] Inventory.

As to locality – the largest Farm is in the Parish of Delting, one in Mid and two or three in North Yell Parish – we have a first class steamer running here once a week all the year round and during the summer we have two steamers a week.

As to rent – this of course must depend upon the wants of the Tenant – all I can say is that it is our wish to give an extra bargain to suitable Tenants.

Being a Tenant myself and a pioneer of Sheep Farming in this quarter (after being in Australia and a native of Aberdeen) I can only say that I know no place where a Farmer can make more money – No disease ever appearing amongst the flock and the prices realised being equal to Orkney or farther South – My last year's crop of Lambs fetched 30/- each here – I'll be most happy to give you any farther information.

The same day he wrote[13] to another prospective sheep-farming tenant, Hugh McKay from Kinlochbervie, who was informed that: *Up till now the grounds have been occupied by small Tenants who graze Shetland Sheep, Ponies and Cattle – We are now enclosing the different Farms and draining them. One of the Farms is above 8000 acres upon which there are two tolerable houses (exclusive of some 30 houses that will be vacant).* Note the future tense. He is confident that the houses 'will be vacant'.

In May, Umphray did an inspection, as we learn from William Pole of Greenbank:[14] *We heard of you making a rapid transit across this District [North Yell] along with another Gentleman whom I see was Mr Umphray. I can only assure you we should have been glad to have seen you both here that night but I see you have had very little time to spare.* Presumably Walker was making Umphray cover as much ground as possible!

Walker to C. Ritchie, 25th May, 1867:[15] *I am much surprised that Mr Umphray had not as promised sent in his Report. It was at considerable personal inconvenience that I went over the ground with him as he should have Inspected a long time previously ... It looks as if one must be endowed with a large stock of patience in these matters.* Patience? Not one of Walker's virtues!

The report[16] was eventually sent to the Commissioners: *They* [the sheep farms] *are said to consist of about 2200 acres uncultivated pasture lands and about 1400 acres arable – hitherto been held by tenants occupying a few acres each of the cultivated land with an unrestricted right to the hill pasture. That this promiscuous occupation having been found to work with little advantage to the tenantry generally and great loss to the proprietor both on account of the overstocking of the ground making it unproductive to them, and for the same cause the surface of the earth being injured was lessening in value to him, while in fact he was receiving very little if any rent for it. That the proposal is to confine the tenantry to the cultivated ground, giving them self-contained farms, enclosing the same, and trenching and draining the waste lands connected with them so as to give a greater breadth of cultivated ground ... and to enclose the hill pasture in connection with some of the cultivated ground for sheepwalks to be let separately.*

That the island of Unst is well adapted for this purpose there being lands connected with or near most of the small holdings capable of cultivation. The pasture land there is also valuable for sheep.

That the same may be said of the holdings in North and Mid Yell, also Delting; but in a few instances the cultivation cannot be increased with profit and it may be seen for the interest of all parties to lay waste townships of this description for pasturage ...

Ah! Surely the commissioners will question the fact that townships are to be 'laid waste'? Hopefully they will investigate how many people live in these townships and what is to become of them?

Back to Umphrays' report: *The uncultivated hill lands of Yell are very varied, much of it broken and mossy but there are some fine grazings about the seashore, hill and burnsides ... In Delting the pasturage is extensive, varied, and generally good for sheepwalks. There are connected with the property fine rich nesses and small islands requiring no expense other than surface drainage.*

News from Umphray in June 1867:[17] *They* [the Commissioners] *are satisfied with the first reports.*

So no objection was made about townships being laid waste; no queries were raised as to what would become of the tenants from these townships. Did they assume that the proprietor would rehouse them? Nor was it made clear that the 'fine grazings about the sea-shore' and the 'rich nesses' was usually where the crofters lived and had their cultivation. Or did nobody – inspectors, commissioners or the government, care?

Although the first report had been approved, Walker was still pressed for more accurate measurements. Frequent underlining shows that his temper is frayed:[18]

GOVERNMENT INCENTIVE

To C. Ritchie, Contract 198
I think Red Tape *is being carried too far with regard to Major Cameron's applications – I have filled them up as nearly as anyone could but they are not* strictly *correct whilst* divided *– hope you will be able to get the Commissioners to pass the present farms – We can give no nearer data as to acreage in Lands being held entirely by the* merk.

By 12th October Umphray was needed for more inspection:[19] *I hope it will be convenient for you in a fortnight or so to Inspect and Report upon about 20 miles of Fencing and 120 miles of surface draining.*

On 2nd November he tried again:[20] *We would like passed this season say 20 miles of fencing and about £200 for drains – the fencing is situated at Garth, Coldback, Swinister, Foraness, Laxobigging in Delting Hill – Lumbister, Kirkabister, Burraness, West o Firth & Cullivoe in Yell and Woodwick in Unst. The draining is in Coldback Ness, Garth, Crookster & Tronaster in Delting (Little Roe too) and Lumbister in Yell. We would like advanced £1500 on fencing and £200 on drains and we could leave the rest till another inspection.* A lot of ground for Umphray to cover at that time of year!

Three weeks later, Walker, restraining his irritation, had to point out:[21] *I am back from my travels and have kept my time at all points to an hour – I have not as yet received the schedules you state were sent to me to be filled up in pencil.* However, when Umphray did send the schedules, his reasons for delay were acknowledged by Walker:[22] *I am sorry to hear that you are not very strong.*

Next month Walker was complaining to C. Ritchie in Edinburgh that Umphray was making *one excuse after another.* To Umphray:[23] *I've been living in hope to have learned that you were in a position to go over the grounds in the North – Is it not competent with a partial advance to give a certificate conditional upon an after inspection? The works are still going on and it would be a saving to have so much borrowed thro the Company instead of a Bank – I am still ready at any day and any hour but am desirous to go South.* And on 30th December: *Hope for cert. of £2,000 by next steamer ... have been relying on advance since end of October, so require something definite at once.*

The same day he wrote to Mr Ritchie:[24] *I expect that Mr Umphray will by tonight's mail report as to an advance of £2,177 under Contract 219.*

That transaction must have come to a satisfactory conclusion as there was a lull in the pressure until 6th May, 1868 when Walker wrote asking Umphray to join him in Unst. Apparently Mr Edmondston and the Messrs Henderson were also anxious for his presence. We can only presume that this invitation did not bear fruit, as, on 25th May, Walker penned a long letter detailing what Umphray would see whenever he did go to Unst:²⁵ *Every part of the Property there are works finished and in progress – At Uyeasound in Unst you'll see a dyke on Ronnan – near the Kirk there are some 14 acres trenched and a stone dyke building – I would draw your special attention to the trenching – at Woodwick and Houlland there is Wire Fencing, Sheep draining [?] and it is there that the proposed steading is to be erected.*

In Yell – there is fencing and draining at West-o-Firth, Lumbister, Vollaster and Windhouse and Fencing with a Sheep Shed in progress at Kirkabister.

In Delting – there is a large extent of Fencing, Sheep Shed at Swinister almost if not completed … Swinister shed to cost £220 – at Garth £200 … so we require special allowance from unexpended Building Grant.

This fank, or sheep shed as Walker termed it, was completed by May 1868 at Swinister, Delting at a cost of £220.   © *Andy Gear*

By August more money was needed *for Draining and Trenching and Stone Dyking in Unst.*²⁶ Followed by a cry of desperation on 19th September: *Name the hour – I'll be there.*

Something must have worked, as on 7th November Walker was, unusually, thanking Umphray for his help. He was in good humour for another reason as we see from the rest of the letter:²⁷ *Midnight, I'm just returned from Yell Sound – I'm gone by steam, against wind and tide, to Delting – been there 6 hours and back since 10am – an improvement upon Packet! The 'Bride' has moved upwards of 80 passengers this week.*

GOVERNMENT INCENTIVE

November 1868, and once more Umphray has not done the necessary:[28] *Hope you have managed to forward the Certificate as by the time it passes the circumlocution offices and we get the needful we'll be put about.*

20th January, 1869:[29] *I do not understand what vouchers we can give for works executed by tenants in virtue of Improving Leases? If the work has been done efficiently it is surely enough Advances under these Heads we require merely to cover extra cost in Sheds, Houses etc. For all which you have had or can have vouchers.*

It sounds as if the work done by tenants (under rule 5 of the lease) was somehow being included in the work being done under the government loan.

Some of the work done on the Estate was detailed later that year:[30] *Houlland Cottage and steading are finished also a sheep shed at Kirkabister. Farther of fencing – 5 miles at Skaw in Unst, three miles at Sandwick, North Yell and 2 miles at Graven, Delting. In Draining – near Dalsetter some 8,000 chains*[31] *are in for the season – outlay in these about £1,670. I would much like if you could go over there at early convenience. In Yell at Basta, Stonsetter, North Garth and West Neep we have continued and virtually finished all our draining in the Estates. In Yell about Basta, Colvister, West Neeps, Stonsetter and North Garth also Delting at Scatsta we have completed wire fencing to the extent of 20 miles.*

By April 1870 it's the same old story:[32] *I am much disappointed that you have not completed a Report, as we cannot do without the contemplated advance owing to our arrangements and the fact that we requested it at* <u>Martinmas</u> *last ... If you cannot pass the trenching why then leave it out but please put in the Swinister Cottage. I again hope that you will manage the Report by Monday as I am put much about.*

Yours faithfully, John Walker

'Put much about' was certainly an understatement. To maintain a polite tongue to someone like Andrew Umphray in order to obtain loans to finance such a major scheme must have been a Herculean task for John Walker. It has to be said that Walker worked hard to obtain funding for the 'improvements'. What a pity it did not bring improvements for the tenants as well.

So who was to blame for the treatment of the tenants? John Walker immediately springs to mind as the person in the front line – the prime mover and the brains behind it all. But the commissioners were not guilt free. The Act of 1845 stated that they had to be satisfied that every application was to have regard for the 'health, comfort and convenience of the inhabitants of any ... villages or populous places'. Being evicted is neither healthy nor comfortable and certainly not convenient. In his

JOHN WALKER'S SHETLAND

initial report to the commissioners Umphray referred to 'townships' being laid waste – presumably the way in which he dealt with the question of the 'existing cottages now occupied'. The commissioners should have looked into any scheme which involved townships being laid waste before giving it the go-ahead. Major Cameron can't escape blame either. After all it was his estate, his tenants.

** ** **

Meanwhile three girls had been added to the Walker family at Maryfield, making a total of eight daughters. Jane Smith on 9th February, 1864, Jeanie Park on 27th July, 1865 and Janet Smith Grey Emily Laurence Lee Octavia on 30th November, 1866.

1 Orwin & Whetham, *History of British Agriculture* 1846-1914, David & Charles 1964, pp.187/8
2 Orwin & Whetham, *History of British Agriculture* 1846-1914, David & Charles 1964, p.195
3 Company Prospectus O.A. D9/7/11
4 Company Prospectus O.A. D9/7/11
5 Company Prospectus O.A. D9/7/11
6 Gardie Papers L.B.2 p.65
7 Gardie Papers L.B.1 p.160
8 Robert L. Johnson, *A Shetland Country Merchant,* Shetland 1979, pp.13,55,61.
9 Gardie Papers 1867/126
10 Gardie Papers L.B.1 p.166
11 Gardie Papers L.B.1 p.97
12 Gardie Papers L.B.1 p.129
13 Gardie Papers L.B.1 p.130
14 Gardie Papers 1867/126
15 Gardie Papers L.B.2 p.33
16 Gardie Papers 1867/219
17 Gardie Papers 1867/258
18 Gardie Papers L.B.2 pp.82 & 144
19 Gardie Papers L.B.2 p.165
20 Gardie Papers L.B.2 p.182
21 Gardie Papers L.B.2 p.205
22 Gardie Papers L.B.2 p.216
23 Gardie Papers L.B.2 pp.249 & 275
24 Gardie Papers L.B.2 p.277
25 Gardie Papers L.B.2 p.383
26 Gardie Papers L.B.2 pp.503 & 530
27 Gardie Papers L.B.2 p.573
28 Gardie Papers L.B.2 p.579
29 Gardie Papers L.B.2 p.640
30 Gardie Papers L.B.2 p.836
31 1 chain = 66 feet
32 Gardie Papers L.B.2 p.892

Chapter Nine

LEAN YEARS

I am thinking often and seriously about the poor fishermen this season and sincerely pray that all may work for the best.
John Walker writing to Alexander Sandison, 20th June, 1868

DURING the 18th and 19th centuries several periods of severe hardship through crop failure have been recorded in Shetland. In 1784 the situation became so serious that the government stepped in with aid in the form of meal, and help also came from charity in the south. The first decade of the 19th century brought poor fishing and failed crops resulting in dreadful privation, and the 1830s and 40s saw a series of bad harvests when labour on road making was paid for in meal to keep families alive. The amount of meal given for this labour was the equivalent in money of about three old pence a day.[1]

As we have already seen, John Walker became factor for Garth and Annsbrae in 1866. That was when the new rules were issued to the tenants, many of whom were obliged to quit their homes and crofts during the next few years, for one reason or another. To add to the misery of that era, bad weather again caused poor fishing, failed crops, resultant debt, and difficulty in settling rent.

As the *Shetland Times* did not start publication until 1872, we have to turn to newspapers further south for correspondence on the subject. In the *Scotsman*, March 10th, 1870, Archibald Nichol, minister of Walls, summed up the weather conditions for the years 1867-69: *The year 1867*

97

JOHN WALKER'S SHETLAND

was unfavourable as to the state of the weather, and a partial failure of the crop was experienced; 1868 was still more so; and worst of all, in 1869 the grain and potato crop was almost totally destroyed. The summer of the latter year continued cold and frosty till the month of July, and ere September was over the snowstorms, with hail and frost, succeeded by drenching rains, prevailed at short intervals till December. He went on to point out that under these circumstances the grain didn't ripen and the potatoes rotted. He had been involved in distributing supplies sent from south in the dearth of 1847, but claimed that the distress suffered in 1869 was greater than that, being the accumulation of three years hardship.

By January 1868 letters were appearing in newspapers signed 'Your Reporter' and 'Our Shetland Correspondent' claiming that the problem was caused through the Shetlanders' laziness:[2] *However incredible it may appear, many, indeed the generality of Shetlanders prefer idleness and semi-starvation to honest labour with its sweet reward.* The writer substantiates this sweeping statement by alleging that he couldn't persuade local men to dig drains and carry out other work for him. He had been obliged to bring in fifty strangers for labouring, and had found it cheaper to import stones and lime from south than to *be at the trouble of coaxing Shetlanders to work, and the still greater trouble – keeping them at work.*

Guess who 'Your Reporter' and 'Our Shetland Correspondent' was? That's right, none other than John Walker himself. He did admit that *the season has no doubt much to do with their deficient crops, but the mode of culture and thriftlessness of the Shetlanders still more so; they cannot realise the fact that man should gain his livelihood by the sweat of his brow; or that, when they spend all their money, they should work for more.*

For a contemporary view of why Walker found it difficult to employ local men we can look at a letter written to *The Northern Ensign* in February 1868 by 'Observer':[3] *It is quite possible that a sheep farmer may have found it difficult to obtain ditchers and drainers ... We are told in very vague terms about the wages offered to Shetlanders for draining ... but while they have crofts of their own, however small, it is not likely that any of them would make a three years engagement; and those who have been warned from their holdings will, no doubt, submit to many hardships before they become the bond slaves of their oppressors.*

We are already aware of resentment felt in the community towards anyone working for Walker. Besides, energy must have been sapped, and apathy bred, by the malnutrition prevalent during those difficult years.

Among the spate of replies refuting Walker's assertions was a clear statement from Alexander Sandison. A merchant and fishcurer, he was one of the four who, as Spence & Co., had taken over the lease of the Garth

and Annsbrae property in Unst – more of that later. He was therefore more directly involved than Walker with the poverty, both in Unst, and in North Yell where his brother Peter was a merchant and tacksman. These two areas were particularly hard hit in the late 1860s. Alexander wrote:[4]
Your Shetland correspondent says 'there is no destitution at present'. As to the points he is ignorant on I shall now try to inform him.
1st, The larger proportion of the Shetland Islands were visited with snow and hail storms, which took away fully three-fourths of the grain crop.
2nd, There are many families at this moment that have not eight days' food in their houses, and some of these have no means to procure it.
3rd, Many crofters have not just now (if they were not to eat an ounce of it) seed enough for their ground in spring.
4th, The herring fishing, on which many depend, was an entire failure. Six hundred fishermen, besides coopers and gippers, were engaged in the north isles alone, and the total catch was three barrels.
5th, The fishings of every kind in 1867-68 were so unsuccessful that, although extra good this year as regards ling and cod, many of the fishermen have not recovered the effects of the unsuccessful years as to be able fully to meet the loss they have now sustained in their crops.
6th, If relief in some way is not obtained, some of the people will certainly die of famine.
7th, I have seen men, heads of families, crying of want within the last eight days, and on the faces of some want is already showing itself.
... Your correspondent may call it rubbish if he so pleases. I am content; truth has been long esteemed ...

But 'Our Shetland Correspondent' of the *Daily Review* wouldn't give in. February 7th, 1870:[5] *We have had a calm in the atmospheric world for the past month, but it seems to have given opportunity for a storm of correspondence anent 'Destitution in Shetland' ... there has been great cry and little wool, and what is worse, we fear that we will hereafter be an apt illustration of the fable of the Boy and the Wolf ... We have made the most diligent inquiries in every parish, we have visited over three hundred houses since the cry arose, and we cannot endorse the statement that the people starve. Nay, more, we assert that, notwithstanding the October storms, the people are able to eat as much of their own grain as they usually do ... from the abundant supply of small fish, they are better off than usual. We therefore denounce the sending of charity, unless the donors insist that a fair amount of work be done for it. Apply the labour test, and the destitution cry will be unheard. Already we perceive pernicious effects in that capable Isle Unst, where the people are absolutely doing nothing to earn an honest penny, being buoyed up with the idea that they are to be fed and clothed by the rich in the South.*

Perhaps because of the labour he hoped to obtain for the chromate quarries which were soon to be opened there, he was especially critical of the Unst folk, declaring that *a few cases of alleged destitution were named to me; on the whole graceless, lazy and extravagant individuals, steeped in debt for years, and with no desire to elevate themselves.*

Included in the 'storm of correspondence' were letters from James Douglas of Cavers, Thomas Irvine of Midbrake, North Yell, church ministers and visitors to Shetland.[6] A few quotes can suffice to give the flavour: *The scarcity of fish on the North Yell coast this winter* (1869-70) *made the deficiency of the crops be more severely felt ... Potatoes were scarcely to be had, and any that I saw were very small and bad in quality ... There was no appearance of* [grain] *ripening, and this near the end of September ... the small fishes which swarmed around our shores have in a great measure deserted us ... no foresight or industry could prevent the failure of the potato crop, as it did not grow ... his* [Walker's] *antipathy to Shetlanders has now become a perfect mania ... It ill becomes any who may have helped to augment the present distress to deny that it exists ... The loss of the pasture has reduced the tenants' circumstances very much ...*

One of the tourists who visited Shetland at this time was an artist, John T. Reid. He leaves us a graphic description of a trip on horseback to Hillswick in midsummer:[7] *The wind was furious ... was dead ahead, and blew in fierce and long continued gusts. Poor Kate* [the pony] *was sadly tortured by the pelting showers ... It was indeed an extraordinary day for summer; and as the saline spray was carried over hill and vale, impregnating the whole atmosphere, and coating the face with layers of salt, it told sadly on the crops of the poor Shetland crofters. The effects were not seen that day; but next morning I surveyed with sorrow the blighted potatoes, with blackened 'shaw', checked thus early in their growth, the blasted grain ... The days were about their longest, and there was literally no darkness.*

That was the summer of 1867, the first of the consecutive bad years. We must also remember how dependent the crofters were on their crops and fish – not like the present day when most of us wouldn't know how to begin to be self-sufficient.

'A Shetland Scot', writing to *The Northern Ensign*, in March 1870, outlined the long hours worked on the crofts when weather permitted: *No one who knows Shetlanders will call them lazy, unless their avowed enemies. In spring they are to be seen in the fields from six o'clock in the morning until ten at night, and in harvest from early dawn till dusk, and when there is moonlight, part of the family work all night when it is dry, if the weather be changeable or squally.*

LEAN YEARS

Women, especially, could never be idle. During the summer months, when the men were at the fishing, they had to keep the croft work going while rearing large families and often tending old, infirm relatives. When walking to fetch peats (carried in a 'kishie' on the back), they would knit as they went – precious time could not be wasted. 'A woman's work is never done' certainly applied to Shetland women in the 19th century.

Walker's letters to newspapers refuting the existence of destitution are too many and too long to quote here, but one more is worthy of mention. By January, when writing to the *Dundee Advertiser,* he had stopped using pen-names: *I represent the properties forming at least one-half of Unst, and of considerable extent in other parishes. In December last I visited every house on the Estates, and I am very frequently in the Island of Unst.*

Now wait a minute. Every house on the estates? We realise he was a super energetic person, but what an achievement that would have been! And he didn't just knock at the door, pay his respects and pass on. No, he claims to have ascertained that all was well: *I found in every house the appearance of plenty ... I found that the average earnings of the fishers for three months were about £17 per man ... that the prices obtained for all kinds of stock were extreme.*

So what would visiting every house on the estate entail? The valuation roll 1868-69 for Major Cameron's property in North Yell, shows thirty-two rentals left, after the clearing of the townships Walker had designated for sheep-farms. These were scattered from the far north in Vigon, through Cullivoe, Gutcher, Cunnister, Sellafirth and on to Basta – quite a trek over boggy hills in December. Travelling, on foot or horseback, would have been easier in Unst – lack of peat on the east side makes the terrain firmer. However, Garth and Annsbrae had at that time almost two hundred households[8] in Unst deserving a welfare visit from their dynamic factor. To visit every house on the estate Walker would also have had to examine about thirty-five[9] rentals still left in Delting, and every household in Bressay.

Furthermore he claimed he took time to note the prices the folk had got for their stock and the fishermen's earnings. In all the correspondence about these disastrous years it has been agreed that the one bright spot was the success of the cod and ling fishing of summer, 1869. It was also agreed that this alone was not enough to lift even these families (and they were not all cod and ling fishers) out of the debt accumulated during the other lean years. So that particular statistic taken in isolation was misleading. Of course his letters were written to influence charitable people in the south, most of whom were not in a position to judge for themselves whether their financial aid to Shetland was really necessary.

101

JOHN WALKER'S SHETLAND

From his rounds of enquiry he argued that *the prices obtained for all kinds of stock had been extreme*. He didn't say whether he meant extremely good or extremely bad. Tagged on to the end of his other assertions we are inclined to assume 'good'. But in letters to William Pennie in the hairst of 1868 he was deploring the fact that the price of lambs had gone down and wrote: *the account of the sheep is very melancholy.*

Furthermore it was in December 1869 that he claimed to have visited every tenant on the Estate. To make his time even shorter for that marathon task, we know from a letter[10] to Jeffray at Belmont on the 11th of that month that he was to be in Aberdeen by the 22nd.

Thomas Irvine of Midbrake wrote to the *Daily Review* on 28th March, 1870: *I am a native of North Yell, and reside in it. I am perfectly acquainted with the circumstances of the inhabitants, and cannot learn that your correspondent visited any houses in the parish to ascertain the state of their provisions.* Irvine sums up Walker and his mendacious attitude towards the Shetlanders with: *Your correspondent has composed and published a work of imagination. It is neither a novel nor a comedy, but had it not passed through the hands of the reviewers might have produced a tragedy by tying up the hands and sympathies of the humane and benevolent.*

Alexander Sandison again:[11] *I have just read the letter from Mr Walker in your issue and ... some parts of it may convey a false idea to your readers.* He then went on to explain the problem of the crops being destroyed by gales before the grain had ripened, and continued: *But admit that we poor ignorant Shetlanders have no foresight, why did not Mr W. tell your readers that the South Country farmers of Belmont, Lund and Uyea farms, on some of the best soils in Unst, lost their crops as well?*

Sandison then turned to Walker's assertion that the average earnings of the fishermen for three months was around £17 per man: *Three months, well it may be so! The ling fishing commences 12th May if weather permits. Herring fishing ends first week in October. The same men are employed at the both, changing from the one to the other from 12th to 20th August. We poor short-sighted Shetlanders count as we like make this fully four and a half months.*

As to the £17 per man earnings. The average earnings of 84 men fishing in 14 boats in the South parish of Unst during the season 1869 was £8:14:11d per man. The herring fishing was an entire failure, nothing even to pay expenses in fitting out.

The average for the same number of men and boats in the same district in 1868 was only £3:11:2d. Average earning ling and herring for the two years – £6:3:0½d.

LEAN YEARS

So why was Walker so set against aid coming to Shetland? We can only guess. Perhaps he started on that side of the argument and couldn't be seen to be wrong. It would appear, however, that the lack of local labour for his schemes really infuriated him. If only we knew what wage was to be offered to any Shetland workers he recruited – that was never mentioned – leaving the suspicion that he was hoping for cheap labour for his ditching, mining (but that's another story), or, to quote 'A Shetland Scot' in the *Northern Ensign*:[12] *to build dykes enclosing the property of which they have been denied the use.*

The same correspondent put forward another reason for Walker's determination that no aid should come to Shetland. Assuming that the factor for Garth and Annsbrae would want to clear more tenants:[13] *famine would be an easier and cheaper way, why not then let it have its course? The obnoxious fish merchants and shopkeepers would then be got rid of in the same manner.* Walker was not the only one who could fantasise!

Possibly the most damaging letter of all, was addressed by Walker to the Home Secretary, dated 16th February, 1870:[14] *I understand that five individuals have sent you a Petition for a grant of Public money (£500) to be spent on Roads etc. and to meet alleged Destitution. I represent as Commissioner & Factor the Estates which comprise above one half of this Parish. I beg to say that I have come here specially to enquire as to the alleged Destitution – that I can find no case – that there is no need for and no Public money (granted as Charity) will be allowed to be spent upon the Estates of Garth ... that any case of Destitution arising hereafter will be provided for by the Proprietors and that it is considered a piece of impertinence on the five individuals (one the Parish Minister lately settled, one the F.C. Minister and the remaining three being partners of one trading firm) without the slightest information or knowledge libelling the Proprietors as unwilling and unable to do their duty towards their Tenants and attempting to excite Public Charity without cause. Altho called upon to do so the individuals referred to have failed to give in the names of any destitute parties.*

On the same theme, he wrote to Frederick Dundas, M.P. for Shetland:[15] *Presuming that your influence has been asked to support a Petition from five individuals in Unst to the Home Secretary praying that a Grant of £500 be made for the relief of alleged destitute on that Isle – I think it right to inform you that on behalf of Garth and Annsbrae I have written to the Home Secretary denouncing the Appeal as an insult to the Proprietors of Unst and quite uncalled for.*

At a meeting of the Parochial Board held subsequent to the sending of the Petition it was unanimously resolved that up to that time no case of destitution had arisen and that the local means were adequate for any emergency. Then he got on to the work he had to offer: *There is at present work to the extent of £1200 offered in Unst and the Chromate Ore Quarries are to be opened within a fortnight.*

** ** **

As Walker pointed out to the Home Secretary he was factor for about half of the island of Unst. As early as August 1866 an unusual proposition had been made to the estate. Walker outlined it to the Major:[16] *Edmondston, Jeffray, Spence, Mouat and Sandison have been at Miss Mouat at Belmont as to letting the Garth properties in Unst to them as a whole ... Tenants might then be used anyhow ... At present any proposition seems premature.* Walker, at that stage, was not keen on the idea.

Three days later Spence and Jeffray had provided him with more detail:[17] *They would like to work them* [the tenants] *under our Rules provided they were allowed to add a clause binding the Tenants to fish for them for 10 years.* But Walker impressed on the Major that this would be *not only impracticable but unjust.*

After some bickering, the estate and the 'Company', as Walker now called them, came to an agreement about changes to some of the rules for the tenants. Jaffray and Edmonston withdrew from the transaction, but in December 1867 four Unst merchants officially set themselves up in business as 'Spence & Co.'. They were John Spence, William G. Mouat, John Thomson and Alexander Sandison. A lengthy circular[18] was issued to the tenants informing them that: *We have, hoping to modify to a certain extent coming changes, obtained a lease of these Estates ... Our desire is to help and benefit the tenants, and as far as we can raise them socially and morally.*

The change in the use of the scattald was to be introduced *gradually and judiciously.* However, there would be a charge for its use – 1/6 per head on byre cattle; 3/6 on horse stock over one year old; 9d a head for sheep, all payable at Martinmas 1868. These rates would be doubled for tenants from other properties. *Thus the benefit of the Scattalds will be secured to those who pay for them.*

As to the 'Rules and Regulations' *when introduced, we believe generally, they* [the tenants] *will see the advantage accruing to themselves. We do not expect that the idle and thriftless will admire them, but it may help them to discover that 'Idleness is the parent of want, while the hand of the diligent maketh rich'.*

Fairness and honesty was the theme of the last two paragraphs of the circular and a warning that any deceit or double dealing would be punishable. Followed by the signatures of the four merchants, the tenants were assured that *our desire is to benefit all under our care, and we will do so, unless the tenants themselves prevent it.*

LEAN YEARS

However, as we saw earlier, unseasonable weather was the adversary they all had to contend with. On 5th March, 1868 John Spence wrote from Haroldswick to Walker:[19] *Some of the Garth and Annsbrae Tenants after agreeing to fish have taken a daft fit and are going to set off and leave their farms and families – I had got them all settled down very well and they and we were trying to face a bad year as well as we could but they, by all I can learn, were advised to this by parties who are doing everything they can to influence the people against you and us.*

On 5th May, Spence & Co. to Walker:[20] *We are indeed both vexed and surprised to learn that it is Miss Mouat's intention to press for her arrears in such a year – when utter destitution and starvation is staring many in the face – and when we are doing all in our power and beyond our power to preserve the tenants from death which but for us must have been the case ere now with very many ... At the same time we beg to say that if stock is taken from the poor starving tenants at this time for arrears – while utter want is in their homes – it appears to us the worst feature in all our correspondence about the lease of the property.*

By 12th September of the same harrowing year, Spence and Co. had changed their tune about at least some arrears, and wrote to ask Walker to arrange the removal of certain tenants:[21] *In reference to Sandwick the rents of which (inc. Mathew Mathewson's) is far on to £50, all the tenants who have been in the habit of making a sort of payment are leaving and those who have paid little or nothing are remaining contentedly so that unless it can be enclosed for a grazing we do not expect to make the Public Burdens out of it. We therefore beg to call your attention and request that you will take the necessary steps for having James Jamieson, Hanna Sutherland, Gilbert Anderson, Andrew Cluness and Ann Nisbet removed at first term and make arrangements with the neighbouring proprietors so that it can be enclosed and used as a grazing next summer. As you are aware we cannot afford to sacrifice such a heavy rent.*
P.S. We need not remind you about the Earl's 12 merk in the middle and at the South side.

Walker replied:[22] *Agreeing with you as to the desirableness of enclosing Sandwick for grazing will issue the necessary Notices of Removal.*

On the 19th September the lawyers W. & W. Sievwright wrote to Spence & Co.:[23] *You have followed the blind leading of Mr Walker in the matter of removing Jamieson, and have thus failed to trust the agents here, particularly ourselves ... We certainly would have nothing whatever to do with the Summons you have sent ... the action itself is bad because it is founded solely upon Acts which do not Authorise the removal of tenants from subjects such as Jamieson occupies.*

As has been pointed out before, William Sievwright frequently defended cases against Walker. Perhaps this time criticism of Walker is unjust. As can be seen from the above correspondence, the first move to clear Sandwick came from Spence & Co. On the other hand Walker rebuked Sandison, by letter, on 26th September:[24]

I sent a Warning *to your brother so as to make sure of clearing Jamieson out.*

In fact Spence & Co. and Walker didn't manage to clear Sandwick, Unst. Some enclosure was started in the form of dyke building, but they hadn't realised, or chose to ignore the fact that at Still, the Jamieson family held udal rights to their croft, and because of that the scheme of enclosure had to be abandoned.

George Jamieson is a great-grandson of the above James Jamieson and he tells the following story about the unusual situation at Still:

Drivin or walkin alang da Hannigarth rod fae da Muness rod, an turning aff ta Hannigarth, a body will notice aboot haaf wye alang da rod, on dir left hand side, a high ston daek dat haeds awa tae da nordert. Da sooth end o dis daek is only twenty space or so fae da side o da rod. A fence runs fae da end o da daek alang da rod tae Hannigarth.

On closer examination dis daek haeds awa tae da nordert as far as Colvadale enclosin da lang deserted crofts o Sandwick. Biggit i da 19th century, hit wis intended tae enclose a lok o da sooth-aest corner o Unst, endin at da banks somewhaar aboot Littlgarth. Da tenant crofters wir tae be evicted tae mak wye fur a sheep farm.

Hooever, while da plan wis pairtly successful, da daek suddenly ended ahint da croft hoose o Bracknigarth i da middle o da hill. Da story A'm heard why dis happened wis dat whin da daek biggers wan tae whit might be defined as da Still scattald, James Jamieson o Still, a udaller in his own right, an a man dat coodna be evicted, guid oot an drave a stake inta da grund an said, 'Boys, yon's as faar as da daek can come becaas you canna enclose da Still scattald.'

I mind my late faider telling me yon story. Noo he wis boarn in 1890, his faider Geordie – my grandfaider – wis boarn in 1857, an his faider, auld James, died in 1897. So, in terms o da time scale da story could weel a bün passed on.

Still wis continuously occupied by da Jamiesons fae at laest da early 1600s until da last resident, Jacobina, better kent as Auntie Jecky, died dere in 1913.

In December 1869 Widow Sutherland wrote to Walker from Uyeasound saying that Sandison and Mouat had warned her with removal. She had given them £3 cash and, to settle her debt, had offered animals which they would not accept. They had been annoyed that she

LEAN YEARS

Da daek suddenly ended ahint da croft hoose o Bracknigarth.
© *Andy Gear*

had bought meal from another merchant. Her final comment was:[25] *The Company* [Spence & Co.] *told the tenants they had 'taken the island to keep out you, a tyrant', but I suppose they are going to act the tyrant first.*

The Company were apparently in debt themselves by January 1869. Walker to Sandison:[26] *I do not regret and cannot withdraw a word I've written to yourself or your firm – You were not in a position to pay the rents when required ... I will not say any more on the matter – than that my business experience will prevent me again making like arrangements, and I hope you will keep this in mind.*

Financial matters did not improve for the company as the year progressed. In December Walker was blaming Sandison's partners for the situation:[27] *As your partners at Baltasound have chosen to insult the property ... for yours and Spence's sake alone I extend the time to accept my offer ... My opinion of your partners is again at a very low ebb indeed.*

And on 2nd April, 1870:[28] *It is more than likely that you might have got some assistance but for the remarks in your P.S. which leads me to fear that were you to be further assisted you would not allow a week to elapse before attempting a similar line of conduct.*

I don't know how imprudent the remarks in the P.S. were, but a week later there had been a change of heart:[29] *After much consideration Major Cameron and myself have agreed to assist you to the amount you asked and stated as sufficient to carry you thro. the season – £500 ... I would now put on record my advice that you at once stop the reckless*

107

credits hitherto given, that you endeavour to buy in *first markets*, that you be satisfied with reasonable profits and if any of your members have forgotten themselves and indulged in intemperate habits that they and all unnecessary extravagances be laid aside ... a disregard of these simple truths will bring ruin on yourselves and others in a very short time ... I expect all the partners to see to this.

P.S. I am sorry that you can get no more seed oats until next week.

The partnership of Spence & Co. as general merchants and fish traders was dissolved on 12th November, 1873, but the lease of Garth properties in Unst still had a year to run. In July 1874 the Major wrote to Walker in Edinburgh:[30] *I hear from Unst that the Company have taken out Summonses against several Garth Tenants to the amount that crop and stock will not meet thus leaving the Tenants Paupers.* He goes on to ask Walker to check the terms of the lease with Spence & Co. as he recalls that *during the last year or so of its currency they were not to harry the Tenants so as to leave them naked at the end of the lease. If Spence & Co. have not the legal right to act as they are doing they should be stopt.*

Two days later Walker wrote to the Company[31] telling them that they must *at once see that such a system is stopt otherwise the Proprietor must interfere.* At the same time he wrote to the Major: *They have no right to act as they are doing if this is to be considered the last year of their lease – that is my reading of the lease.*

It looks as if Spence & Co. ignored these warnings as, a few weeks later Walker received a letter from Unst. It was written on the 17th August by Douglas Sinclair on behalf of himself and John Clark:[32] *As we have been warned by Mr Spence to leave the farms we hold on Skaw at Martinmas first we beg to ask if you will still allow us to hold them afterwards as we would like to do so if agreeable to you. If you cannot do it will you please allow us to remain all winter as there is severe sickness and trouble in our families.*

Apparently contradicting the above correspondence is a letter of 22nd August from John Spence [of Spence & Co.], Haroldswick:[33] *There are two of the Skaw tenants going to New Zealand and the other two have warned or rather I have warned them to leave at Martinmas as you wished me.*

When the lease of the Unst properties of Garth and Annsbrae ended in November 1874, Major Cameron received a long letter from Spence & Co. explaining why they had not made a success of the venture. The failure of both fishing and crops during the late 1860s meant that much of the rent due had not been forthcoming and they had been obliged to give a considerable amount of credit.

The lean years had taken their toll.

Croft house at Still. The dyke which was to enclose Sandwick seen below the ridge of the hill. © *Andy Gear*

1. Andrew T. Cluness, *The Shetland Isles*, London 1951, p.67
2. S.A. D 6/292/8
3. S.A. D 6/292/8
4. S.A. D 6/292/24
5. Ibid
6. Ibid
7. John T. Reid, *Art Rambles in Shetland*, Edinburgh 1869, p.14
8. S.A. CO 8/1/14A/1
9. S.A. Valuation Roll for Delting 1868-69
10. Gardie Papers L.B.2 p.842
11. Sandison's Archive, draft of letter, no date or paper named
12. S.A. D 6/292/8 p.18
13. S.A. D 6/292/8 p.17
14. Gardie Papers L.B.2 opposite p.861
15. Gardie Papers L.B.2 opposite p.869
16. Gardie Papers L.B.1 p.15
17. Gardie Papers L.B.1 p.17
18. S.A. D 16/393/5
19. Gardie Papers 1868/104
20. Sandison's Archive L.B.3 Mar.1868-Dec.1870
21. Sandison's Archive L.B.3 pp.89-90
22. Gardie Papers L.B.2 p.524
23. Sandison's Archive
24. Sandison's Archive
25. Gardie Papers 1869/583
26. Sandison's Archive

JOHN WALKER'S SHETLAND

27 Gardie Papers L.B.2 p.831
28 Gardie Papers L.B.2 p.891
29 Gardie Papers L.B.2 p.895
30 Gardie Papers 1874/144
31 Gardie Papers 1874/146
32 Gardie Papers 1874/155
33 Gardie Papers 1874/160

Chapter Ten

STEAM

I'm just returned from Yell Sound ... I'm gone by steam, against wind and tide, to Delting, been there 6 hours and back since 10am. The 'Bride' has moved upwards of 80 passengers this week.
John Walker writing to Andrew Umphray, Midnight 7/11/1868

ON 24th August, 1868, in the middle of the lean years, a meeting was held in George Reid Tait's office in Lerwick, of subscribers to a company for placing the first steam powered vessel on the Shetland inter-island trade.[1] Present were, G. R. Tait, John Robertson, Dr Cowie, John Harrison, Dr P. D. Loeterbagh, John Airth, C. Robertson, Robert Irvine, C. Merrylees and John Walker. Capital was £5000 divided into 500 shares of £10. Robertson and Merrylees were appointed company's agents.

Walker was unanimously appointed chairman and authorised to take all necessary steps for carrying through the preliminary arrangements, and to arrange that a meeting of shareholders be held in Lerwick within the next few weeks. Members of the Walker family were prominent shareholders – brothers Robert, Alexander and James being involved and Alexander taking shares for his sons, James and Alexander, and also for his daughter Mary.[2]

About a week after the first meeting, Walker updated Major Cameron:[3] *The steamer matter is a settled question. Everybody has gone into it and although I've booked you for 5 shares it will only take £25 out of your pocket as so many subscribed that I raised the capital from 300 to*

111

John Walker's Shetland

500 shares thereby necessitating only £5 per share ... I hope ere you return [the Major was on one of his many trips south] *that you'll hear of her being regularly in the trade. We've got the vessel for £2000 the captain keeping one half. My father is still alive so I don't move as Mrs Walker is not better yet.* Mary Walker was about to give birth to their ninth child.

Although he did remain a shareholder, it would seem that Major Cameron was not particularly enthusiastic, as we can read between the lines from Walker on 10th September:[4] *I am duly favoured with yours of 7th and note contents. If you desire it I can have no difficulty in transferring the shares I had put you down for in the Steam Co. But I looked upon it that your name should appear at the starting of it however long it remained.*

There was exciting news in his next letter to the Major, on the 17th, which perhaps explains why Walker's handwriting is less legible than usual![5] *First let me thank you for the three nice birds sent to Mrs Walker thro. Gardie. They will come in very opportune for Mrs Walker this morning about 12.30 duly presented me with a <u>son</u>* (the tables seem turned at last). *Both seem to be getting on well.* After discussion of problems about the North Yell Division, the last paragraph deals with the Steam Co.: *Please sign and send me by return of post the enclosed* [?] *forms for the Steam Co. I would like you, J. Bruce, G.H.B. Hay, G. Tait, the Captain,* [?], [?], *and myself to be elected Directors. I hope you'll have no objections.*

The first Directors[6] appointed were, Major Thomas Cameron, Thomas Edmonston of Buness, John Bruce of Sumburgh, John Harrison, Charles Robertson, John Tait, George Reid Tait, William Irvine and John Walker (Interim Manager). At the first general meeting of the company held in the Subscription Rooms on the 26th September, the following motion was passed: *The meeting then adopts the circular issued by Mr Walker as a prospectus and agrees to purchase the S.S. 'Chieftain's Bride' upon the terms defined in Sale Note from Hugh McLean, late owner, also approved the names Hugh McLean, George Reid Tait and John Walker being registered as owners for and on behalf of the Company.*

The vessel cost £2,000 and with extra expenses – outfit at Glasgow, foresail, chains, buoys, etc., the total initial expenditure was brought up to £2,159:17s.[7]

The crew[8] appointed in October 1868 –
Captain McLean – Master, £3 per week.
Magnus Robertson – Pilot and to act as Mate, 20 shillings per week.
Laurence Johnston – Seaman, 18 shillings per week.
Andrew Anderson – Seaman, also to act as Clerk, 18 shillings per week.
James Bolt – Stoker, 10 shillings per week.

STEAM

And at the same time, details of summer sailings[9] to the North Isles and North Mainland.

Monday – leave Lerwick at 6am, call Whalsay, Mid Yell, Uyeasound, Brough Lodge, Whalsay, Lerwick.

Tuesday – Whalsay, Swinister, Mossbank, Ollaberry, Lochend, North Roe, Westsandwick.

Wednesday – from Ollaberry, West Yell, Ulsta, Mossbank, Burravoe, Whalsay, Lerwick.

Thursday – 10am Whalsay, Gossabrough, (Fetlar when required), Mid Yell, Basta Voe (once a fortnight), Cullivoe, Uyeasound, Baltasound, Uyeasound, Brough Lodge, Mid Yell, Whalsay, Lerwick.

In addition the *Bride* would call anywhere she may be required such as Vidlin, Neep and Girlsta. With a schedule like that, the stoker certainly earned his 10 shillings a week!

The fares decided on at the October meeting[10] seem quite high, especially when compared with the crew's wages.

	Cabin	Steerage
Symbister	2 shillings	1 shilling
Mossbank	3 shillings	1 shilling & 6 pence
Burravoe	3 shillings	1 shilling & 6 pence
Ollaberry	3 shillings & 6 pence	1shilling & 9 pence
Mid Yell & Fetlar	ditto	ditto
Lochend & N. Roe	4 shillings	2 shillings
Cullivoe	ditto	ditto
Uyeasound	5 shillings	2 shillings & 6 pence
Baltasound	5 shillings & 6 pence	2 shillings & 9 pence

Until the formation of the Steam Company and the purchase of the *Chieftain's Bride*, trade to the North Isles had been carried out by sail. In theory steam would be quicker and more dependable and of great benefit for shifting cargo, especially animals – hence John Walker's interest. It must have been an exciting time. Imagine how impressed the bairns would have been when she came puffing in the voe! And she likely had plenty of critics too, including believers that vessels should proceed by *the Almighty's ain wind and no' wi' the devil's sunfire and brimstane.*[11]

The Unst Shipping Company, for which Alexander Sandison was agent, owned the *Imogene* and *Matilda* which were to be replaced.[12] Walker had instructed Sandison on 29th August:[13] *You will require to call a special meeting of Unst Shipping Co. to ratify taking a £500 interest in the Shetland Steam Shipping Compy. Limited.*

And again on 5th September:[14] *With regard to the Unst Shipping Co's Meeting I have merely to advise that the meeting should resolve to take say 60 shares in the Shetland Steam Compy. Ltd.*

113

Alexander Sandison with his wife Margaret and their family c.1870.
Courtesy Duncan and Jan Sandison

The Unst Co. agreed to invest, but Alexander Sandison held grave reservations about the *Chieftain's Bride*. He made his opinion known to the Steam Co., when writing to notify them of the Unst Company's decision to buy shares:[15] *You must not think that any of us are against Steam, but at the same time, I wish hereby to record to you by this letter, my firm belief that the 'Chieftain's Bride' is unsuitable for the trade ... A vessel of 130 tons burden with a 25 horse power; she is a trash and would be thrown aside where either speed or power is required.*

Walker was furious. To Alexander Sandison, 8th September:[16] *Rumours are current that there are some wise heads in Unst who consider that the 'Chieftain's Bride' is too like themselves <u>slow</u> and I think it right to state that the vessel has never had any sort of a fair Trial here having always been too heavily ladened and there seems no doubt but that she'll come up to her speed of 8 knots. This rate is quite fast enough to begin with and I've no doubt when once in the passage that those who now think her slow will admit as Mr Shepherd has done when he saw her cleave thro Whalsay Sound against an ebb tide – that she is far better than he thought.*

Yours truly, John Walker.

Four days later he had calmed down, and, believe it or not, actually sounded slightly worried – most unlike our over-confident entrepreneur. To Alexander Sandison:[17] *But now as to my remarks about what you call <u>my steamer</u>. It has surely not escaped your memory that all my Unst friends when I was there thought well of her ... I will be truly sorry if you are right as you and others are placing so much confidence in the matter that I for once begin to feel nervous ...*

Sadly, tragedy was about to hit the Maryfield household. 30th December:[18] *A good New Year to you! Our house is bung full of measles caused thro: muckle Milne's*[19] *stupidity ...*

On the 17th January, 1869 the Walkers' much-longed-for son, William, died of measles at Maryfield, aged four months. Some of his eight elder sisters were very ill too, but the girls all survived. In a black-edged letter to Alex Sandison, *Saturday, Midnight:*[20] *I have only time to thank you for your warm sympathy in our sad bereavement – loss to us but gain to our dear Boy.*

Another black-edged letter, 20th February, was addressed to the Shareholders of the Aberdeen, Leith & Clyde Shipping Co.:[21] *I beg to draw your attention to the accompanying copy of correspondence just concluded between your Directors and myself anent a charge against your Manager or other Officer of allowing a man suffering under an infectious disease to travel by your vessel and thereby causing death and misery to many families in Shetland.*

It seems possible from the timing of this correspondence that the infectious disease referred to was measles, often fatal in those days. From the rest of the February letter it can be surmised that the directors of the Aberdeen Shipping Co. would neither admit their error nor promise greater care in the future. He urged the shareholders to censure this mismanagement. It has to be said of Walker that he was not afraid to speak his mind, but would he have held himself responsible for an infectious passenger on the North Isles circuit for which he was a director?

Meanwhile the *Chieftain's Bride* was laid up with serious boiler trouble. Alexander Sandison was right – the vessel was fit neither for the route nor the gruelling time-table, and because of her lack of speed had earned the nickname *Crab*. By the 30th the problem had still not been resolved and the Steam Company's agents, Robertson and Merrylees sent an apology from the Office of the Aberdeen, Leith & Clyde Shipping Co., 62 Marischal Street, Aberdeen, to Alexander Sandison:[22] *We regret that the 'C. Bride' having been withdrawn has created so much inconvenience in your quarter. Had the Directors imagined that the time required for putting the vessel in order would have been so long they would probably have chartered a sailing vessel. The expense to the new Company will be very considerable ... We are sorry to tell you that the steamer will be unfit to go north this ensuing week yet. The repairs to the machinery and boiler have been extensive but the Directors are determined now to have her put in first rate order before she again commences to ply ...*

It was noted at a directors' meeting on 1st February that the boiler makers from Aberdeen were still at work, and it was the middle of that month before the *Bride* was back in service. Meanwhile Robertson and Merrylees had intimated their resignation as company's agents and Walker and Tait had been appointed joint managing directors and were authorised to take over all cash books, papers etc. in the hands of the previous agents. In April, Robert Scott was appointed to act as agent, at a salary of £45 per annum. Repairs to the boiler etc. cost £58:4s:3d which the directors considered was an overcharge.[23]

By the 12th April the *Bride* was again out of service with boiler trouble and was at Hall Russell's shipyard where the boiler was to be enlarged. Blame that time was laid upon the engineer, as orders were given that he was to be paid off at Aberdeen. A clue to the neglect involved comes from the directors' meeting of 19th May, when *the Captain is specially enjoined to see that the Boiler is always supplied with water to prevent a repetition of the late disaster but in no way to relieve the Engineer of his responsibility*.

On a lighter note, at the same meeting Dr Loeterbagh's attention was drawn to the quality of liquor available on board the *Bride*. It was confirmed that at least the beer and brandy were inferior, and that the passengers' complaints in this respect were correct. About the same time it was agreed that *the cook is to be allowed his food in consideration of making himself generally useful in working the cargo on board*.

And *a boy to be engaged as a deck hand at wages not exceeding 10s.* [a week].[24]

STEAM

The rest of the summer of 1869 passed uneventfully. It was agreed in July to send the *Bride* on a pleasure trip to Muckle Flugga, and in August a complaint was received from Lady Nicholson – a shareholder[25] – about the length of time the steamer was prepared to wait at Brough Lodge, Fetlar. In February 1870 the Captain was instructed to be *as attentive to Fetlar as possible.* The previous year Walker had written, somewhat brusquely, to *The Lady Nicholson.*[26]

Dear Madam,

It has now been resolved to place a steamer betwixt Lerwick and the places in the North whose inhabitants shall take a suitable interest in the undertaking. My own personal friends and interested parties in Unst and Lerwick have in two days subscribed £1650 and I have now to ask you to join with them and thus secure that the Steamer makes Fetlar one of her ports of call – The Company will be registered under the Limited Liability Act. An early answer will oblige.

Carriage of mails to the North Isles was an ongoing subject of negotiation between the Post Office and the Steam Company. In February 1870, agreement had still not been reached, as we learn from a directors' meeting: *The matter of carrying the mails to the North Isles for a sum of £50 per annum after due consideration was declined as being too low.*

And in September 1870 *it was resolved to discontinue the sailing of the Steamer to Cullivoe in consequence of the withdrawal of support from that quarter.*

There must be a story there. Unfortunately, no further detail is given.

Later that year the company's office flit to 44 Commercial Street, rent £9 per annum.[27] Walker owned several properties in Lerwick, including Nos. 40, 42 & 44 Commercial Street. In the Valuation Roll for 1872-73, No. 40 is described as a shop occupied by Robert Scott (Brown's Representative), No. 42 was a house also occupied by Robert Scott, here described as Shipping Agent, with rooms and cellars below the house rented out separately.

Early in 1871, Mr Mouat, Board of Trade Inspector, reported that he had never seen engines so dirty as those of the *Chieftain's Bride*. About the same time there was a problem with the balance sheets. At a meeting of shareholders on 29th February, 1872, the chairman (Walker) expressed the opinion that a majority of shareholders were in favour of selling the vessel and winding up the company. By April the *Bride* was in Glasgow for sale at a reserve price of £2,500. But some of the shareholders purchased the *Bride* at her reserved price and were anxious to continue the company. Directors, including Walker, George Bruce, George Reid Tait and John

117

Bruce left the company that year. In October new shares were called at £5 and Major Cameron was elected to the chair.

And so the *Bride* continued to serve the Isles in her crab-like fashion for a few more years. Captain McLean was replaced by Captain William Nicolson, a Shetlander, born in Whiteness, who had worked his way up from his first voyage as a cabin boy on a Leith ship employed in the Faroe and Iceland cod fishing.[28] In 1876 the *Bride* was sold and the Shetland Steam Company wound up. They were replaced by the Shetland Islands Steam Navigation Co. Ltd., and temporarily by the *Lady Ambrosine*.

In April 1877 the first *Earl of Zetland* arrived in Shetland to take over the North Isles trade, which she plied valiantly until the end of the second world war.

A last word on the *Bride*. After her 1874 Board of Trade Inspection the surveyor decreed that the following be provided to satisfy the test requirements:
One Life Boat
Two new Life Buoys
One set of Signal Rockets and Blue Lights
One Cannon of 3½ inch bore

Curious about the cannon, I made enquiries as to its use, and discovered that it was probably used for signalling purposes. By 1874 John Walker was no longer living in Shetland and I must confess that I rather liked the suggestion made by one witty historian that they had installed the cannon in case he came back!

S.S. *Chieftain's Bride* photographed in the 1870s by J. Irvine
© *Shetland Museum*

STEAM

1 S.A. D 1/251/1 Members' Minute Book,
2 S.A. D 1/251/3 Register of Members, 1868-76
3 Gardie Papers L.B.2 p.506
4 Gardie Papers L.B.2 p.513
5 Gardie Papers L.B.2 p.527
6 S.A. D 1/251/1 Members' Minute Book, 1868-76
7 S.A. Shetland Steam Shipping Co., Balance Sheet at 31/12/1868
8 S.A. D 1/251/2 Directors' Minute Book, 1868-76
9 Ibid
10 Ibid
11 Adam Robson, *The Saga of a Ship,* Lerwick 1982, p.35
12 Charles Sandison, *Unst, My Island Home and its Story,* Lerwick 1968, p.58
13 Sandison's Archive
14 Ibid
15 Charles Sandison, *Unst, My Island Home and its Story,* Lerwick 1968, p.58
16 Sandison's Archive
17 Ibid
18 Gardie Papers L.B.2 p.602
19 John Milne, Manager at Aberdeen of Aberdeen, Leith & Clyde Shipping Co.
20 Sandison's Archive
21 Gardie Papers, L.B.2, facing p.684
22 S.A. D 1/251/2 Director's Minute Book, 1868-76
23 Ibid
24 Ibid
25 S.A. D 1/251/3 Register of Members, 1868-76
26 Gardie Papers L.B.2 p.499
27 S.A. D 1/251/2 Directors' Minute Book, 1868-76
28 Adam Robson, *The Saga of a Ship,* Lerwick 1982, p.19

Chapter Eleven

POLITICS

> *Mr Walker moved a vote of no confidence in Mr Dundas, which was seconded by Mr John Harrison, merchant. During the course of Mr Walker's remarks he attacked Mr Dundas for the part he took in regard to the Shetland Road Bill.*
> 'Mr Dundas at Shetland' *Orkney Herald* 25/7/1867

ONLY 340 men were eligible to vote in Shetland in 1868 and, of course, no women.[1] That was an increase in the electorate over previous elections because householders of £10 a year rental had now been granted the vote.[2] The ballot was not secret, the voter having to declare his allegiance verbally to the polling-sheriff. This system is illustrated by a story from Orkney in the *Herald* of 8th December. When asked which candidate he wished to vote for, a Shapinsay man replied, 'Mr Balfour's man' and then 'the other man'. He either didn't know or couldn't remember the name of the man he had been sent to vote for. It is easy to see how corruption like threats of eviction could go hand in hand with elections in those days. The 1868 election was rife with rumours of eviction, but, as most Shetland crofters did not pay a high enough rent to make them eligible to vote, these rumours more likely applied to the Orkney farmers with their bigger holdings and higher rent.

Frederick Dundas, Liberal, had been M.P. for Orkney and Shetland since 1837 with only a break from 1847 to 1852 when he lost the seat to Arthur Anderson,[3] and he seemed to have earned a certain respect in his island constituency. However, he incurred the wrath of John Walker through a disagreement over the Zetland Roads Bill, and Walker was henceforth hell-bent on discrediting Dundas.

In 1864 a vote of censure was passed on the M.P. at a meeting called by Walker. To counter this, another meeting was organised by the Dundas supporters. John William Spence, who attended that meeting, wrote in May 1864 to his uncle,[4] describing how Mr Hay had proposed a motion to suspend the judgement on Dundas until he could have the chance to speak for himself. Walker then moved that the censure be approved. Spence continued: *Mr Walker made a very long and in fact a very clever speech and the result was that Mr Walker's motion was carried by a sweeping majority. There were fully 150 people present and out of that number Messrs Hay, Sievwright, Saunders, myself and one or two others were the only supporters of Mr Hay's motion. Walker is now going to do what he can to induce some candidate to oppose Mr Dundas at the general election which must take place this year.* Yet another example of Walker's powers of persuasion. Although Spence was supporting Hay's motion, he had to admit a grudging admiration for Walker's rhetoric.

Dundas was returned in that election, but in 1868 Walker was equally determined to unseat him, and, after several unsuccessful attempts to find a Conservative candidate to stand for Orkney and Shetland, a committee was formed, calling themselves 'Independent Liberal'. They too had little success at first in procuring a candidate but eventually did secure the assistance of a certain Colonel Taylor from the Treasury. He provided the pseudo-Liberal Committee with four sheets of Stationery Office foolscap listing Dundas' attendance and votes in the House with a view to discrediting him. Taylor also promised that the Treasury would grant generous financial aid to compensate for years of Whig neglect of Shetland. One of several schemes set to benefit from these assurances was the recently formed Shetland Steam Shipping Company, which was to receive a postal subsidy.[5] As we saw in the last chapter John Walker was a prime mover and financier in the formation of that Company.

Walker's name was strongly connected with the Independent Liberals. 'An Independent Elector', Shetland, wrote to the *Orkney Herald* on 16th November, 1868 claiming that the 'Independent Liberals' who supported the Conservative candidate were disappointed at the small amount of encouragement they were receiving from the electorate. He suggested that this was either because the voters *detest dishonesty of profession and practice* or because they felt degraded *as puppets in the hands of the agricultural adventurer who presides in the 'Shetland Clearances Office', Bressay.*

JOHN WALKER'S SHETLAND

In the same newspaper of 1st December the readers were warned, under the headline *INFAMOUS TORY TACTICS ... Do not be duped by Turncoat John or any other trifling individual.* Walker had earned the nickname 'Turncoat John' by posing as an Independent Liberal when it was well known that he was Conservative.

At last, less than four weeks before the election, the Shetland group persuaded the Orkney Conservatives to join them in nominating a candidate by the name of Henry P. A. Riddell. The *Orkney Herald* again: *From week to week since the beginning of August rumours have reached us of the doings of the clique of malcontents in the sister group* [Shetland], *headed by him of Bressay whose name is Walker ... For some time the Orkney Tories, not wishing to be led ignominiously by the nose, looked askance at the overtures from Shetland ... but they seem, unfortunately for themselves, to have been unable to resist any longer the persistent badgering of the malcontents, who form only a petty portion of the Shetland electors.*

Practically nothing was known of Mr Riddell: *The Conservative candidate remains a man of mystery, and some people are inclined to consider him a myth altogether. He has not yet ventured to show his face or issue his address ... All we can learn about him is that his name is Riddle* [sic], *he has bushy whiskers and a nose, that he made a lot of money in India, that he resides in London and is known to a few members of the Carlton Club.*[6] Another rumour claimed that all Shetland was to be turned into a sheep farm![7]

Riddell proved his existence just prior to the election when he made his first visit to Orkney and Shetland. In a humiliating start to the campaign he was seasick on the crossing from Scrabster to Stromness and had to be nursed by his rival, Dundas.[8] On his arrival in Shetland *people looked at him with curiosity, in order to discover whether there was any similarity between him and Mr Walker before they should venture to hold communication with him.*[9]

In Lerwick a meeting was held in the Court Room, Fort Charlotte, chaired by Major Cameron. He introduced Riddell to the electors and non-electors present as someone he had known in India. It was feared there might be some disturbance at this meeting as feeling was running high due to the methods used by some of the canvassers: *There was a display of feeling when the horses and gigs were landed from the mail steamer, sent here it is said for election purposes. The sums spent about this election would have been of very great benefit if laid out in another way.*[10] Perhaps destitution relief? They were in the middle of the 'lean years'. But the folk who were hungry didn't have a vote, so assisting them made no difference to the election results.

POLITICS

In 1868 there were only two Shetland polling stations, one in Lerwick and the other in Burravoe, Yell. The election was held in early December and the weather was very stormy. The *Flying Meteor* paddle steamer which Dundas had chartered from the Clyde to transport his North Isles followers was held up, and the sloops *Naiad* and *Gossamer* were dispatched from Lerwick in the teeth of a flying gale to carry Dundas' brave men to Burravoe. Meanwhile, Riddell, not to be outdone, had the smack *Imogene* manned to face the storm. At one stage of the journey north the skipper of the *Naiad* was knocked from the wheel by a huge wave which also half filled the cabin, but they made Burravoe safely and at the close of the first day's voting in the North Isles the result was six to Riddell and twenty-eight to Dundas. But the next day the *Chieftain's Bride* arrived with a batch of Riddell supporters from Unst. The *Orkney Herald*, an overtly Liberal paper, described Unst on this occasion as *the only benighted island in the group*. The votes of the Unst contingency put Riddell ahead by seven at the end of the second day in Burravoe. Polling continued the following morning and when the poll closed at 1pm Riddell was still ahead, now by five votes. Apparently Riddell's supporters had anticipated a larger majority in the north as this result was seen to auger well for Dundas in Shetland. The *Flying Meteor* had weathered the storm in time to take voters home, *astonishing the dreary solitudes of the North with a display of rockets.*[11]

Much excitement was engendered by the continuous counting of votes and there were fireworks, songs by the children, and what is

Shipping in Bressay Sound 1872. Smack *Gossamer* on right of photo. Also in the picture is the Dutch frigate *Admiral Van Wassenaer* and the stern of the mail steamer *St Magnus I* on the left. Photographer J. Irvine.

© *Shetland Museum*

123

described as *the exercise of a natural perversity on the part of the non-electors of bawling out 'Dundas for ever' when they met a known supporter of Riddell, and 'Riddell for ever' when they met a supporter of Dundas.*[12] So even the non-electors had a part to play!

Of the 340 eligible voters in Shetland 137 voted for Dundas and 101 for Riddell. So the Shetland result was quite close. It would be interesting to know what the result might have been had more of the crofters been able to vote. Would they have been worried by Walker's association with Riddell or scared to vote for the 'wrong' man for fear of reprisals? We will never know. A bigger proportion of the Orkney farmers could register at the polling stations at Kirkwall and Stromness and Dundas had more support there. The Orkney result was 578 for Dundas and 345 for Riddell. Dundas was returned with an overall majority of 269.

Naturally John Walker wanted to become involved in local politics as well. The nearest equivalent to the Shetland Islands Council in those days was the body called the Commissioners of Supply (see appendix). Walker wrote to George Smith, Clerk to the Commissioners of Supply for Zetland on 15th September, 1868:[13] *I now beg to claim to have my name enrolled as a Commissioner of Supply in virtue of the following qualifications.*
As Commissioner and Factor for Major Thomas Mouat Cameron of Annsbrae etc under Deed of Factory dated 30th April, 1867.
As Commissioner and Factor for David Dakers Black Esquire of Kergord under Deed of Factory dated 18th January, 1865.
You will please take the necessary steps for the due admission of my claim.

Factor for David Dakers Black! He was the proprietor responsible for clearing the crofters from the Weisdale Valley in the 1840s and 50s. That was too early for Walker to have been involved, but possibly he got ideas from Black's policies. So far, whatever work, if any, he did for Black has escaped me. It also seems to have escaped the lampooners, and there were plenty of them around at that time (see appendix). I did find mention of Black's name in a letter to a William Grant of Wick in October 1870:[14] *D. D. Black esq. has informed me that you were anxious to get a Sheep Farm in this County – if so – I am prepared to let nine large Farms on reasonable terms.* Note that there were still nine farms available for rent in 1870. Demand had not lived up to Walker's expectations.

Apparently his application to become a Commissioner in '68 was turned down on the grounds that being a factor and commissioner for Cameron and Black did not entitle him to sit as a Commissioner of Supply.[15] Needless to say, he appealed, and in January 1870 we find Major Cameron writing to John Phin,[16] solicitor, with details of Walker's appeal and pointing out that *Mr Walker is not bona fide* [genuine] *factor for Mr Black,* which, no doubt explains the dearth of documentation on this

POLITICS

imaginary factorship! D. D. Black, being a Commissioner of Supply himself, must have been in on the intrigue – whatever it was.

However, Walker was eventually admitted as a Commissioner in 1874. The minutes for18th August list those present:[17]
George Thoms – *Sheriff of the County*
D. D. Black Esq. *of Kergord*
Joseph Leask *of Sand*
Arthur James Hay – *Factor for Earl of Zetland*
John Robertson sen. *Lerwick*
Charles Duncan – *Chief Magistrate*
John Walker Esq., *Factor for Major Cameron of Garth, who for the first time took his seat and signed a declaration in terms of the Act.* And, of course, had something to say: *Mr Walker instanced the treatment of the Zetland Parishes by the Government in the matter of allowances for their Schools and Schoolmasters' houses as a matter to be taken up by the County.* More about that in the chapter on school boards.

John Walker was not present at a meeting of Commissioners held in October 1875, but a letter was read from him on the subject of telegraphic communications with the islands, another topic in which he was keenly interested: *The Clerk was directed to reply to Mr Walker that under the Telegraphic Acts no new lines can be laid.*

He attended the A.G.M. of the Commissioners of Supply in May 1876 and was appointed convener of a committee to prepare plans for a new pier at Lerwick. As he was then resident in Edinburgh it must have been a considerable inconvenience to have the convener living so far away.

According to *Peaces Orkney and Shetland Almanac*, 1876 was the last year he served as a Commissioner of Supply in Shetland.

1   *Orkney Herald*, 25th August, 1868
2   R.D. Woodall, *Shetland Life* No.83
3   R.D. Woodall, *Shetland Life* No.83
4   S.A. D 12/142/34
5   *Orkney Herald*, 20th January, 1868
6   Ibid
7   *Northern Ensign*, 10th December, 1868
8   *Orkney Herald*, 10th November, 1868
9   Ibid
10   *Northern Ensign*, 10th December, 1868
11   *Orkney Herald*, 8th December, 1868
12   Ibid
13   Gardie Papers L.B.2 p.518
14   Gardie Papers L.B.2 p.990
15   Gardie Papers 1869/563
16   Gardie Papers 1870/6
17   S.A. Minute Book of Commissioners of Supply

Chapter Twelve

WALKER AND THE COMMISSIONS

The London gent now writes that he is ready
to advance £20,000 or more to check <u>Truck</u>.
John Walker writing to Major Cameron

BY THE 19th century fishing tenure in Shetland was developing into a system of truck where tenant fishermen were usually obliged to sell their fish to the specific merchant who was acting as agent for the laird. They were not told, on delivery, how much their catch was worth. The settlement of the price did not take place until November or December, after the fish had been cured and sold. Then rent had to be deducted from the fisherman's share of the catch and accounts settled for goods purchased and other debts which had accrued since the previous season. Frequently, the fisherman did not manage to clear his arrears. Because of the increased population most of the crofts could no longer sustain a family for twelve months, even in a good year, and so, increasingly, meal and other necessities had to be purchased from the merchant. The women bartered butter, eggs and hand-knitted articles, but somehow it never seemed quite enough to keep many families out of constant debt. A poor fishing season or failed crops, often happening in the same year, was enough to ensure that even more debt was carried over to the next season with little chance of escape from the trap.

Charles Bowen and Alexander Sellar were appointed as commissioners in 1870 to investigate the truck system. In January 1871

When carrying peats home in a kishie the women usually knitted as they walked along. Behind this knitter/peat carrier we see a poan-roofed outhouse. Photographer G. W. Wilson. © *Shetland Museum*

Thomas Edmonston, Arthur Hay, George Smith and John Walker travelled to Edinburgh to present to them the need for a commission of inquiry into truck to be held in Shetland.[1]

When asked by Mr Sellar how long he had lived in Shetland, Walker replied:
About eleven years permanently, but I have been acquainted with Shetland since I was a boy.
Are the shops good?
No, I consider them second rate.
Do you yourself deal with them?
No I do not, except for what I cannot help. We get all our stores from the South.

Walker was passionately opposed to the system of truck used by the merchants. In fact, generally speaking, he seemed to dislike the Shetland merchants – or was it that the merchants disliked him? After all, the more tenants Walker forced off the isles, the fewer customers the merchants would have left to truck. Or maybe Walker felt that if the merchants stopped their system of barter, more crofters would be unable to pay their rent and therefore be forced to leave.

When questioned on the subject of Shetland hosiery he explained that, in the town, the merchants gave out worsted to knitters, but when they brought back the finished goods, the knitter did not get any cash but was remunerated in fancy goods such as dresses, ribbons etc. He maintained that the women had no option but to accept these goods and I wonder if this explains references made by visitors to the islands in the 19th century about the excessive dressiness of Shetlanders, especially on Sundays. After all, if they were obliged to take fancy goods in payment for their knitting, they might as well make use of the stuff.

When Sellar asked about the system of payment in the country districts Walker replied: *When you leave the town you come to the middlemen merchants, or merchant factors, or merchant proprietors, in which case the knitters are their tenants. All worsted goods taken and sold in town are virtually taken surreptitiously, or on the sly ... I think there is absolute compulsion. If it is continued to any extent, the tenant will be walked off.*

When asked about the fishing, much the same picture was painted: *Boys of the family are engaged as beach boys, and each boy is established in the books of the firm, and he is allowed to draw his coat to go to church with. By the time the fishing is over, that boy has overdrawn his account, in bank language, to such an extent that he is 'thirled' to be engaged for the next season. This will go on for two or three seasons, till he is a grown lad, and then he has to go into some boat, and he is trucked away till he is an old man, and then he is trucked into his grave.* As regards the boats and fishing gear: *They get the advance of lines in the same way, and it is debited to their account, or they pay a hire for the lines. The generality in Shetland pay a hire for the boat.*

When researching family history I found in one of Sandison's account books[2] that my great-grandfather William Spence, in the summer of 1860, paid a hire of sixteen shillings for four-year-old fishing lines. William was then only eighteen, but went on fishing, and survived the 1881 tragedy known as the Gloup Disaster. Although Walker was full of sympathy for the fishermen when putting his case to the Truck Commission, we must not lose sight of the fact that he was responsible for evicting many fishermen, including William Spence, who had to leave his croft in Bigsetter (or Bixter) in 1868, presumably for failing to report who was damaging the enclosure fences. Walker's compassion was fickle.

Later in the questioning Walker, naturally, got on to his own achievements during the eleven years he had been resident in Shetland: *When I went there* [Shetland] *a few years ago, I considered it* [the truck system] *was so highly injurious that I came to a special arrangement with the proprietor as to working his properties. I saw that the hosiery was doing the female portion of the community no good whatsoever, and that the commons were of no use to the people, and were doing them harm. I at once resolved to take the commons from them, but I offered every tenant on the property a lease.*

Admitting to Sellar that his policy of leases had not been well accepted, Walker laid the blame for this failure on the merchants: *With Delting and Yell, I commenced it at once, and gave every man the opportunity of taking a lease. But they were so acted upon by the merchants, that about half of them refused to take leases. In my opinion that was the sole cause of their refusing.* As we know the leases were unacceptable to the crofters for many reasons, but any part played by the merchants must have been minor compared to the practical problems set by the terms of the lease itself.

Walker had with him a copy of the Garth and Annsbrae Estate 'Conditions of Lease' which he then handed over to Sellar for examination and there follows a question and answer session on the terms of the lease. It is not difficult to imagine the underlying brag with which Walker expounded the so-called 'benefits' which the loss of the scattald and other terms of the lease were supposed to have brought to the tenants. The many ways in which the scattald was necessary for the survival of the crofters has already been discussed. To these could be added the uses made of the soft wool from the native breed of sheep, including barter of knitted goods. In the country districts hosiery was usually exchanged for household goods. The fact that the knitter got increased value by accepting goods instead of cash was unprincipled but obviously tempting.

When Bowen and Sellar presented their report to Parliament later that year, they stated that they had received information from four Shetland witnesses *tending to show that the existence of Truck in an oppressive form is general in the staple trades of the islands.*

The following year, on 1st January, Mr Guthrie, the commissioner appointed by the government to inquire into the truck system in Shetland, opened his investigation in the Queens Hotel, Lerwick. There was a good attendance by the general public. Sittings were held in country districts too – knitters and fishermen as well as merchants coming forward with their evidence.

John Walker's Shetland

John Walker was recalled on 30th January and asked if he wished to give any further information, and replied that he merely wished to reaffirm all that he had previously stated except for one item about the price of shawls. However, once he got underway, many other points were raised both by him and Guthrie, amounting to a further one hundred and eight questions and answers.

It seems to me unfortunate that Walker's evidence was given in such a way as to leave him wide open to criticism. Much of what he said was true – undoubtedly the merchants were in a position of power over the fishermen/crofters but Guthrie managed to wrong-foot Walker in such a way as to make some of what he said appear invalid. For example, when referring to *the largest establishment in this place for the manufacture of blubber*, Walker claimed that the superintendent and manager were illiterate. Later Guthrie produced a ledger from Hay & Co. (the blubber establishment), kept by one of these men, and Walker had to admit that it was written in a fair enough hand. Sidestepping, he continued: *The reason why I mentioned this matter at all was to show the subserviency of the people in Shetland – that they are accustomed to do what they are bidden – that they are ready to sign their names to what they really cannot understand, if they think it is doing a favour to anyone above them.*

As he stated to the commissioners he had been instrumental in setting up a fishing company which would be free from the truck system – the Shetland Fishing Co. Ltd. At this point in his life he does seem genuinely anxious to put an end to truck. Writing on 30th August, 1871, probably to Gilbert Goudie,[3] about the problem in Shetland: *I saw Lord Neaves address upon the subject and agree with many of his ideas especially that Legislation on such a matter will likely be powerless in Shetland ... the only hope for the poor people here lies in their feeling our interest in them assisting them to get out of the trammels of the shopkeepers and working under some co-operation system.*

** ** **

John Walker's name cropped up several times at the Highlands and Islands Commission in 1883, although by that time he was resident in the southern hemisphere.

Gladstone's Irish Land Act of 1881 gave the small tenants in Ireland the three 'F's – fair rents, fixity of tenure, and freedom to sell their tenant right. Other crofting communities were aware of these reforms and hopes were raised. Poor harvests and fishing in 1881 and 1882, followed by unrest in Skye, forced the government to appoint a Royal Commission to investigate conditions of crofters and cottars in the Highlands and Islands of Scotland. Leading this commission was Francis, Lord Napier who had previously enjoyed a distinguished diplomatic career in India.[4]

Because all, except one, of its members were either landlords, or sons of landlords, it was generally considered that the crofters could expect little from the commission.[5] However this was far from the case. Now, for the first time, crofters were encouraged to hold public meetings and elect spokesmen to voice their grievances to a commission set up by parliament and in the name of the Queen herself. Notices, headed by the Royal Coat of Arms, were pinned on church doors intimating the time and place of meetings and stating:-

THE INHABITANTS ARE REQUESTED TO ELECT DELEGATES FOR EXAMINATION BEFORE THE COMMISSION[6]

The commission proposed to collect information in two ways. By holding public meetings where they would listen and record all that was said, and by requiring each estate to provide information about tenants, their rent, land cultivated, animals etc. The Admiralty supplied H.M.S. *Lively* on which the Commissioners would travel from place to place, and the Post Office provided a team of telegraphists to keep them in touch with London. Living on board ship the Commissioners were free from pressure from either landlords or crofters.[7]

The first meeting was held in Skye on 8th May, 1883. By 7th June many meetings had been held in the Western Isles and they were shortly to head north for Shetland. But disaster struck that evening on the way back to Stornoway when the *Lively* ran on to Chicken Rock. No lives were lost and the papers were saved, but several of the passengers lost all their possessions. That was the end of the *Lively*, but the Commissioners carried on with their investigations. The *North Star*, hired by the government at considerable expense,[8] took them to Shetland where the first meeting was held on Friday, 13th July in the Lerwick Court House. Meetings were also held at Hillswick, Mid Yell, Baltasound and Foula. On arrival in Foula, the commissioners treated the twenty-five bairns to sweets[9] – this was to be seen as a friendly commission.

Saturday 14th saw the *North Star* anchored in Mid Yell Voe, and a meeting being held in the church. Our John Omand from chapter four enters the story again.[10] By that time he was living in Kaywick, Yell, proprietor Lady Budge, paying £10 for three and a half acres cultivated ground and a four roomed house with a leaking roof. When asked if they kept up the thatch on the byre roof themselves, he replied:

Of course we do. We build byres and barns to ourselves.
But not the dwelling house?
No; it was always considered that the proprietors should do that.

John Walker's Shetland

What induced you to come here and take a place without a lease?
Rise of rents where I came from.

Where he had come from was Garden in Unst, and previous to that Vigon in North Yell, both properties on the Garth and Annsbrae estate: *I went there [Vigon] and took a farm from him [Major Cameron] for £7:10s of rent. The first two years I settled the rent with him myself, but the next three years I was on the property he put his lands into the hands of the factor Mr Walker, and the rent he took from me was £8 – that was 10s of a rise; the second rent he took was £9:16s and the third rent was £14 ...*

Asked what notice he got of the rent rise from Walker, Omand said: *I never got notice at all until I came to pay the rent.*
And then he asked you for more for that same year?
For that same year.
And had you the extra money in your pocket?
No, I had to go and get the loan of the money until I came home. I had to go two miles from the place where I settled with him, and had to borrow money from another until I could pay it back.
Was this Mr Walker John Walker?
Yes; there are not many under the British flag who do not know him.

The valuation roll does not show rent for Vigon any higher than £7 at the time when Omand was tenant, which raises a few questions. Is the valuation roll inaccurate? Was £14 really the rent charged? And if so, what became of the money?

When the Omands left Vigon they moved across Bluemull Sound to Garden, in Unst. There, in the 1871 census we find John, head of the family, aged 45. His father and mother are there, also his sister, her husband and daughter, two other nieces and a servant. A typically crowded Shetland croft house of the time. John continues his evidence at the commission: *I went to Unst and took a farm at £7:10s. I was there nine years, and after the improvements I made on the property – over £50 worth – the rent was raised to £9:10s and I left and came here.*

Major Cameron referred to Omand in his written statement to Napier:[11] *John Omand left my property about five years (ago), but while the property had been under my management his rent had not been raised – certainly not since 1874, when John Omand's and G. W. Williamson's rent at Gardon was £8:3s. If John Omand is the same person I refer to, I have now a scroll lease made out for him when my tenant in Vigon, North Yell, which he refused to accept. In short, any evidence given by a crofter must be accepted with a certain amount (and that a pretty large one) of salt.*

Omand's evidence covered a wide range of subjects – housing; crofting; life in the colonies. When asked which was the best country he had visited he answered:

Victoria [Australia] *was the place I would have approved of.*
Are many people from Shetland there?
A great many.

He was questioned at length about the fishing, and when asked which improvements the Government could introduce, replied: *When the boats are out, and it comes very rough weather we cannot see, and there is no light to direct us, and the men might be cast away. We have great need of a light to lead us in.*

On Monday 16th evidence was heard in the Reading Room, Baltasound. James William Bruce told what happened to his father who was a crofter in Ballista:[12]
... the proprietor leased his lands to a company of merchants and then the scatholds were taken from the tenants. My father then had to pay this company some 30s for the right to graze his animals on the scathold, and about the same time the proprietor also deprived him of the right to the meadow. When the company broke up in 1876 and the farms were again in the hands of the proprietor, the same rent was exacted as he had been paying to this company, notwithstanding the loss of scathold and meadow grass.

William Spence, also living in Ballista, had moved there from Woodwick even although there was no scathold available at Ballista. When asked why he had made this unfavourable change:[13] *My croft was laid in a sheep farm, and I was warned out of the place ... the town was laid in with hill as a sheep farm.*

Another Unst crofter, Archibald Smith from the Westing, said he only had one complaint – he was paying 36s a year for scathold, the greater part of which had been taken from him:[14]
When was it taken off?
When Mr Walker became factor.

Two North Yell men appeared before the commissioners at Baltasound. Daniel Moar, a young Cullivoe fisherman, gave clear and knowledgeable information about the local fishing. His landlord was Major Cameron and he spoke of the hardship his father suffered when the scathold was taken away:[15] *There was £1 put on the land when Mr Walker came and looked over the scathold; he raised the rent £1 on account of the stock pasturing, and then he took away the scathold and the £1 was never taken off.*

Neither he nor Andrew Spence, the other North Yell representative, were able to keep any sheep because of lack of scathold. Andrew Spence was asked if this was a loss:[16]
A great loss.
Did you use the wool of the native sheep for making clothes at home?

JOHN WALKER'S SHETLAND

Yes, stockings and blankets, and the old people made outside clothes of it also.

He too had a few words about Cameron's factor: *Walker, who took away the hill, left some years ago; and the gentleman who is in it now just has it something as he found it. Walker wronged every person, and would not have cared whether the sheep were put under a dyke or what we did with them. I believe he spoiled the Major.*

Looking again at the report which Major Cameron sent to the commission: *From my point of view, the crofters in Shetland have very little to complain of, but the Landlords have a cause of complaint against their crofters, viz. – Houses are expensive to begin with, costing from £30 to £40, and are repaired by the landlord.*

That's clear enough, but he muddies the water with his next statement: *repairs, such as yearly thatching, incumbent on the tenant, are not always executed.*

Looking towards Lerwick and Clickimin in the 1880s. The thatched croft house in the photograph would be typical of those quoted by Major Cameron as costing £30-£40. cf cost of sheep-sheds/fanks in Chapter 8. Photographer G. W. Wilson. © *Shetland Museum*

We'll let sixty-nine year old Mathew Robertson, crofter and ex-fisherman, have the last word on Walker at the Napier Commission. His complaint at the Mid Yell meeting was that the fences erected between Lady Budge and John Walker were not sufficiently stock proof:[17]

134

Did you represent that to John Walker?
No.
Do you think, if you had represented it to him, he would have seen that the fence was so erected that it would keep in your sheep?
I could not say; he was a very stiff kind of man.

Again and again we see Walker, the factor, rather than Cameron, the proprietor being held responsible for the removal of scattald and clearance of tenants. In stories from that era, Walker is sometimes referred to as the land-owner. This probably reflects the fact that he was travelling about among the tenants (no doubt with a proprietorial air), talking about his plans etc. On the other hand it seems unlikely that Major Cameron was known personally to many of his tenants, other than in Bressay. He did spend a lot of time out of Shetland.

And so the crofters came forward and gave their evidence, much more confidently than they did for the Truck Commission. The Napier Commission listened to 775 people in 61 places in Scotland, mostly in the Highlands and Islands. Answers were given to 46,750 questions, translated if necessary, taken down in shorthand, and printed for presentation to Parliament and sale to the public. A report was written and published in 1884 along with five volumes of evidence.[18]

However the five commissioners were not fully agreed on the outcome of their investigation. On the land question, Lord Napier felt that the solution lay in improving leases, township organisation and assisted emigration:[19] *The occupiers in an existing township should have the right to claim from the proprietor an enlargement of the existing township, in regard to arable land and common pasture.* He suggested that, if the crofter's claim was not accepted by the landlord, the Sheriff Substitute should be called in to decide whether the claim was a reasonable one.

On the other hand, two of the commissioners, Cameron of Lochiel and Sir Kenneth MacKenzie argued that the township system would damage proprietorial rights.[20] Irrespective of whether the commissioners agreed or not, the government paid little heed to the proposals put forward by Napier. It seems that the main achievement of that commission was to air the crofters' grievances.

Two years later, in 1886, the Crofters Holdings (Scotland) Act was passed, giving crofters security of tenure, subject to certain conditions, and a Crofters' Commission was set up to adjudicate on rents.

Of course only a fraction of the evidence gathered in Shetland, from either of the commissions, referred to the Garth and Annsbrae estate. By the time of the Napier Commission the Walker family had been resident in South Africa for three years. John certainly would have known about Napier as he frequently made business trips to Britain, and kept in touch

JOHN WALKER'S SHETLAND

with friends and family. However, he likely felt safely removed from the critical report on his policies in Shetland. Besides, by 1884, his energy had been diverted into schemes and contracts at the Cape.

1 S.A. 12/126/6
2 Sandison's Archive 1860 : 24
3 Shetland Library, Reid Tait Collection 18/33
4 William Thomson, *The Little General and the Rousay Crofters,* Edinburgh 1981, p.123
5 A.D. Cameron, *Go Listen to the Crofters,* Stornoway 1986, p.3
6 Ibid, p.xii
7 Ibid, p.30
8 Ibid, p.35
9 Ibid, p.79
10 Highlands and Islands Commission, minutes of evidence, pp.1235-42
11 Highlands and Islands Commission, Appendix A, LI. pp.226-232
12 Highlands and Islands Commission, minutes of evidence, p.1312
13 Highlands and Islands Commission, minutes of evidence, pp.1311/2
14 Highlands and Islands Commission, minutes of evidence, pp.1287/88
15 Highlands and Islands Commission, minutes of evidence, pp.1280/87
16 Highlands and Islands Commission, minutes of evidence, pp.1278/80
17 Highlands and Islands Commission, minutes of evidence, p.1247
18 A.D. Cameron, *Go Listen to the Crofters,* Stornoway 1986, p.x
19 Brian Smith, *Toons and Tenants,* Lerwick 2000, p.54
20 Ewan A. Cameron, *Land for the People,* East Linton 1996, p.23

Chapter Thirteen

SMACKS, BLUBBER AND OTHER SCHEMES

The only hope for the poor people here [Shetland] is in their feeling our interest in them assisting them to get out of the trammels of the shopkeepers and working under some co-operation system.
John Walker, writing on 30th August, 1871[1]

THE Shetland Fishing Company Limited was registered in Glasgow, on 5th February, 1872. From the *Memorandum of Association*[1] for the company we see that their principal aim was *to afford, through the medium of the co-operative or any other system, facilities and opportunities to the people of Shetland for the prosecution of fishing, free from the Truck system.*

By March 1873 twenty shareholders held a total of forty shares of £250 each in the company. None of the shareholders lived in Shetland. Among them were merchants, bankers, a doctor, a minister, a dealer in musical instruments, an M.P. and R. Scott Skirving, who, the following year, was to write a glowing report of Walker's farming in Bressay.

John Walker held three shares in the Company and was also a director. The fishing smacks were named after the directors – *John Walker, Robert Miller, Robert Kirkwood, James Stevenson, Henry,* etc. They were to fish for cod round Faroe, Iceland and Rockall.

The *John Walker*, 77 tons, was built at Halls shipyard in Aberdeen in 1873. Three years later tragedy struck. She had been sighted on the 26th March, 1876 by the smack *Henry*. The next day a severe gale was blowing off the coast of Faroe.[2] But it was not until 20th May that a meeting of ship owners, and others interested, met in the Queen's Hotel, Lerwick to discuss the matter.[3] The meeting was convened by Mr McGregor, secretary of the company, who had been sent north by the directors to get advice from men who understood the fishing. The directors were prepared to send a vessel to search for the missing smack, if this was considered advisable.

The master of the *John Walker* had written to his wife on 23rd March, from Faroe, saying that the fishing there was a failure and that he intended to go to Rockall. A French lugger had reported passing a waterlogged, dismasted vessel, painted the same colour as the missing smack, a short distance from Faroe. However, the interested parties at the Queen's Hotel decided that, since the smack was known to have provisions aboard for perhaps a fortnight yet, there was still a chance that she might be at Rockall, and that in any case no good could be done by sending a vessel to search. Walker apparently attended the meeting, as, at the end of the newspaper report we read: *Mr Walker remarked that the money which would be spent by the company for such a purpose would be better expended in relieving the widows and children.*

It would seem that Walker's suggestion was not taken up. On 2nd December, 1876 the following letter appeared in the *Shetland Times* written by the Shetland agent for the Fishing Company, Robert Scott: *The smack 'John Walker' was lost on the coast of Faroe early in the spring of this year with a crew of thirteen hands all of whom must have perished with her. The wives and children and relatives of some of the crew were left very destitute and it was hoped something would be done for them by those interested. But nothing of any consequence was done for these poor people and they have now appealed to me to help their cause, it being with me the men were engaged, and most of them well known to me.*

I have been unable to find a record of whether or not any aid was given to the dependants.

** ** **

Robert Scott's association with the company ended unhappily. He had a lengthy letter published in the *Shetland Times* of 27th July, 1878 clarifying his side of the trouble: *The Shetland Fishing Company (Limited), of Glasgow, was started in 1871, and was (as I afterwards understood) to be conducted on cash principles in opposition to the old system or, what the Company choose to term, truck. I fortunately, or otherwise, was connected with the Company from the beginning until May 1876, hence the reason why I deem it necessary to protect myself seeing the Company choose to make public what to them appears of interest to Shetlanders.*

SMACKS, BLUBBER AND OTHER SCHEMES

He was referring to an involved case which had appeared in the *Shetland Times* the previous week, where doubt was thrown on Scott's integrity over a sum of £6:5s which he may or may not have paid to a workman on behalf of the company.[4] In his letter to the paper Scott went on to claim that the company had forgotten to publish the many cases they had already lost. Until the end of 1873 he had been acting under the instruction of the managing director and all had gone well as far as he was aware *and not until the Directors choose to disagree was I asked to become the Company's agent, which offer I accepted in ignorance of what had caused such a change in their management.*

Before long he began to suspect that something was radically wrong at headquarters, but he had soldiered on, hoping for the best: *Not until the time for settlement for the fishing for 1874 did any real difficulty arise. Cheques for the fishermen's earnings (or share) were dishonoured, etc. etc., but in order to save the Company's credit, still believing in the veracity and honour of my employers, I continued to increase my borrowing powers to the extent of getting my friends to cash the men's dishonoured cheques and thus save the Company's credit.*

The books from Scott's office were all removed to Glasgow before the settlements for 1874 were completed, but Scott carried on until January 1876 when he intimated his intention to resign whenever a replacement could be found. He was still agent when the fishing boats returned from the first voyages of 1876, and his letter exposed the sorry situation: *I had not a farthing to give the crews, neither could I get credit for them, consequently as a last resource I guaranteed, along with the masters of 'Robert Miller', 'Robert Kirkwood', 'James Stevenson', and the bank, and got the necessary sums to enable the crews to purchase provisions, and thus enable them to prosecute the fishing.*

In May 1876 the company's secretary removed papers from the office and told Scott his only redress was through the law. Scott wrote: *I protested and tried my utmost to gain justice, but for want of means to carry my case through, I suffered. Thus my connection with a Company, I am sorry to say, has in all its dealings acted so unfairly, and it cannot but be asked what has such a Company done to abolish the ghost truck? Simply nothing farther than that I was trucked myself with a vengeance from first to last.*

** ** **

The Company had a policy whereby the fishermen signed 'Articles' at the start of a season agreeing that if they should fail to join the vessel, or fail to continue to work for the company, they would be liable to pay damages of five shillings per day from the time such failure began until the following 12th of August. This did not apply in a case of sickness.

Under that contract the company took William Twatt, Stensland, Walls, to court for desertion in 1878.[5] He had signed the said articles in February and gone to the fishing in the *Robert Kirkwood*. When the smack returned in May with her first catch both William and Thomas Twatt left her, taking with them property they considered to be their own. Ogilvy Jamieson, who had succeeded Robert Scott, informed Duncan and Galloway, their solicitors in Lerwick, and they wrote to the Twatts warning that steps would be taken against them unless they returned. The Twatts did not return to the *Robert Kirkwood* and so were liable to pay the Company a £24:10s penalty for 98 days, also £8:6:10½ on account.

By January 1880 the company was in serious financial difficulties and went into voluntary liquidation. The final winding-up meeting was held on 8th June, 1896. Hance Smith, in his book *Shetland Life and Trade* points out that the company had invested in the most up-to-date fishing techniques at a time when the cod fishing was in decline.

** ** **

During the early 1870s Walker chartered vessels to trade to and from Iceland carrying tourists, emigrants, ponies and sheep. In the *Shetland Times* we read brief reports of these trips involving the steam ships *Queen*, *Pera* and *Wicklow*, and there may have been others. A surprising number of people took part in these voyages. On one trip the *Queen*, besides twenty-seven tourists, carried a hundred and sixty emigrants en route for Quebec and the United States. On another the *Pera* arrived at Lerwick with twelve emigrants and a hundred and ninety-two ponies. Ponies were also imported from Canada. Later in the 70s he set up a business importing fish from Norway to Shetland to cure for export. Other speculations are listed in the bankruptcy statement (see appendix). None of these ventures appear to have been financially successful.

** ** **

In December 1871 Walker purchased, for about £470, a huge 'caa' of whales which had been stranded at Uyeasound, Unst. Believing them to be bottle-nosed whales, two men from Peterhead joined him in the speculation. The whale bodies were flenched, the unflenched heads cut off, and for £50 the fishing smack *Petrel* was chartered to transport the blubber and heads to Peterhead. With twenty tons of coal aboard, provided by Walker to be ballast for the journey north from Lerwick, the smack arrived at Uyeasound. The blubber and heads were then rowed out to the *Petrel* in small boats and her master signed a bill of lading acknowledging delivery of 32 tons 19 cwt of blubber and 213 whale heads.

This photo of the smack *Petrel* was taken by J. Leisk on 1st November 1888, the day before she sailed for Norway on what was to be her last voyage. Caught in rough seas she turned completely round, righted herself, and amazingly no lives were lost. However, on arrival in Norway, her condition was such as to constitute her a total wreck.
© *Shetland Museum*

No hitches so far, so what can go wrong? Yes, the weather. It's midwinter, in Shetland. The smack left Unst on 31st December, but a strong head wind forced them to take shelter for three days. They then managed to reach Lerwick where they had to anchor to be cleared at the Customhouse before going south. Unfortunately the weather deteriorated again and the *Petrel* and several other vessels were obliged to wait for abatement of a long period of stormy weather in the shelter of Bressay Sound.

Meanwhile the cargo on board the *Petrel* was not taking kindly to the delay. Oil was running off the blubber, putrefaction was setting in and the stench must have been obnoxious. Walker provided some casks to hold the whale oil pumped from the bilges, but not enough to contain the ever increasing flow. He wired to Peterhead for more casks which arrived eventually, after considerable delay. Peter Garriock, merchant, principal owner of the *Petrel*, sought advice from people he knew to be experienced in the handling and manufacturing of whale oil. As it was clearly unsafe to continue the journey with much of the blubber in a liquid state and also impossible to load it into casks on board the smack, Garriock decided to land the cargo at Messrs Hay's premises. There, the decomposing matter on the blubber had to be cleaned away and the skin removed. The whales' heads had to be flenched – having been packed into the bottom of the vessel they were in an advanced state of decomposition. Lastly, the blubber had to be cut into narrow strips, as apparently the usual way of loading these casks was through the bung-hole. I hope the men who did this unsavoury work were well remunerated!

Although the weather had eased by the end of January, this reorganisation of the cargo took until 26th February. All the casks could not be stowed aboard the *Petrel* so some were sent to Aberdeen by the steamer *St Clair* and then to Peterhead by rail. Still short of casks, some of the whale heads were left behind in Lerwick where they created such an offensive stink (and remember this is the days before proper sewage disposal) that they were sold for ten shillings for manure.

We likely wouldn't know so many details of this story had it not ended up in the court rooms. Garriock and the other owners of the *Petrel* took Walker to court for expenses of £213 (£50 for freight; £113 for expenses at Lerwick; £50 for detention of the vessel). In a counter action Walker tried to sue Garriock for £1200 for breach of contract, pleading that the owners of the vessel had delayed the cargo and, having landed it at Lerwick, had dealt with it improperly causing great loss. At the Court of Session Lord Shand considered that all Walker's defences were unfounded and declared Garriock and the other owners entitled to their expenses. Garriock had followed the best advice he could obtain and Lord Shand maintained that the delay caused by treating the cargo was to Walker's advantage as it prevented further deterioration. Not unreasonably, Walker's defence argued that the tops of the casks should have been removed instead of filling them through the bung hole, but it was accepted that the latter was the method always used and had been proved less wasteful. Another of Walker's defences was that the skin of the whales could have been preserved and was of value. Lord Shand's reply to that was: *If the skin be valuable, it yet remains for someone to show – first, how it can be preserved, and then to what use it can be put.*[6]

The Court of Session heard a third case, in 1873, concerning the same, by then infamous, whales. This time it was an action raised by John Walker against Langdales Chemical Manure Company in Newcastle. He had sold the whales to the manure company for fifty shillings a ton, payable on delivery at their wharf. However, as we know, the delivery was two and a half months late and by then the blubber was so putrid as even to be unfit for making into manure. The local Board of Health at Newcastle prevented the cargo from being landed, then had it condemned and destroyed as a nuisance and injurious to health. Furthermore, the owner of the *Mars*, the vessel which had transported the casks from Peterhead to Newcastle, was claiming £40 from Walker for the expense of destroying the cargo, also £84 for his failure to discharge the charter within the time specified. Lord Mure upheld both the latter claims but not Walker's against the manure company. The verdict was summed up by Lord Ardmillan thus: *It is important that we should adhere to the well-established rule of the law of Scotland, that when a contract is made for delivery of a specific quantity at a particular port, if the article perishes before it is delivered at the port it perishes to the seller.*[7]

Listed among Walker's losses in his bankruptcy papers:- *Whale Speculation, £1,000.*

Caain/Pilot whales caught at Weisdale in February 1903. Photographer A. Abernethy. © *Shetland Museum*

1   N.A.S. BT 2/346
2   *Scotsman*, 22nd May, 1876
3   *Shetland Times*, 21st May, 1876
4   *Shetland Times*, 20th July, 1878, Laurence Mouat v The Shetland Fishing Co. Ltd.
5   S.A. SC 12/6/1878/43/2
6   *The Scottish Law Reporter*, Garriock v. Walker, 31st October, 1873, p.20 and *Shetland Times*, 17th March, 28th April, 17th November, 1873
7   *The Scottish Law Reporter*, Walker v. Langdales Chemical Manure Co., 16th July, 1873, p.635

Chapter Fourteen

CRISIS IN BRESSAY

In 1871 or 1872 my Bressay tenants, in consequence of the regulations contained in my leases, rose in mutiny. Having passed the Indian Mutiny of 1857 I did not wish a second, and therefore, at a great sacrifice, I sold the island.
Statement by Major Thomas M. Cameron at Highlands
& Islands Commission in Lerwick 20/7/1883

ON THE 31st July, 1871, Major Cameron's mother, Margaret Mouat of Garth, died at home at Gardie, Bressay, aged 92. This meant that the tenants on Bressay were no longer protected from Walker's 'new rules' as they had been while Mrs Cameron Mouat was alive. Although tenants on Garth and Annsbrae in other areas of Shetland had suffered to make room for sheep farms, Bressay had hitherto been unaffected.

The *Saturday Herald & Shetland Gazette* of August 5th reported Mrs Cameron Mouat's death and picked up on the fears of the Bressay folk: *The death of this venerable and much respected lady has been awaited with mournful anticipations by the whole tenantry of the large isle of Bressay, who not unreasonably dread the advent of the new regime ...*

Not unreasonable. They would have been well aware of what had happened in Yell and Delting. But what's this about a flag? *Great astonishment was expressed in Lerwick to see, immediately after Mrs Mouat's death, a flag displayed from one of the most elevated points in Bressay, where it floated as in triumph for the greater part of the day.*

CRISIS IN BRESSAY

August 7th – Major Cameron to John Walker:[1] *Will you write a very short note to the Editor of the 'Shetland Gazette' explaining that the Flag hoisted on Bressay on the 1st inst. was a signal agreed on between Mrs Walker and you if you had to be recalled and not as printed in the Lerwick news letter. The less said the better – but I think some explanation should be given and I think by you as you are hinted at throughout said letter.*

A week later the paper printed a profuse apology blaming an *anonymous communication* for the misinterpretation: *We learn that there was no unbecoming exhibition at Bressay, but on the contrary that there was an appropriate and marked expression of respect immediately paid to the memory of the deceased.*

By September the tenants on Bressay had been introduced to 'The New Rules'. New to them, but all too familiar to the crofters on the estate elsewhere. The difference now was that there was a local press to take up the cudgels on their behalf. Again we read from *The Saturday Herald & Shetland Gazette*: *Last week the tenants in Bressay were given to understand distinctly the terms on which they will be allowed to remain in their present holdings ... now that the demise of the last Mouat to whom the property belonged has put them under a new regime, and one which they believe must end in their destruction, though attempts are made to persuade them that it is only for their benefit. This is much like the boy who, while pelting the young ducks, kept saying, 'It's all for your good, little duckies, it's all for your good.'*

As we already know, one of the new rules involved the loss of the scattald. The paper comments: *When the poor peasants are prevented from having a sheep in the pasture, or a quey or cow outside the dykes, how is it possible they are to keep their crofts, or live on them?*

The island of Bressay lies just across the harbour from the town of Lerwick, so the Bressay folk were in a prime position to draw attention to their plight: *At the corners of the houses here in town, many of them may now be seen standing crying, and telling their sad tale, enough to make any heart softer than steel to bleed.*[2]

And in the same newspaper the following week: *The excitement in Bressay is every day getting worse, and it is reported, as a result of the new decree, that one man has been brought over here* [Lerwick] *quite deranged. On the 10th inst. there were only a mere handful of people at the Parish Church, out of a population of about 1000. The people do not know where to go. Some have agreed for a season, but the majority have declined to accept the proposed terms ... The price of stock continues high, and is not likely to come down, notwithstanding that the tenants in Bressay are selling off every day.*

145

Annsbrae House, Major Cameron's residence in Lerwick.
© *Shetland Museum*

An anonymous letter written in reddish brown substance had been sent to John Walker early in September:³ *Sir I heard Magnus Yorston saying that he wold be your death on bord the Stemer. he is a Scamp & cannot deny it. & says he will do what he likes in spite of you.* He likely meant 'do what he likes' with his croft in spite of the new rules.

The Major, wrote to his factor on September 18th from Boyndlie, near Fraserburgh, where he seemed to spend a lot of time. He had heard something of what was happening and was beginning to worry. Luckily for him there had been little publicity when the 'new rules' were first introduced and imposed on his more remote tenants. Besides, he had probably taken at face value what Walker had written to him on 30th August, 1866:[4] *The 'Northern Ensign' honours us by inserting in full our pamphlet and devotes a <u>Leader</u> to abuse it. His arguments are so absurd I don't intend to reply.*

Walker was referring to a forthright article in the Wick newspaper, *Northern Ensign,* where readers were urged to study the conditions of lease described as – *remarkable alike for cool confidence and selfish assumption.* After analysing the pitfalls of complying with the terms of the lease, it was pointed out that *if it had been intended to carry out a system of wholesale eviction on any estate in Shetland, without having recourse to the inhuman system of systematic legal removals, scarcely any means more effectual could have been devised than the drawing up and adhering to the articles and regulations under reference.*[5]

Also, of course, it saved the expense of 'legal' removal. The article ended: *We hope there is public spirit enough in Shetland to meet by strong moral feeling this movement, which, whatever may be its real intention, will have most assuredly the effect of converting Annsbrae and Garth into unpeopled estates.* Sadly, 'public spirit' didn't rise to support the North Isles and Delting in 1866.

But it was different in 1871. Attention was drawn to events by the local newspaper, helped by the proximity of Bressay to the town. The Major seemed genuinely troubled as he wrote to *My dear Mr Walker,*[6] *I have yours of 14th inst. and am very vexed to hear of what has occurred in Bressay for it has perhaps in a measure been caused by the Tenants getting too short notice of the proposed changes in mode of farming etc ...*

He went on to emphasise that 'truck' – carrying off earth for manure – must be put a stop to, but insisted that the tenants be given until the following year before they were compelled to accept the lease agreement or remove. *You will do this as most agreeable or rather least disagreeable to your feelings, for eating humble pie is not pleasant but my name would be ruined for ever, were it supposed that only a few weeks after my Mother's death I warned off on 40 day notice some hundreds who had for generations been tenants on the property ... I do not uphold the tenants in their foolish childish ideas and actions but I must consider if my own actions as a large landed proprietor are just and humane.*

Yet he could not bring himself to offend his energetic factor: *You must not look on this as finding fault with you, as I believe you thought you were acting for the best ... sincerely hope no violence will be offered to you that of course could not be overlooked on any account ... I may mention that one reason why I never contemplated any change to take place as from Martinmas 1871 was that you had spoken about co-operative farming and that would take some time to consider and talk over. I consequently never supposed you would think of warning for this year.*

Or perhaps Bressay could have received special treatment: *I had also hoped the rules might have been so modified as to avoid such extensive enclosing as in Delting etc. for except a small portion Bressay is surely not worth very heavy outlay for hill pasture.*

And the cause of all the trouble: *So long as there is a Walker at the helm things must keep moving.*

Major Thomas Mouat Cameron. *Courtesy Mr & Mrs John Scott*

CRISIS IN BRESSAY

Walker's reply,[7] on 21st September, is difficult to read, an indication of his mood when writing. First he shows surprise at the contents of the Major's letter, then: *I understood your orders to be simply to stop truck, equalise rents and consult Dr Hamilton as to Co-operation Farming this season.* Carrying out the order to stop 'truck', he wrote: *I placed a notice on the Kirk's door forbidding 'truck'.* Perhaps this explains the poor kirk attendance reported in the newspaper. If word of the notice got around it's possible the folk reasoned that what they didn't see, they didn't have to obey.

However, he had gone a step further than the above 'orders'. He had given a copy of the 'New Rules' to one of the tenants, Laurence Smith, who had called to make enquiries about future labouring. That was when the trouble started: *On the same day I discovered that the Tenants from some unknown cause were in a panic selling off their stock right and left and talking the most outrageous nonsense as to the future of the Isle . . .*

He had made arrangements to meet the tenants and talk matters over. At first they refused but *by Friday they had seen their folly and made their appearance – to one and all I tried to speak with them in the kindest manner – telling them again that you did not wish to see one out of the Isle and that every reasonable sacrifice would be made to accommodate every one according to his circumstances.*

Also, there had been a signing of documents: *I caused the West Side men to all sign a Title of Removal of this Martinmas – just to make a distinction between them and the East Side men – but telling them distinctly that it would not be put in force if there was any reasonable good behaviour.* So was that how he persuaded the North Yell crofters to sign those blue slips? By making promises, then using some so-called offence (like failure to betray neighbours) as an excuse to remove them.

Meanwhile Walker had sent a reassuring telegram to Boyndlie to which the Major replied:[8] *Your telegram of Saturday last was at Fraserburgh the same evening. I am very glad indeed to find the people have quieted down.* Arranging for the two of them to meet, the proprietor rather pathetically reveals how dependent he was on his dynamic factor: *I should like to see you on Thursday – as no end of questions will be put to me on return. I should like you to draw out such answers as you think will be likely to be suitable – rent for instance, enclosing or anything else you think of.* Then, presumably referring to the incident of derangement mentioned in the newspaper, adds a compassionate touch: *It's a pity you looked at his farm or said anything to the poor body – for we need not think of getting him even when in his senses to do much and he could have been provided for somewhere as a number of poor bodies will have to be.*

149

By October the Major had obviously had enough, was thinking of selling Bressay and had confided his intentions to his factor. Was that wise? Walker wrote to him from London on 12th October:[9] *About settling Bressay – I do not think I will have any difficulty in getting it bought in fair terms and if you'll let me know the price you have set upon it I could see to the matter ere I returned – I still believe that Bressay is capable of being made a good deal of.*

A week later Walker was still in London and we find out why in his next letter to the Major:[10] *Trying to arrange some special matters about the Truck – I have duly received yours of Monday – of course I will say nothing to anyone that can repeat your wish as to selling Bressay but the price you quote is surely out of the way too high – it surely would be 40 years purchase – I will see what I can do ...*

The year is 1871, and besides the trouble in Bressay and all the other problems involved in the day-to-day running of the estate, we are reminded here that Walker was also involved in giving evidence to the Truck Commission. Furthermore he was fast becoming embroiled in strife about the chromate mines in Unst. On the positive side, his farm at Maryfield, according to contemporary reports, was going from strength to strength.

In the census of that year Mary, aged 35, was at home in Bressay with – Mary, aged 13; Isobel, 11; Catherine, 10; Helen, 9; Jean, 8; Jane, 5; Janet, 4; and son John, 5 months. All the girls, except four-year-old Janet, were described as scholars and had a resident governess at Maryfield – Christion Cabel from Forfarshire. Two house servants were employed – Ann McKay and Alexandria Manson, both from Caithness. The oldest daughter, Amelia Mary 15, was spending the census night in Aberdeen beside her Uncle James at 3 Adelphi Court, the family home where John spent his childhood. We don't know whether she was on holiday there or perhaps attending school. I haven't been lucky enough to track down John senior's whereabouts for that census but this is not altogether surprising considering how much he travelled around.

By October the Major had heard rumours of the trouble brewing in the Unst mines:[11] *I am afraid you have allowed your quick temper to get the better of your sober judgement in these matters and caused you to forget you were acting for another – It is most unpleasant to me to hear such reflections made about you and indirectly on myself. So I beg these disputes may be amicably settled.*

In the next letter written only a few days later:[12] *One of the latest reports ... refers to you – viz. bribing the wives of certain Chromate proprietors by promising them so much per ton on ore quarried if their husbands would vote for you being appointed factor for all* [i.e. for all the proprietors of the Haroldswick and Balliasta mines in Unst. G.H.B. Hay was at that time their factor] *An idea seems to be abroad that you have a greater interest in the sale of ore than your mere commission and brokerage.* Little did Major Cameron know how true the latter rumour would prove to be!

Reading Walker's two lengthy replies, from Edinburgh, exonerating himself in the most indignant and hurt tones, anyone could be excused in thinking the poor man was being utterly maligned. For example:[13] *My connection with you has prevented my entering into many profitable transactions & it seems hard to have denied myself that and yet find slanders of my conduct ... a reflection on your part ought to convince you that my strong feelings are entitled to vent when I am constantly assailed in this cowardly manner. As on all occasions I am ready to give you the fullest information upon every point you wish.*

These two letters are annotated with pencilled notes in the Major's hand, a record of his reaction to Walker's allegations. These notes clearly reveal the disillusionment Cameron was beginning to feel about his trusted factor. I have included the Major's notes in square brackets and bold print. Walker writes: *I think I have arranged matters to submit you a favourable offer for Bressay.* And the Major adds **[is already sold]** . . . *You can believe me when I say that I have never either directly or indirectly spoken **[nor written]** to a Chromate Proprietor's wife nay it would not suit me to act for these dirty wretches should even Hay give up **[nor led anyone to suppose Mr E would vote for you]*** . . . *I note what you say as to Bressay & will, I think, be able to offer you an acceptable sum . . . in addition to paying off all Improvements but of this we can talk when we meet **[I cannot allow a wholesale disruption of Tenants causing Misery to all. Poors rates & loss of peace of mind to myself alone forbids harshness or injustice]*** ... *I have arranged for a fleet of smacks etc to break up the Truck so far and will ere long have responsible parties in every part of the Shetland business.* **[good, but you will be beaten in the long run by the Merchants or my name is not T.M.C.]**

Through these notes we can see the Major shifting from worrying about his own reputation, to allowing his conscience to drive him.

Making use of his pencilled comments, the Major replied to Walker.[14] He first comments on the Unst chromate mine situation: ... *not to define Mr Hay's powers but yours the proprietors thinking that particularly in retaining Millers payments you were exceeding your powers, this is also my opinion – and if you will have the goodness to give up the Cheques, Drafts, Bills or whatever the proper term may be I shall feel obliged.*

Strong words from the Major! Then he gets on to Bressay: *I have no doubt if there were no Tenants in Bressay to get rid of, the Island would pay far more as a Sheep Farm but as there are Tenants left for the Proprietors to care for & look after I could not be a party to summarily removing these & causing misery to poor people who have been all their lives in the Island.*

At this point it is tempting to wonder how different the distribution of townships in the North Isles and Delting would now be if Walker and Cameron's 'New Rules' had been applied to Bressay first. Would the Major subsequently have taken more interest in what was happening to his other tenants? If he had done, perhaps Burraness and Kirkabister in North Yell, for just one example, would still be a thriving community. Or did his sympathy extend only to those with whom he had a closer association?

Agonising again over his own discomfiture, the Major continues: *What I have suffered since returning is just indescribable.* Could he be suffering guilt pangs about tenants already removed? No mention of that. Then he drops what was probably a bombshell for Walker: *I therefore decided to sell and ... I have done so to my sister Miss Mouat – my relations could not think of the property going to strangers.* On the Major's death, his son is to have the option of buying the property back.

Tongues would certainly have wagged on the subject of the sale of Bressay. For example, we find R. Neven Spence writing from Lerwick to 'My dearest Mrs Craigie' in November 1871:[15] *Have you heard that Miss Cameron Mouat has bought Bressay from her brother, and sent word to all the people that during her life-time they shall remain as they have done and know no change. The poor creatures are half mad with joy, and once the bargain is concluded every house in the island is to be illuminated and bonfires on every hill or summit in commemoration of their deliverance from the hand of Walker.* This letter is among Thomas Irvine's papers from Midbrake in North Yell and it is annotated in his handwriting: *Bressay and Walker, the Director General of Shetland.*

Walker's reaction to the news was positive and probably extremely rash. He's leaving! In two letters, written on 7th November to the Major, he states his case.[16] As always, in times of stress, his handwriting is not as legible as usual: *I saw your sister last night and told her my resolve – she seemed surprised ... and anxious that I should stay ... I will at all times place my best advice at her service ... if what I hear is true the Bressay Tenants already admit that they have acted foolishly ... However I am not the man to yield my opinions to anyone ... I desire to put all except a reasonable return for my labour & Capital in your hands – if unsuccessful I want nothing ... I've no doubt your mind will be at ease ... my greatest comfort will be in having overcome these disgusting uncertainties and help to put your Estate on an improved footing.*

In the second letter he was trying to sort out the conditions and outcome of the joint working of the farms:- *Having finally resolved to insist upon being relieved of Maryfield.* He pointed out that the existing agreement was fixed for ten years and at the end of that period it was to cease if his plans had not proved advantageous to the Major. It had been understood that, if successful, the agreement would be renewed. If the Major wanted to terminate the partnership Walker was prepared to accept three months notice at any Martinmas provided the Major took over Walker's share of stock and plant at a valuation, and allowed him half the profits for the unexpired period of the agreement. He ended by declaring that he didn't want to enter into a formal agreement *until all the liabilities I have incurred on your account are provided for and the permanent position of the undertaking seen.*

From his reply of the 8th the Major gives the impression that he was more or less coerced into the original agreements:[17] *I have every wish and intention to do all that is just by you but seeing that you most urgently pressed the undertaking on me and at last I yielded against my own opinion ...*

We know from other deals Walker made that he seemed to be able to persuade people to agree to whatever plans he had in mind, and perhaps Thomas Cameron took the easy way out and closed his mind to what was happening to his tenants during the 1860s. Belatedly, he is trying to be assertive: *A bargain is a bargain all the world over and you keep people to theirs so I only ask you to put yourself in my place but rest assured that so long as you act fairly by me I shall do the same by you.* He goes on to dispute some of Walker's suggestions as to the conditions under which they would part company and points out that his leaving Maryfield would be a breach of the lease and so Walker should expect no remuneration.

In his reply, written the following day, Walker didn't seem at all put out:[18] *I am quite satisfied ... When I act unfairly towards you you are at liberty to treat me as you choose ... Your sister has agreed to relieve me on equitable terms (involving however a loss of some £1,500 to myself) ... I assure you I only wish to advance your interests.*
                Yours very faithfully,   John Walker

** ** **

So the year 1871 drew to a close. The Major has begun to lose faith in his go-getting factor, but the partnership was to last for yet a few more years. By the summer of 1872 the Walker family had left Bressay and were resident at Marine Terrace, Aberdeen. In spite of that John appeared to be more deeply involved in Shetland affairs than ever, and in 1873 was elected to several school boards. He continued his work on some of the

Parochial Boards, and every year at Christmas sent gifts of tea and sugar to the poor of these parishes. And, of course, he was deeply involved in mining and other business ventures based in Shetland.

The Marquis of Londonderry, who took the lease of the Isle of Noss and Maryfield farm after Walker, had his estate at Seaham, six kilometres north of Sunderland. Scott Skirving, in 1874, refers to the transfer of the lease and writes that the Marquis *intends to devote them* [Noss and Maryfield] *to the rearing of ponies in order to supply in some degree the increasing want of these animals for his coal-pits.*

The Marquis was also one of those active in founding the Shetland Stud.

The Island of Noss. © *Andy Gear*

It seems that the Major considered that Mary Walker deserved a rest from childbirth. On 17th August, 1873 he wrote to John.[19] After remarking how glad he was to hear that Walker's *Iceland Pony Spree* was not likely to be so bad as reports were making it out to be, he passed comment on Mary's condition: *I had hoped that Mrs Walker's troubles that you refer to as likely to occur next month were at an end – I trust however she will get well over them.*

Next month, on 25th, a son, Thomas Mouat Cameron Walker, was born at Marine Terrace, Aberdeen. Major Thomas Mouat Cameron declared himself 'honoured' to have the boy named after him.[20]

SHETLAND

SHETLAND.—To Let, Furnished, from 1st June, Maryfield House, Bressay, opposite Lerwick, and connected therewith by a private telegraph cable. House is New, and suitable for a Large Family. Apply to John Walker there.

Notice from *The Scotsman*, 10 April, 1872.

CRISIS IN BRESSAY

1   Gardie Papers 1871/229
2   *Saturday Herald and Shetland Gazette,* 16th September, 1871
3   Gardie Papers 1871/291
4   Gardie Papers L.B.1 p.31
5   *Northern Ensign,* 23rd August, 1866
6   Gardie Papers 1871/309
7   Gardie Papers 1871/313
8   Gardie Papers 1871/315
9   Gardie Papers 1871/335
10   Gardie Papers 1871/339
11   Gardie Papers 1871/340
12   Gardie Papers 1871/344
13   Gardie Papers 1871/345 & 348
14   Gardie Papers 1871/349
15   S.A. D 16/388/196
16   Gardie Papers 1871/357 & 358/1
17   Gardie Papers 1871/359
18   Gardie Papers 1871/363
19   Gardie Papers 1873/223
20   Gardie Papers 1873/261

Chapter Fifteen

HAAF GRUNIE

*What a difficult pack you have to deal with. I trust
Mr L. will manage to put down the women in this case.*
Robert Miller writing to John Walker 27th June, 1872

O N 21st February, 1872, George Leisk of Uyea, Unst, wrote to John Walker with the plea that he was 'pressed for funds'. He had been informed by Alex Sandison that Walker might be interested in taking a lease of the chromate ore mine on nearby Haaf Grunie which Leisk described as 'my island'. Haaf Grunie, nearly half a mile long by a quarter of a mile at its widest, lies east of Uyea, at the south end of Unst.

When the geologist, Samuel Hibbert, visited Shetland in 1817 he did not venture to Haaf Grunie but was so impressed by the *ore which was strewed over the hills* [in Unst] *in astonishing abundance,* that he returned to Shetland the following year *to render the proprietors of the land aware of its distinctive character.*[1]

The yellow pigment extracted from chromate of iron was used in paint and for dyeing fabrics. Hibbert tells us that, before the Unst discovery, chromate was imported to this country from America, at considerable expense. So the Unst mines were no doubt quite profitable, especially in the early stages.

The offer which George Leisk made to Walker was for a nineteen year lease of the mine on Haaf Grunie on condition that he paid Leisk fifteen shillings per ton royalty on all chromate ore lifted. A week later Walker replied, accepting the offer.

Walker had, four years previously, shown interest in the ore from Grunie. In May 1868 he wrote to Miller, Son & Co., Glasgow, offering them samples of the ore. He also informed Miller that the agent for the proprietor had offered a cargo of ore from Haaf Grunie to Messers White. Miller replied that they were anxious for it to pass through Walker's hands so that they could monopolize sale of the ore. Miller did not process the ore but sold it on to Stevenson of Glasgow (White's rival). Walker duly sent the samples, with a note to say that he couldn't get Leisk to set a price although he thought he had quoted to Messers White, adding that Leisk was 'peculiar'. Walker agreed to pay half the cost of analysing the samples.

Many letters later, in 1872, Walker secured the lease and offered Miller a half share. He had spent nearly £300 in his endeavours so far, but assured Miller, *it is estimated that there is any amount of fine ore, and I think it gives a complete pull over Balleasta* [a mine on Unst].

On 22nd March an agreement was drawn up whereby Miller made available £2000 on the understanding that Walker guaranteed that the profits on the mine would amount to at least that sum. After the £2000 was paid back the profits would be equally divisible. The business was to be worked on a joint account, and they agreed to jointly purchase Lawrence Moncrieff's property in Scalloway for the erection of a store or any other building.[2]

However, work at Grunie had only just begun when Leisk's sister, Ann, put the metaphorical spanner in the works. She claimed that as the property had been left to George in life-rent only, he could not legally issue a lease to anybody without her consent. In a long letter to her brother she tried to persuade him that he had *fallen into bad and unscrupulous hands ... They may pretend to be your friends,*[3] etc.

And her lawyer was? William Sievwright!

In the Lerwick Sheriff Court on 3rd June, 1872 it was revealed that, under Peter McKay's supervision, a large booth for the accommodation of the workmen, a crane and various tools and appliances, had been taken into the tiny island of Haaf Grunie. The case presented by Sievwright for Ann Leisk/Spence was that her consent for this work had neither been asked for nor obtained.

From his home in Aberdeen Walker explained the situation to Miller: *I am getting a good deal of bother with this. After being at work a week, Leisk's heirs-at-law took out an interdict against him and me from working – really because Leisk had given us too good a bargain.*[4] Walker didn't pay off the workmen as he thought he would be able to sue for the delay, and he didn't foresee the waste of time that would result from the interdict.

Bombarded by letters from Millers during July and August demanding word from Haaf Grunie, Walker was powerless as long as the interdict was in operation. At last he had good news on 26th August: *The Grunie case has been decided in our favour, and we are commencing to work.*

On such a small, exposed island it was most unfortunate that the interdict stopped all work during the summer months. Mining during the winter was difficult and dangerous. In the *Shetland Times* of 16th September the lifting of the interdict and resumption of work was noted: *It is hoped that a considerable amount of ore may be raised ere the winter storms set in when we understand, during easterly winds, the quarry would be liable to be filled by waves breaking over the island.*

The tiny island of Haaf Grunie with Fetlar in the background.
© *Andy Gear*

By 4th November work was halted by a second interdict which was not lifted until spring. Constantly urged by Miller to make up for lost time, Walker must have been relieved to be able to write on 19th March, 1873: *It was only last week that the Court of Session declared in my favour about the lease, and you are aware that little was done last year on account of the Sheriff-Substitute's interdict – however the matter is now all right.*

But matters turned out to be far from all right. Miller got increasingly impatient with the lack of production from Haaf Grunie. Walker stopped the work in September because he considered the foreman inefficient, and decided to wait until a more experienced man was free to supervise. By March 1874 communication between Walker and Miller had broken down and was being conducted by their lawyers. The dispute was

HAAF GRUNIE

mainly over finance, each side disputing the other's accounts. Work was again halted on Haaf Grunie until such time as the disagreements were settled.

In April 1875 Messrs Miller took Walker to court on the grounds that after three years' trial no profit had been made. They alleged fraud on the part of Walker in that, they maintained, the island contained no ore and that Walker had known this all along. Walker's defence was that the lack of profit had been due to various temporary hindrances and that there was every chance of profit in the future. Therefore he was still entitled to the use of the £2000.[5]

Robert Miller did not visit Haaf Grunie until July 1874 when he sailed there on the *Blue Bell*, a yacht belonging to Stevenson the ore buyer. Giving evidence he described the island as *perhaps a mile in circumference, which you could walk around in twenty minutes. It is well covered in grass, and we found a number of cattle on it. There was no human being except an old woman who attended to the cattle, and who lived in a bothy which seemed to have been put up some years ago for the working of the chromate mines ... I am positively certain there is no chromate to be got in Haaf Grunie.*

Although it seems strange that Miller had not checked out the island at the start of the deal, we must remember that Walker had sent samples (four boxes) in June 1868 for which Miller acknowledged receipt and asked him to share in the cost of analysis.[6] But Miller made no mention of that in court.

In a letter to Alexander Sandison dated 21st January, 1875, Walker recalled:[7]

Strange I find that in 1868 Miller got samples of the Grunie ore (last cargo was shipt about August 1868) and had them analysed and urged me then to secure it.

When cross-examined in court, Miller was asked about his company's book-keeping.

Question – *Were there not two years during which he* [Walker] *was pressing for his accounts and could not get them?*
Miller – *I am not aware.*
Question – *Was there not confusion in your book-keeping through the conduct of some of your clerks, which may explain that?*
Miller – *It may have been. A book-keeper of ours was dismissed because he had been acting improperly. He was in our employment at the time Mr Walker and I had our differences.*[8]

On 10th March, 1875, Andrew Mure, Sheriff-Substitute, with his clerk, Peter Slater, travelled to Unst on the *Chieftain's Bride*. The following day they went to the Mansion House of Uyea to take a statement from George Leisk as a witness for the pursuers (Millers). Also present were William Sievwright, agent for the pursuers and James Kirkland Galloway, agent for the defender (Walker). Leisk was described as *suffering from paralysis and his tongue affected*[9] – probably a stroke – and Walker was anxious that he should not be questioned. On 24th February he had written to Alex Sandison:[10] *In Miller's action a Commission has been issued to examine George Leisk and from his condition it seems neither fair to himself or us that he be examined – so on receipt hereof I would like you to get from Dr Smith a certificate that George is not in a fit state of health to be subject to any examination ... If George is really better and can be examined you'll just need to explain to him that he has to adhere to what he used to tell you and Edmondston, that he believes there is the chance of plenty of ore in Grunie.*

Considering that Leisk's income from the lease agreement was fifteen shillings per ton royalty on the ore lifted, it seems obvious that he believed there was ore to be had on Haaf Grunie, otherwise he would surely have insisted on some other form of income from the lease. Back to Walker's letter to Sandison: *Of course as you cannot trust to George it will be far better to avoid getting him examined.*

When the legal party arrived at Uyea the medical certificate was duly produced, but Mure interviewed Leisk alone and decided he was fit for examination. Leisk's servant, Jean Manson, understood his indistinct speech, so she was sworn in as interpreter, and the interrogation went ahead. Questioned by Sievwright, Leisk declared: *I told Mr Walker there was no chromate in Grunie worth while.* But when asked by Walker's lawyer if he had often expressed the opinion that there was chrome ore in Haaf Grunie he replied: *Oh yes! I have never given it up but that there was chrome ore in Haaf Grunie.*[11]

In Mure's notes for the Lord Ordinary and the Court he claims to have understood the witness, and that, although Jean Manson was asked to verify each answer, there was no real need for her assistance. Mure ends with: *His examination had no apparent evil effect on him* [Leisk]*, but on the contrary, it appeared to raise his spirits and do him good.*[12]

Perhaps we see here a lonely, paralysed old man who had enjoyed playing along his solicitor visitors with his conflicting evidence, and it seems Walker was right that Leisk was unfit to be a reliable witness.

At the Court of Session in April 1875 Lord Gifford decided to relieve Miller of any interest in Grunie. Walker was to return the £2000, with interest accrued, and Millers were to receive expenses. Lord Gifford ended with the tongue-in-cheek statement that *the defender's* [Walker's] *present defeat will be a great gain to him, as he remains in possession of the lease, and firmly believes in the existence of large quantities of ore in the island.*

HAAF GRUNIE

Walker immediately wrote to Alexander Sandison:[13] *Millers' Case a victory and yet not a victory ... I give back the £2000 and Millers get modified expenses — well it can't be worse – may be better and so I appeal.* Then in August: *I hear that Gardner has struck ore on Grunie – I hope it may be a good beginning.* Next, a reminder of other business ventures and possible problems: *Sandlodge moves slower than I expected but keeps up to expectations as a mine – your countrymen are not able for full work but like full pay.*

His appeal was heard in December. After the Lords Gifford, Deas, Ardmillan and Mure had passed judgement at length, they still found that Millers were entitled to withdraw from the 'joint adventure' and recover their £2000, but without interest or expenses. Walker was cleared of fraud. Pleased, he wrote to Sandison:[14] *The result of the Millers' case is good – I get as much interest from him as should pay my costs and I get out of a bad bargain – I am quite satisfied especially that my character has been vindicated.*

I don't suppose Lord Ardmillan realised how neatly he had summed up Walker and all his other ill-fated ventures when he opined: *The eager and sanguine disposition of Mr Walker may sustain his own efforts amid discouragement, but cannot justify the Court in compelling the pursuers to continue a hazardous speculation which they apparently, not without some reason, expect to be disastrous.*[15]

The *Shetland Times* of 30th September, 1876 has the last word I have found on the Haaf Grunie affair: *Mr Walker, Edinburgh lessee, is promising fair to repay all the trouble and expense connected with the prospecting and quarrying. The workmen, under the energetic and able superintendence of Mr George Gardner came the other week on a very fine vein of rich ore which appears to run South and West to a considerable distance and will no doubt recoup Mr Walker for his indomitable perseverance and steadfast purpose. A considerable breadth of ore has been exposed; the extent and quality of such can only be brought to light by time and work. There is thus a prospect of giving employment to many who stand in need to do something to make up for the deficient fishing, and not less – to all appearance – deficient crop.*

Couldn't be a more optimistic report if Walker had written it himself!

1   Samuel Hibbert, *Shetland Islands,* Edinburgh, 1882, p.592
2   S.A. D 12/171 Appendix to reclaiming note for John Walker against Lord Gifford's Interlocutor
3   S.A. D 12/156/6
4   S.A. D 12/171
5   *The Scottish Law Reporter,* Miller v Walker, 10th December, 1875
6   S.A. D 12/171

JOHN WALKER'S SHETLAND

7   Sandison's Archive
8   S.A. D 12/171
9   S.A. D 12/171
10   Sandison's Archive
11   S.A. D 12/171
12   S.A. D 12/171
13   Sandison's Archive
14   Sandison's Archive
15   *The Scottish Law Reporter,* Miller v Walker, 10th December, 1875

Chapter Sixteen

CHROMATE CONTRIVANCE

*I am glad your counsel think the Chromate Proprietors
have not a shadow of a case against you, but ...*
Major Cameron writing to John Walker 2/2/1876

IN 1871 Major Cameron was worried about rumours of corruption and bribery involving Walker and his factorship of the chromate mines in Unst. Walker had hotly denied these suggestions, describing the other chromate proprietors as 'dirty wretches".

Five years later, on Saturday, 1st July, 1876, the *Shetland Times* published a special supplement on a case being heard at the Court of Session in Edinburgh. The Earl of Zetland and other proprietors of the minerals found in the scattalds of Haroldswick and Balliasta, Unst, were suing John Walker for £2,538:15s:8d, with interest from 1873 until payment. A large sum of money at that time. What's been going on?

Since 1858, Mr. G. H. B. Hay of Lerwick had been factor for all the proprietors of these Unst chromate mines. He disposed of the minerals and divided the proceeds among the proprietors. But in 1869 Major Cameron and his mother, Mrs Mouat of Garth, appointed their factor, John Walker, to represent their interest in the minerals, with Mr Hay still representing the rest. However, as Walker professed to have a good outlet for selling the ore in the south, for a time he acted for all the proprietors – with Mr Hay's, somewhat reluctant, consent.

John Walker's Shetland

Walker's outlet for this chromate, as with the Haaf Grunie ore, was with James Miller, Son, & Co., Glasgow. Back in March 1868 he had written to them:[1] *I am only now able to give you information about Shetland Chromate of Iron. The best rock seems only to contain about 45% of ore ... the best stone is fetching about £4:10s per ton.*

When Garth and Annsbrae opted out of Hay's factorship, Walker wrote a long epistle to Thomas Edmondston of Buness, chairman of the United Chromate Properties.[2] The content of this letter was 'to be communicated' – presumably to the other proprietors. The first four paragraphs were devoted to how well he, Walker, had done in the marketing of ore compared to the other factor (Hay's name was never actually mentioned). Next he strongly refuted a rumour that all his work had been done in order to become factor for all the mining proprietors, ending with: *Garth and Annsbrae now merely wish to do the best they can with their own, they cheerfully grant this right to others and might even assist them in their difficulties, but they are not prepared to sacrifice their interests wholly.*

The events which followed are detailed in that special supplement of the *Shetland Times*, and, as we read extracts from a few of the letters published, the wheeling and dealing emerges.

22nd April, 1869, Miller to Walker: *We hope the meeting on 28th will result in giving you the control of all the mines.*

3rd May, 1869, Walker to Miller: *There is no doubt that the other proprietors' share of the ore are now being offered to the Whites, and if you can by any means foil this attempt, the whole ore would at once come thro your hands and I could deliver the 1800 tons this season ... Where in Norway are the chrome ore quarries? If near here, I would go and see them to ascertain their mode of working.*

12th May, 1869, Miller to Walker: *Is Mr Hay the party who is trying to sell the ore for the other proprietors? Is he resident in Shetland, and does he deal with an agent here? Please fix us on this. What is the reason for the other proprietors not going in with you? Is it a matter of price or what? ... We are making enquiries as to where in Norway the chrome mines are.*

17th May, 1869, Walker to Miller: *Mr Hay is a merchant here, and was until lately agent for all the proprietors, but is now only for a part indeed he is at present only representing one; but several, if they thought he could secure a good market, would put their ore into his hands, but if he cannot within a few weeks show them favourable terms, they would allow all their shares to go with ours – hence his exertions to sell; but I believe he is doing so direct with the Whites.* Evasive about Hay's representation! Meanwhile Miller is urging Walker to ship the 1800 tons ore already bargained for. And there's another scheme afoot.

21st June, 1869, Miller to Walker: *It is understood and arranged that we give you one-third of the profit we have on the 1800 chrome ore, bought from you on 3rd March last, and that for the future all business in chrome ore from Shetland be one-half joint account between you and us.*

Meanwhile Walker wrote to G. H. B. Hay saying that he was willing to buy the ore belonging to Hay's constituents at a price within reason of the market value, assuring Hay that he would be unlikely to get an alternative, suitable market unless at great sacrifice. Hay replied cautiously, pointing out that Walker had the advantage of having had access to all the accounts of his transactions and suggesting that Walker was concealing his hand. He also questioned the three per cent commission, remuneration from the proprietors to Walker as payment for his trouble in negotiating the contract.[3] Needless to say neither the proprietors nor Hay knew about the profitable financial deal Walker had made with Miller.

By January 1870 Walker was in Glasgow (at the proprietors' expense).[4] From there he sent a lengthy epistle to Hay about his negotiations. Later that month Miller sent two letters to Walker, one private and one official. In the private letter Miller wrote: *You will now, we hope, bring Mr Hay to book, and thus close the affair ... We enclose letter as drafted by you. We send it under separate cover.* The latter was the official letter which could be made public – composed by Walker himself.

Eventually Hay was reluctantly persuaded into accepting the terms of the contract. 7th March, 1870, from Hay & Walker to James Miller: *On behalf of the Balliasta and Haroldswick chrome ore proprietors we accept your offer for the first 1500 tons chrome ore to be mined and if possible raised during the next two seasons.*

During the summer of 1870 disagreements arose over alleged short weight and inferiority of the ore being sent to Millers. In August Robert Miller (partner of James) visited Shetland. Something was bothering him, judging from a letter to Walker after he returned to Glasgow: *The remittance was sent to your own house and I trust you received it all right. You know it was my partner that first arranged the business with you, and in consequence I don't like to interfere in his particular boat. Only, I wish you had not mentioned about the future. You have written your letter in anger, and that is always dangerous ... it would be a great pity if the business was spoiled and your friend Hay got his revenge.*

By January 1871 relations between Hay and Walker were worse than ever, Walker describing Hay in a letter to Miller as *very peppery, and unreasonably unwilling to sign the letter sent you ... I'll now work Hay up gently as to future contract.*

JOHN WALKER'S SHETLAND

In February he had the nerve to write to Hay asking that consideration be made as to whether his (Walker's) services had been adequately remunerated by the other proprietors, and also: *I have now to point out that our great difficulty in correctly deciding upon the terms of a new contract lies in the fact that foreign ores are interfering much with our trade, and to ascertain the resources of the foreigners I have to suggest that you join with Garth and Annsbrae in paying the expense of my running out to Smyrna* [now Izmir, Turkey] *and collecting information as to ore found there (I am willing to give my time for the sake of still further developing Unst) ... I can spare the time, say three weeks hence.* It seems unlikely that he made the journey to Smyrna – but it was a good try.

Not surprisingly Hay had been worried for some time because he was increasingly aware that correspondence was passing privately between Walker and Miller. In February he wrote to Miller himself, setting out his own case: *You seem to attribute to me whatever may have been unsatisfactory in your transactions with the Unst chromate proprietors. Allow me to say that misunderstandings might have been avoided had you addressed all your communications in reference to the contract to Mr Walker and me jointly, instead of to him alone. Representing as I do two thirds of the one set of quarries, and four fifths of the other, this would have been the ordinary course.* In March he informed Walker that he did not wish to continue the joint working of the mines.

Meanwhile Walker, on another of his trips south, started a letter to the Major by declaring that he had made an unsuccessful trip to Peterhead in an attempt to procure some of the Major's special tobacco. However, the main theme of the letter was complaints about Hay's attitude:[5] *Hay has put the Glasgow men all wrong again in fact worse than ever – to save himself makes nasty insinuations against me.*

He had received a letter from the Major with some rebuke about the chrome working and replied: *You can believe that I am not well satisfied with your remarks about Chrome Ore matters ... However to me there is a pleasant satisfaction that no Shetland Ore can be sold except thro myself. Upon my return I will show you the exact position of Glasgow matters. I have nothing to keep you in the dark about ... Hay cannot object to any part of our accounts – I take the responsibility of these all upon myself too and all I want is that your Property and your representation command the respect I humbly think the latter deserves ... Like the other volcanic eruptions that occasionally threaten to swallow me – you'll find them collapse when boldly confronted and recoiling upon the authors – If I gave the signal Hay's constituents would undo their connection with him – he at present serves our purpose best to keep him in.*

CHROMATE CONTRIVANCE

The volcano did begin to erupt in the summer of 1871 when letters from lawyer William Sievwright began to appear in the correspondence. To Walker: *Your position is certainly a very anomalous one and I do not understand how you can act consistently in a double capacity. A private correspondence between you and them about joint transactions, and in regard to the settlement of these transactions, puts you in a dubious position.*

Needless to say Walker penned a testy reply: *I hardly understand your remarks as to my position with the Messrs Miller ... were it not on my account they would do no business with Mr Hay ... besides, Messrs Miller are my friends, and, I believe will continue such.*

By August the intrigue was deepening. R. Miller to John Walker: *As you desire it we enclose a note addressed to 'Messrs Hay and Walker', worded as you dictate, but we scarcely know your reason for asking such a letter. We trust you won't need to use it.*

30th January, 1872, John Walker to Robert Miller: *About chrome, you'll need to send me a note, after the enclosed, which I will reply to, stating that it is Mr Hay who is detaining shipments, and then you'll reply to H. and W. upon that.*

29th April, 1872, John Walker to Robert Miller: *You have done well in sending copy of Sievwright's letter before answer. I enclose a sort of scroll of what your lawyer should answer, and see that he does so by return post. Before yours arrived I had written Hay that I was to ship off the ore quarried whether he consented or not. I at once got a thunderer from Sievwright that he would on Hay's behalf interdict us ... The Major is fairly roused, and will now fight them keen ... Do not go beyond what I indicate in scroll, but let your agent threaten boldly, as Hay is a coward.*

17th May, 1872, John Walker to Robert Miller: *I now send drafts of what should be sent to Hay and Walker in answer to Sievwright's last ... you keep from distinctly stating more than that, upon the assumption that my view of matters is correct, you have nothing to do with the money.*

27th May, 1872, Robert Miller to John Walker: *In Mr Hay's absence cannot you call a meeting of the other proprietors and open their eyes as to real state of ore business? We are being very badly used.*

The last letter quoted in the *Shetland Times* is one of the strangest. 6th August, 1872, Walker (from Aberdeen) to Messrs Jas. Miller, Son & Co: *The longest day and darkest night have an end, and from Hay's you now see that we have worked him out in the right way. I send you a scroll of what Mr Watt should write. The quarries stop on Saturday first. I leave tonight, and will no doubt Hay work up ere I return.*

JOHN WALKER'S SHETLAND

At the Court of Session, in 1876, Walker was sued for £2538:15s:8d – the amount by which the proprietors' proportion of the proceeds of the minerals sold would have been increased if Walker had accounted for all the profits.[6] In court Walker admitted that he had received certain sums from Millers as a share of the profit on the ore, but said that he transacted in these matters solely as factor for Major Cameron and Mrs Mouat and that they were fully aware of the interest which he had along with Messrs Miller.

The *Shetland Times* was authorised to publish an excerpt from a letter written by Major Cameron, as he had not had the opportunity to make a statement in court: *I repudiate with scorn the idea that I participated in Mr Walker's chromate profits. Until the case Miller v Walker was published, I did not know the nature of the latter's profits further than supposing them to be his factor's commission on sales, the same as Mr Hay and the chromate factors had always been.*

The reason why the Major was unable to make a statement in court personally is revealed in correspondence between him and his factor in February 1876. The Major was relaxing in a villa at Cannes, in the south of France. To Walker's inquiry whether he would attend court on 20th March, he replied:[7] *My present plan is to remain here till about 1st April to which date I have taken this Villa and then ... to go on into Italy for three weeks or a month.* Doesn't that serve to remind us of the disparity of lifestyle between lairds and crofters in 19th century Shetland!

Although Major Cameron was not prepared to forgo his long vacation, he was becoming increasingly upset and disillusioned:[8] *That you had a profit by Commission I believed, but that you were not accounting for the full price for which you sold the ore I did not know till the case was published. The imputation on my Mother's and my integrity is too serious to be passed over in silence.*

The end of the Cameron/Walker partnership is in sight: *As the period of the close connection that has existed between us since 1866 is so soon to expire I am very much grieved you should have said or done anything to mar the harmony that I would wish for in winding up what may be called our Co-partnership in the sheep farms but I may be advised to clear my character in the eyes of my friends who do not look on some sharp dealings in the same light – as many people do in the present day.*

The case of *the Earl of Zetland and Others v. John Walker and Others* cropped up again in Walker's bankruptcy statement of 1880. Among his many *Losses and Investments etc*, is included – *Action Earl Zetland & others. R. Miller Son & Co should pay ½_____£2000.*[9]

** ** **

At Hagdale, Unst, the site of a disused chromate quarry which has been largely filled in. © *Andy Gear*

While all the wheeling and dealing was going on, ore was quarried, washed, carted to the piers, weighed and shipped. George Gardner was foreman at the quarries in the early 70s and he was sent his instructions in a stream of letters from Walker. Gardner carried a load of responsibility as we can gather by reading extracts taken from some of these letters:[10] *I herewith send you Forty Pounds (£20 in gold and £20 in silver) to pay the last fortnight's wages to workmen and advance to McKay in a/c of the washing. P.S. Bag of money is sealed ... I've sent for four quarriers who I trust will be fit to keep the squads at work and relieve Magnus Coutts ... With regard to shipping the ore you can offer Andrew Anderson 8d per ton and he is to be responsible for the boats ... I had heard of the accident at the Quarry. You have not stated whether or not the man is married – but in any case I think you should make all those engaged in the folly contribute weekly an amount equal to half the man's earnings – I hope the men's conduct does not indicate continual trifling when you are not present ... It seems that the washing the stuff has got by machine is nothing equal to hand washing and until all the sand and dirt is removed we cannot ship more ... I expect to send three vessels up to you next week so push on the carting ... Tell Sinclair to give good fair weight so that there is no room for complaints but to be just for all parties ... The House for your Engine is promised on Thursday – see that it gets a coat of coal tar ... You will push on with sorting the Ores and get as much of the 2nds done from the Upper*

JOHN WALKER'S SHETLAND

Quarry as you can, for I expect one of the Buyers here next week ... Lay the No.1 beside Edmondston's No.1, but don't mix ... And so on. John Walker was keeping his finger on the pulse of several other projects at the same time as this one. Wouldn't he have appreciated present day means of communication!

**   **   **

Before we leave Unst minerals, a last letter on the subject. After the Court of Session case he wrote to Alexander Sandison on 21st June, 1876:[11] *I had to compromise the great case ... Well so be it – I am vexed that I did not manage better but it's always easy to be wise after the fact – I am about disgusted with Shetland and feel inclined to forswear it altho I believe I have many true friends – but we'll see. I'll be North with this but not sure if I'll get to Unst.*

Even though he was obviously disturbed by the result of the case, the P.S. to Sandison's letter shows that School Board matters were on his mind:- *Look out for Prof. Ramsay and watch Smith.*

1   Gardie Papers L.B.1 p.310
2   Gardie Papers L.B.2 p.713
3   Reid Tait Collection : 16/19: Vol. 2: Law Papers
4   Ibid
5   Gardie Papers L.B.2, no number, loose at back
6   Reid Tait Collection : Vol. 2 : Law Papers
7   Gardie Papers 1876/42
8   Gardie Papers 1876/26
9   N.A.S. CS 3181371321
10 Gardie Papers L.B.2 Extracts from letters to Gardner pp.927-999
11 Sandison's Archive

Chapter Seventeen

WALKER AND THE SCHOOL BOARDS

The financial condition of the islands [Shetland], as regards education, must be gauged not merely by their poverty in rental, but by their wealth in children.
From Professor Ramsay's report on education in Shetland, written in 1874.

THE Education (Scotland) Act of 1872 should have revolutionised children's lives because it made attendance at school compulsory until the age of thirteen, thereby lifting many out of drudgery for at least part of the year. The school environment should have been improved by the Act for those who did manage to attend. However, at first it brought nothing but controversy, and a deterioration in the sparse education system which did exist.

Previously the responsibility for education in Shetland had mainly depended on three bodies – the SSPCK (Society in Scotland for Propagating Christian Knowledge), the Churches, and the Heritors (landowners). This led to a patchy provision with no establishment carrying overall responsibility. The quality of education depended largely on the enthusiasm and dedication, not only of those teaching, but also of influential personalities in the community. Funding was always a problem. As attendance was not compulsory many children only attended when there was no work to be done on the croft.

At first the new system was to be controlled from London by the Scotch (as it was then known) Education Department, but, after strong protests from north of the border, a temporary Board of Education was set up in Edinburgh. School boards were to be elected to manage matters at a local level. They were to take over the old schools and organise the provision of new accommodation where needed. Some Government Grant assistance would be given to help in the cost of new buildings.

The economic and geographical problems of the remote rural areas were completely overlooked by bureaucracy in the south. The expense of providing education for all, in widely scattered districts, threatened to place an impossible burden on the parish. The Government Grant only covered about half of the cost of building, taking no account of teachers' salaries or maintenance costs. When Professor Ramsay was sent to Shetland in 1873 to compile a report for the Scotch Education Department he realised that about sixty new buildings, costing upwards of £1000 each, were needed to carry out the provisions of the Act. However he recommended that, to save money, the buildings should be designed to accommodate only three-quarters of the children eligible to attend, on the assumption that, in spite of the compulsory attendance clause, at any one time a quarter of the school roll would be absent because of distance and bad weather.

By spring 1873 School Board elections were in full swing. John Walker was elected to boards for Unst; Fetlar & North Yell; Mid & South Yell; and Bressay, Burra & Quarff. He was made chairman of the three North Isles boards. In spite of the fact that he was by then living in Aberdeen, (and Edinburgh by 1874), he attended meetings at least as regularly as most other board members. He also stood for Delting, Lerwick and Scalloway, but was not elected. No doubt he had the improved education of the children at heart, but to stand for so many boards is also evidence of his power-hungry nature.

The aftermath of the Lerwick school board election in May 1873 provides a typical 'Walker' story when he claimed he had been deprived of a seat because an invalid paper had been allowed, and took Andrew Mure, the returning officer, to Court. The case rested on a dubious number '4' on a voting paper which could possibly have been read as '11'. As each voter was allowed to cast seven votes on his voting paper, a number '11' would have caused that paper to be null and void. Walker had been defeated by only three votes, so a decision to scrap the questionable paper would have given him a seat on the board. A sealed packet of ballot papers was held in the court, but although Walker repeatedly moved that the packet be opened and inspected, the Sheriff, on Mr Mure's objection, refused the motion. The decision of the court went against Walker.[1]

However he came top of the poll in North Yell with 58 votes; William Pole – 52; Rev. C. S. Murray – 48; Mr. P. M. Sandison – 44; Thomas Irvine

– 42.² Walker was an excellent choice. As we will see, it took his bold tenacity to deal with the Education Department of the time.

In a letter published in the *Shetland Times*, he thanked the electors for their confidence in returning him, stating that he had been honoured with chairmanship of the three North Isles boards: *I feel that a deep responsibility rests upon me, especially owing to my residence in Aberdeen. I shall however do my utmost to ensure the full benefit of the Education Act at the least possible expense to the rate-payers.* He goes on to say that, in his opinion, the Bible should be read and its principles taught in every school, but he wasn't so sure about the Shorter Catechism. The last paragraph of the letter is addressed to the electors of Scalloway *who, unsolicited, nominated me as a member for their board, and only failed in their wishes to secure my return by some 5 votes (in a contest with 17 candidates for 7 seats). I am equally bound to express my gratitude for their exertions.*³

The plight of the remote areas as regards education was taken up by Sir Alexander Grant, Principal of Edinburgh University. Extracts from a speech he made at the University were printed in the *Shetland Times*, where it was pointed out that Sir Alexander was a member of the Select Education Board and that he seemed well informed as to conditions in Orkney and Shetland *and the special difficulties which attend the working out of the new law in our islands.*

The first part of Sir Alexander's address was full of the promise expected from the new Act and praise for the work of most of the school boards. He gradually introduced the difficulties inherent in the outlying areas: *But I had hitherto left out of consideration the Highlands and Islands of Scotland. In these regions the educational wants are clamant, and the difficulty of meeting them great beyond anticipation. Take, for instance, the islands of Orkney and Shetland. In these islands there are children of school-going age to the number of 10,000. There exists nominal school accommodation for about 6000 children. But this nominal school accommodation consists for the most part of wretched, ruinous hovels; ... in Shetland the net rental may be stated at £22,500, which would give only 1s per child. It is clear then that the adequate education of these districts cannot be provided locally ... An Act of Parliament has been compared to an egg, which after being laid needs hatching. The Education Act for Scotland has on the whole been very well laid, but it will need a long incubation ... During that period school boards will themselves be under a process of education.*⁴

He finished by asking whether educational endowments should exist merely to relieve the pockets of ratepayers or should they benefit the nation as a whole by providing technical or scientific instruction or providing bursaries to carry poor but talented scholars through a High School and University career. Remember, this man was talking in 1873!

Criticism of the Education Act was a popular subject for letters to the Press. In the *Scotsman* of 17th August, 1874, George Stewart writes from Levenwick: *Permit me ... to call the attention of friends of education and the public in general to the deplorable condition of these islands in the matter of education, arising from the operation of the late Education Act. This Act, though neither anticipated nor intended, has had the effect of depriving the islands of the most important means of education which existed, and left nothing to replace it but what is utterly unworkable and unsuitable, and must have been framed either in entire ignorance or disregard of the peculiarities and circumstances of the islands.*

He went on to illustrate the problems of financing the new buildings and paying teachers without imposing crippling rates: *The Government Grant of 14s. 6d. for each scholar who shall attain to the proper standard in the three R's will not help the case. As there has been no school of any kind in the village for the last ten years, the teacher in most cases would have to begin with the alphabet ... It is next to impossible to enforce the compulsory clauses here, as the people are so poor they require the assistance of their children more or less in the farm and bringing home fuel, so that the number of proficient scholars, even after three or four years' work, will be very small indeed.* No doubt his last statement was true enough, but it was hardly a valid argument for retaining the old system.

The wrangling continued for three years and meanwhile the building work was delayed. Walker's ability to write hard-hitting letters proved useful as he kept up a lively correspondence with the Scotch Education Department, in his endeavour to sort out costs of building the new schools and schoolhouses.

From 1 Polwarth Terrace, Edinburgh:[5] *My board will not move further in the way of building (so much needed) until they are assured that the assistance to be granted will be in accordance with the reasonable interpretation of the Act. The matter of maintenance of these buildings must form an after question. I shall be glad of an early reply as I have ordered special meetings to consider same.*

Your obedient servant,
John Walker

The building grant sought (or offered) was £300 per school and £100 for teacher's residence.

The *Shetland Times*, 26th October, 1874: *On Tuesday last Mr. Walker, chairman of the school boards of Unst, Fetlar & North Yell and of Mid & South Yell, had a lengthened interview with the Scottish Education*

Board for the purpose of stating the serious difficulties encountered by these School Boards in carrying out the provisions of the Education Act, and requesting advice and assistance as to obviating these difficulties.

And again on 16th November: *On Wednesday the 4th inst., the Lord Advocate received a deputation, consisting of Sheriff Thoms, Mr Peacock as representing the Western Isles, and Mr Walker as representing our North Isles School Boards ... At his Lordship's request Mr Walker sent in details as to the present burdens upon property, and the probable increase to carry out the Act as at present, and to meet the ever recurring difficulties that must arise between a Board sitting in London and unacquainted with the peculiarities of Shetland.*

Since the election of the school boards bad feeling had developed between John Walker and Rev. William Smith, one of the Unst ministers. Perhaps the result of the Unst school board election had something to do with it, viz. – Rev. John Ingram, 173 votes; Mr W. G. Mowat, merchant, 144; Thos. Edmondston Esq. of Buness, 109; Mr John Spence, merchant, 94; Mr Alex. Sandison, merchant, 75; Mr John Walker, Factor, 74; Rev. George Makin, Methodist Minister, 71. Rev. Wm. Smith and Mr Jas. Jeffray were unsuccessful candidates.[6]

The disagreement started between Walker and Simon S. Laurie, Secretary to the Education Committee of the Church of Scotland, as to whether certain schools should remain under the jurisdiction of the General Assembly. In so far as their argument epitomises the general chaos in Scottish education after the 1872 Act, it is worth a mention here.

On 15th October, 1874 Simon Laurie wrote to the *Scotsman* on behalf of the Education Committee of the Church of Scotland, Edinburgh, defending the actions of their committee since the Act: *The policy ... was to continue the Assembly Schools, as long as furnished with the means of doing so, mainly for the purpose of easing the transition from the old system to the new, partly as a standing protection of religious instruction.*

Walker replied:[7] *Whenever the Committee [church] could continue a school to humour their own ideas they have been quite indifferent as to the interests of the Parish – instance Norwick, Burrafirth, Sellafirth, etc. In the two former the buildings were quite inadequate in every respect, in the later inadequate at least in size, and therefore in all cases not relieving the parishes from having to provide other schools but retaining them so far as I can see for no other reason than opposition to the Act. I am a Churchman, but the manner in which our Education Committee are acting is in my opinion only aiding those who desire disestablishment.*

'A Shetlander', Leith, pointed out, among other things, that the nine Assembly schools left *would barely meet the wants of two of the smallest parishes in Shetland. It is not difficult to estimate the amount of educational destitution which exists when it is known that those nine schools are spread over twelve parishes, containing a population of nearly 30,000 inhabitants.*

So the dispute raged on, the complexities of the situation often eclipsed by personal gibes – Walker calling Laurie, 'Simple Simon', and Rev. William Smith writing:[8] *Mr Walker's words, like himself, sound large and loud – but, like himself, are of little weight.*

When George Stewart recovered sufficiently from a serious illness to catch up on the correspondence in the papers, he neatly summed up the situation:[9] *I am sorry to find that the dispute between Mr Laurie of the Education Committee of the Church of Scotland and Mr Walker late of Bressay has assumed such a bitter and personal character. These gentlemen ought to remember that in their official capacity the great question is not who may be right in any particular point, but whether the great command 'feed my lambs' has been obeyed to the utmost. Whatever errors may have been committed in the past cannot now be recalled, and mutual recriminations can do no good. It is surely therefore wise to lay aside this spirit and make the most of present and future opportunities to further the common cause.*

Sensible advice! He continued by tactfully suggesting how the strengths of both individuals could best be used: *Mr Laurie, as representing the Church, can do something to mitigate the hardship which the withdrawal of such a large portion of its aid has caused, and Mr Walker, as representing the School Boards so largely can do much in aid of carrying the matter before Parliament, where now only proper and permanent help can be obtained ... I earnestly trust that School Boards and others who have now taken action will not allow their efforts to flag.* To give John Walker his due, he did not usually allow his efforts to flag on any cause that he supported, whether it was a popular one or not.

Andrew Dishington Mathewson, by then 76, had been teaching in East Yell since 1822.[10] When he wrote to his son, Arthur, in March 1875, he was worried:[11] *through fear of Barclay's Plans to throw me out of House and Office without any annuity*. He does not entirely blame Walker for his plight: *He* [Barclay] *has twice had me called to the School-Board and both times shewn the Members how he was merely getting Walker to do his bidding.*

However, we can tell that Mathewson is neither a fan of Walker nor of the local proprietors: *And now Walker has a charge of Two Thousand against him in the Court of Session, and is beginning to find his Shetland Sheep Farms not likely to pay – so he is Resigning some of the Chairmanships of the Parochial Boards which he had got by the carelessness of the Proprietors and their untaught Ignorance.*

Next comes an uncanny piece of prophecy: *Who knows but the diamond fields of Africa may not open for him* [Walker] *to deceive some poor easily led persons as in his sheep farming here; to make him Manager of a new Joint Stock Company for Diamond in Africa.* Substitute railways for diamonds – but that story comes later.

Lastly an intriguing piece of gossip: *Till he can decamp with a few thousands as he is reported to have done from Australia.*

By 1876 Professor Ramsay was proposing to further reduce the school building required in Shetland, to now accommodate only three fifths of the total number of children aged between five and thirteen. Walker pointed out that,[12] although attendance would be sparse in bad weather, on fine days there could be almost perfect attendance with children over thirteen present as well, resulting in unacceptable overcrowding *thus rendering it impossible for the teacher to give, or the children to receive the requisite instruction, whilst the additional expense for an efficient school will practically be nothing in cost of building.*

None of the Walker children, who were said to have adored their Papa,[13] would have attended the local schools, they were educated by a governess. However, he insisted that the needs of the pupils took priority: *You also object to the apparently expensive nature of the plans, &c., which have been sanctioned ... As to lavatories, I do not see why the children here should be deprived of such a luxury (if such you call it) ... The play-sheds I hold are also absolutely necessary in this climate. It is a piece of refined cruelty either to keep children in an unaired, stuffy school for six hours on end, or to leave them out in all weathers without some efficient shelter. The Legislature has ordered that children shall be educated, but it never meant that this should be accomplished at the expense of their constitutions.*

You intimated that certain schools in Shetland were being erected without these arrangements, and that you thought them sufficient. The difference is, that I do not ... any competent architect will confirm my opinion that the cheap and nasty is not the most economical ... as yet more has been spent upon inspections, special reports, etc., than upon Educational Grants for this district.

An amusing follow-up to this letter came from Robert Cogle, Cunningsburgh, who used the original meaning of lavatory (place for washing hands and face) to show up Walker's lack of provision at the Sandlodge Mine:[14] *As to lavatories, if Mr Walker would be at the expense of erecting one in the 'oor pit' at Sandlodge, it would be a most useful appendage to clean the workmen before they come up to the daylight, but in the case of schools they are quite superfluous, since it would be a sheer waste of time to keep children doing that while at school which they should do before leaving their homes.*

JOHN WALKER'S SHETLAND

In the summer of 1876 the second round of School Board elections took place, with Walker re-elected to his previous boards, and adding Tingwall to his list. The latter was decided without a poll, having only the necessary seven nominees. He was not a popular new member according to one 'Ratepayer and Elector of the Parish of Tingwall', who wrote to the *Shetland Times* bemoaning the loss of George Hay who had withdrawn from the election: *And what have we got in exchange? Shall I say 'Mr John Walker, farmer, 1 Polwarth Terrace, Edinburgh', and congratulate ourselves on the change? Surely hearty thanks or <u>something</u> is due to the nominators of this apparently ubiquitous personage, from whom, living in Edinburgh, and having the important stake of £8 : 5s rental in the district we may expect full attention to the interests committed to him! But if we should fail to get attention, I do not think we will fail to get bluster.*

In a complete reversal of fortune, the Rev. W. Smith came top of the poll in the 1876 school board election in Unst, and immediately moved that Walker resign the chair of the board. Writing to Alexander Sandison[15] from Sandlodge on 28th August, we learn that Walker felt that, because the matter of the chairmanship ought to be settled in his absence, he would not attend the Unst Show that year. Three days later, in another letter to Sandison this time from Aberdeen, he is pleased to have learned that *Smith's motion fell to the ground.* But asks Alexander to let him know the <u>feeling</u> *of the members as I have really no wish to continue Chairman if there is the least wish that I resign.*

He has even more than usual on his mind at this time because, as we know, in June of that year he had been taken to court by the proprietors of minerals in Haroldswick and Balliasta and had been found guilty of fraud. In August he was *much bothered by the men here* (at the Sandlodge mine). By October he was no longer Factor for Garth. In the middle of it all he got stuck in Fair Isle for five days and then was housebound with a bad leg which he hurt getting into a boat. Pouring out his troubles to his friend Alexander Sandison:[16] *There are many small reptiles that are annoying and I don't just now feel inclined to stand even annoyance upon School Board matters.*

However, in spite of that, he did carry on with the struggle to improve the school buildings. Correspondence in the *Shetland Times* in 1877 indicates that the delay in school building in Unst was dragging on, with Walker, as representative of the school board, blaming the Board of Education and vice-versa. In one of his letters to the Scotch Education Department[17] he pointed out that during the first three months of 1876 he had submitted twenty-one plans etc. for schools and teachers' houses.

WALKER AND THE SCHOOL BOARDS

Sixty new board schools were erected in Shetland as a result of the Education Act, most of them by 1880.[18]

The schools and schoolhouses erected at that time were built of stone with slate roofs and well-lit, airy classrooms. Most of them are now occupied as private dwellings. Certainly Walker specialised in bluster, but we must give him credit for the success he had in his work on the school boards. He devoted a great deal of time and energy to achieving what would be best in the long term for the education of children in Shetland.

Now a private dwelling house, the Ulsta School and Schoolhouse was one of those built after the Education Act of 1872.   © *Andy Gear*

1. *Shetland Times*, 19th May, 1873
2. *Shetland Times*, 12th May, 1873
3. *Shetland Times*, 19th May, 1873
4. *Shetland Times*, 17th November, 1873
5. *Shetland Times*, 5th October, 1874
6. *Shetland Times*, 26th May, 1873
7. *Scotsman*, 19th October, 1874
8. *Shetland Times*, 17th December, 1874
9. *Shetland Times*, 23rd November, 1874
10. Margaret Robertson, *Sons and Daughters of Shetland*, Lerwick 1991, p.123
11. S.A. D 23/150/34/4
12. *Shetland Times*, October 1876
13. Private correspondence – Betty Ambrose
14. *Shetland Times*, 4th November, 1876
15. Sandison's Archive
16. Ibid
17. *Shetland Times*, 24th March, 1877
18. John J. Graham, *A Vehement Thirst After Knowledge*, Lerwick 1998, p.142

Chapter Eighteen

SANDLODGE COPPER MINE

I had been aware that copper ore existed at Sandlodge from 1852 and being on very intimate terms with the Bruces, I early in 1872 got a 19 years lease.
from examination of John Walker, bankrupt,
at Edinburgh on 10th December, 1880

IN 1872, John Walker obtained a nineteen years lease, from John Bruce of Sumburgh, for the Sandlodge mine at Sandwick, fourteen miles south of Lerwick. Almost a hundred years earlier, in 1789, copper prospects had been discovered there, and at Garthsness. By 1800 the Shetland Mining Company had been formed and Cornish miners were brought in to work at Sandlodge. Two years later a steam engine was transported north to pump water from the mine. In 1803, at a depth of 22 fathoms, hard rock prevented the miners from reaching a rich lode they expected to find, and the company ran out of money. However, in 1805, a new company was formed, and a shaft sunk, 40 fathoms deep, at a cost of £1050. Unfortunately, very hard rock was still a problem and ore was sparsely distributed. By 1808 the mine was full of water and the engine dismantled.[1] The elusive, supposedly rich vein of ore had won the first round.

In his Sandlodge endeavour John Walker was originally in partnership with Henry Aitken and Robert Miller – probably the same merchant who featured in 'Chromate Contrivance'. After two years the partners withdrew and John carried on himself until 1879, when the

SANDLODGE COPPER MINE

Sumburgh Mining Co. was formed.[2] Shareholders, mostly from addresses in Aberdeen and London, were persuaded to invest. John's five brothers were all shareholders. In fact, the six Walker brothers among them held about half the shares in the mine[3] and Alexander was a director. At considerable expense, machinery and furnaces were installed. It is estimated that during the eight years of Walker's lease he raised about 10,000 tons of iron and copper ore.[4]

In Victorian times safety of workers was certainly not top of the agenda, so it is hardly surprising that miners were injured, often fatally, and Sandlodge was no exception. By looking at the records of these tragic events we can incidentally learn quite a lot about procedures and conditions at the mine.

6th February, 1875:[5] *Scaffold had been erected five fathoms below the surface of the shaft for the purpose of getting some water pipes out.* R. Beatty (manager), William Jamieson (joiner), Alexander Smith (miner) and Laurence Sinclair (miner), were standing on the scaffolding working with the pipes. It was the first time Laurence Sinclair had been engaged in that kind of work. He slipped, and the other three couldn't prevent him from falling down the shaft. At the police inquiry all the witnesses said that the scaffolding was quite secure and nothing gave way. Laurence Sinclair died of his injuries a few days later.

We get a hint of trouble with the workforce at the mine later the same year from a case brought before the Assize Court – Walker v. McGuffy. Walker had chartered McGuffy's vessel, the *Frankfort* to carry ore from Sandlodge to Newcastle in July. But there was a delay in the charter being carried out:[6] *some difficulty at the Shetland Islands – a strike or something of that sort going on – which created some difficulty in getting the ore.*

By 5th February, 1876 the *Shetland Times* was optimistic about progress at the mine: *Operations at the Sandlodge mine are being carried on with considerable activity. Two additional steam engines are soon to be put on the works, as also a crushing apparatus. While the iron ore will be sent away in the same condition as formerly, the cupreous ore will be crushed and washed, before being shipped, and by these means the expense of transporting it to the smelting furnaces at Newcastle will be greatly reduced.* The spongy brown iron oxides which occurred in the upper part of the vein were extracted and sold for use in gas works as a desulphurising agent. The richer copper ores were treated separately.[7]

By April, a stalk was being erected at the works, high enough to carry away smoke which had been causing some annoyance. Also a rich deposit of copper had been struck and handbills were advertising for more workmen at four shillings a day.[8]

181

Sandlodge Copper Mine, 1905. Photographer J. Manson.
© *Shetland Museum*

On 20th May, a correspondent to the *Shetland Times* described the happy mood in the Sandwick area: *Since the mine at Sandlodge has offered employment to so many people ... everybody in the parish seems to wear a different countenance ... almost everybody is becoming cheerful and altogether different to the feeling which pervades the mind when there is nothing talked about but landlords planning as to how they may get people away and such-like depressing gossip.*

In the same year, on 31st May, the schooner *Prince of Wales* bound from Bo'ness to Sandlodge with a cargo of coal and machinery for Walker, foundered off the Bard of Bressay.[9] The schooner had arrived at Sandlodge early in the evening of the 30th, and after anchoring, the master, John Williams, went ashore with two of the crew to make arrangements for unloading the cargo. He left the men in charge of the boat at the beach, but, on his return, they had disappeared. When he finally got on board the mate reported that the vessel was leaking badly. They tried the pumps, but the water was gaining, so they hoisted a light for assistance and sent out distress signals. No help was forthcoming, so the master decided to run for Lerwick.

He had with him mate, Robert Williams and a boy, Thomas Jones. These two continued to work the pumps, but the water was increasing so rapidly that eventually the vessel refused to answer the helm and at 3.30am the three men took to their boat to save their lives. They remained alongside the schooner until the hull was under water, then pulled for Noss where they landed safely and were looked after by the shepherd. By then the wind was freshening and the *Prince of Wales* sank with her cargo of machinery and coal.

As an agent for the Scottish Fire Insurance Company, let's hope John Walker had the mine well insured, as another catastrophe was just around the corner.[10]

FIRE AT THE SANDLODGE MINES

A FIRE of a very disastrous description took place on Sunday morning at the Sandlodge mine ... The first appearance of fire was observed at six o'clock. Soon after the alarm had spread, the Manager arrived with a number of people whom he had roused out of bed, who willingly rendered every assistance to quench the fire. A large quantity of debris having fallen on the chain attached to the safety valve, and the flames raging fearfully at the time, it was considered unsafe to approach near, for fear the boiler should burst. After some delay the chain was got clear, and the steam flew off quickly. The fire now spread very rapidly, and caught on the pithead frame. No sooner was this observed than an endeavour was made to subdue the flame, which fortunately proved effectual. Luckily there was a good supply of water in the engine pond, which, with the exertion of people with buckets, the pithead frame and seat of the stone crusher were saved. Had the wind been in any other direction at the time of the fire, the loss would have been much greater: in all probability the smith's shops would have gone too.

The valuable machinery at the mine has been much damaged. The loss from the fire is very great, but is said to be covered by insurance. The origin of the fire is not known. When the engineer left everything seemed to be as usual.

It will be about two weeks before the engine can be repaired, so as to pump the water out, which is now rapidly rising in the mine. In the meantime Mr Walker and his manager have put the men on to raise hematite in the upper sections of the mine, until the water be got out.

During the last two months a good many improvements have been made at the mine. A wooden pier of 200 feet long has been built, on the point of which a powerful steam crane is in process of erection, so that vessels may come in and the ore be put on board by the crane. There is also being put up a stone breaking machine, to crush the ore as it comes out of the mine, and all is being done in a systematic and business-like manner. (From an Occasional Correspondent.)

The wooden engine house had burned fiercely, the materials in and around it being inflammable. Damage was estimated at about £300.

A month later, trouble of a different kind was brewing at the mine:[11] *Almost the whole of the men had left work because, as they thought, all* they made could not keep them living; while, on the other hand, their employer [Walker] thought that if they wrought as they ought to do it would pay them well enough. We learn, however that six men have agreed to work underground on certain terms, and that Mr Beith, the manager, is to act as overseer so as to ascertain what steady working can do, and after a week an offer will no doubt be made to all. Job assessment?

Next comes the blackmail: *If it so happens that master and men cannot agree, men will have to be brought from a distance, and that as there is no market in the parish where milk can be purchased, each family will require to keep a cow and must therefore have land along with their houses, and in that case tenants will have to leave in order to give place to new hands ...*

Perhaps Walker's threat was just scare-mongering on his part, but it is easy to understand how worried the Sandwick people would have been, in light of the recent history of clearances in Shetland.

And there was a final cautionary reminder: *Let us hope that master and men will study each other's interests, and that our own people will remain in the parish and receive such pay as they deserve; not forgetting, however, that while they earn their bread by the sweat of their brow others must do the same thing by the sweat of their brain.*

A meeting was held at Sandlodge in an attempt to sort out the problem.[12] It was attended by miners, fishermen, crofters and other interested parties and, of course, John Walker, the employer.

Mr Duncan, Hoswick, was invited to take the chair, but declined. He then spoke at some length, starting by saying that he was there at Mr Walker's suggestion. He had recently been in conversation with Mr Walker who had stated that if he could not recruit local labour he would have to import workers who would need houses, land for cows, etc.

After pointing out that miners in the South did not have land for cows, Mr Duncan got down to brass tacks. Sandwick had got along very well in the past with farming and fishing. He admitted that large sums of money had been laid out on the mine and, if carried on, it could be a great boon in the way of employment to the parish: *But when Mr Walker commenced mining operations here he was certainly aware that he was doing so not in the midst of a mining population; and however much we may desire to see this branch of trade successfully carried on amongst us, we are determined that it shall not so interfere with our farming and fishing as to compel the crofters to give up their houses.*

Mr Duncan concluded his heartfelt speech with the assurance that, should there be any 'ejectment' for mining purposes, as representative of the *Shetland Times*, he would first publish it there, next in the *Scotsman*, and thereafter in every newspaper in the United Kingdom.

Mr Bruce declared that he was unaware of any unease in the parish and in his opinion Mr Duncan should not have referred to it at all. After further discussion on the pay and conditions at the mine, employer and men appeared to reach some agreement and the meeting closed. John Walker was heard to say that it would do no harm.

A week later the *Shetland Times* reported further anxiety, but also a promise of support: *It is said that the men working at the mine at Sandlodge cannot live at the wages offered, and all are threatening to leave come what may. All the crofters seem determined to keep their houses and lands, banishing their fears as to the rumours about them being forced out, and it has been said that the west side men have sent word to their neighbours in the last that they are ready to defend them against any unwarrantable proceedings.*

Late in 1876, Mr Beith who had managed the mine for a few years, left, much to the disappointment of *the people who presented him with a testimonial of respect when he went back to his home in the South.*[13]

In December 1876 John Walker's smack *Dryad* was wrecked on the beach of Meal, South Cunningsburgh. According to the 'Register of Wrecks' she was at anchor waiting to load when the storm came on, but the *Shetland Times* described her as *laden with ore.* Laden or not she drifted broadside on to the beach, and fortunately the crew reached the shore safely in their boat. Apparently Walker's smack *Farmer* had gone ashore at almost the same spot on November 14th. She was taken off and repaired,[14] and we can presume that the *Dryad* was not a total wreck either, as in 1880 she is listed in his assets at the bankruptcy court to the value of £400.

Also in December:[15] *At the present time there is very little employment in the mine. It looks as if the company care little as to doing much just now, the ore being very low in price, but as the mine is considered to be a good one it is thought that there will be a fresh start by-and-by. Indeed building is still going on, which looks like business.*

By July 1878 progress at the mine must have been sufficient for Walker to feel that the time was ripe to host a public relations exercise, and the *S.S. Earl of Zetland* made an excursion to Sandlodge.[16] The weather was fine for the hundred and forty excursionists, *the sea being calm and smooth as a millpond.*

Having admired the scenery round Noness Head and through the bays of Sandwick, and noted the beaches crowded with stacks of drying fish, they anchored off Sandsair where the passengers were treated to a meal with roast and boiled meats, then: *All were safely landed at the pier below the house of Sandlodge. Mr Bruce, by way of welcome, displayed a splendid large flag from the Manor House, and the mines were also* decorated with bunting ... the great attraction was the mine. The more adventurous spirits were by the kindness of Mr John Walker the lessee, permitted to descend the main shaft of the workings, a depth of about 240 feet, and those who remained above had the pleasure of seeing a furnace opened and its contents of molten copper run out into the moulds. Another shaft about fifty yards distant and descended by ladders leads to the old workings, which are still wrought for Hematite iron. At one time the ore was sent to the market as taken from the mine, but to save freight it is now smelted on the spot and sent to market in that condition. A very considerable sum must have been spent in buildings and machinery and we hope the energetic and pushing lessee finds his profit in it. All have to heartily thank Mr Walker for the trouble he took in showing everything that was to be seen.

Sandlodge House and the coppermine with the island of Mousa in the background. Photographer J. Smith.   © *Shetland Museum*

Another serious accident occurred on 4th September, 1879. We can hear what happened in the injured man's own words, from his statement made at Sandlodge on 3rd December.[17] He was Malcolm Duncan, residing at Houlland, Sandwick, aged 36 and married: *Previous to 4th September last I had been employed at the Sandlodge Mines for about four years. I wrought as a labourer above for three years and during the last year I wrought below. The mine has been for sometime under the management of John James Hamilton who resides close by the works. John Walker, 1Polwarth Terrace, Edinburgh, visits the mine at times and directs the working when he is present ... After I went below I wrought on wages and*

Sandlodge Copper Mine

was employed in shovelling ore and at times at heaving up ore from the inclining shaft to the foot of the main shaft from where it was taken up by steam. I never saw any rules published at the works and none were ever read to me ... John Murray, Alexander Murray, Francis MacPherson, Nicol Laurenson and I entered into a contract in the spring of last year to 'cut out' at £7 : 10s a fathom length, the drive of which was five feet by six. We did not have a written contract as far as I am aware. I was not present when the terms were agreed on. We wrought by turns two at a time and on a stretch of eight hours at a time ... We paid for the powder and the other requirements and for the sharping of the tools. The tools used in boring were 'pumpers' or drills made of steel and hammers. After the powder had been put in we put in wadding and rammed it with an iron tamping rod or stemmer which we had for the purpose.

On 4th September last John Murray and I went below at 2 o'clock and after boring three holes we stemmed two and set fire to them. One of these charges missed fire and after waiting about an hour we went to it and commenced to unram it with the drill ... When we had bored about nine inches it went off and severely injured my hands (I was holding the drill at the time and Murray the hammer). The explosion also seered Murray's hands and arms and the hammer drove out three of his teeth. Doctors Burgess, Scalloway, and Macmillan, Dunrossness were called. They found it necessary from the extent of the injury received by me to amputate both my hands ...

Twenty-four-year-old John Murray corroborated Malcolm Duncan's evidence, adding that he was present when the bargain about the 'cut out' was entered into with John Walker: *It was verbal. No rules as to working was mentioned.*

Meanwhile, Alexander and George Smith had been working about forty yards away at the foot of the main shaft, on the same level. They realised that one of the fuses had not gone off and after an hour were aware that Duncan and Murray had gone back to unram the hole. When they heard the charge go off they knew it had gone off by accident. Alexander immediately gave seven pulls on the communication wire to signal to the engine driver that all was not well, then ran to the scene of the accident. They carried Duncan to the foot of the shaft and were astonished to find that the cage had not come down. After laying Duncan on a large box and covering him with some clothes, Alexander signalled repeatedly but got no reply. Meanwhile George climbed up through the ladders and found that the engineer who should have been in attendance at the top had gone home for his supper. George had to fetch him from his house – a distance of three or four hundred yards – before the cage could be let down for the injured men.

JOHN WALKER'S SHETLAND

In Alexander's evidence we hear the awful extent of Duncan's injury: *His hands were hashed and burned all over and during the time he lay below the blood was coming from the sores on them. He was taken to the cottages belonging to the company and messengers were immediately despatched for the Scalloway and Dunrossness doctors. Both Duncan's hands were amputated ... I am not engaged at the mine now. I left the work on Saturday last.*

A fortnight later, the *Shetland Times* took up the question of financial relief: *A poor man having an aged mother, a wife and young children depending in him for the most of their support, to be deprived of both his hands is an awful calamity, and then the great expense incurred in endeavouring to save his life is not little. We are aware that a collection is being taken up in the parish to assist him, but why not have a fund in connection with the works out of which a sufferer, such as this man, can receive something weekly, and into which those employed at the mine should pay something as regularly as they receive their wages? In order to lessen the expense, we understand the man has to be removed to Dunrossness where the doctor resides. This is increasing his sufferings, having to be away from his own home.*

It is difficult for us, who have enjoyed a welfare state for half a century, to grasp the implications of a situation where a breadwinner with no hands can expect little or no financial assistance, but still have doctors' bills to pay for saving his life.

Writing to John Bruce, Thomas Cameron raised the question of compensation for injury:[18] *I saw a subscription list for the unfortunate injured miner – whether such a case should be left to the generosity of the Public or undertaken by the Proprietors of the mine is a matter of opinion.*

In November 1879, John Walker made one of his trips from Edinburgh to visit the mine, in his role of managing director. Among the miners employed at that time were brothers John and Hugh Harris from Yorkshire.

At mid-day on 11th, Walker descended the shaft to give orders to the miners, coming up again about 2pm. At 5pm the two Harris brothers came up the shaft and refused to go back down unless they could have the pump kept on continually. Walker insisted that ten minutes every hour was sufficient for the pump. He then gave the brothers ten minutes to resume their work, but they refused, and so he dismissed them on the spot.[19] Walker's statement to Procurator Fiscal Charles Gilbert Duncan continues: *During the remainder of the day they* [the Harris brothers] *were parading over the mining ground abusing me and giving me a great deal of annoyance.*

SANDLODGE COPPER MINE

Remember that the month is November, the location is Shetland, and the Harris brothers did not come up the shaft until 5pm. So by the time they were parading and abusing we have to wonder what Walker meant by 'the remainder of the day'.

It would also be interesting to know what depth of water accumulated during the fifty minutes each hour when the pump was not working. In 1805 at a shaft depth of 38 fathoms they were pumping out 6000 gallons a day.[20]

Next day Walker told John James Hamilton, the manager, to prepare a statement of the Harris' accounts as they were demanding money. Henry and William Andrew, also miners from South, were to get statements as well. Like Malcolm Duncan and his workmates, they had all been working together on a contract where they were paid a certain amount per fathom of 'cut out'. With the four miners, Hamilton went down the mine to measure the work done, then, half an hour later, they all gathered in the office where Walker himself read the accounts to the men, showing that they in fact had no money due to them but owed the company about £11 for advances made to them. Walker handed the paper to John Harris asking that the account be settled as soon as possible. At that point we can take up the story as told by John Hamilton in his evidence to the Procurator Fiscal:[21] *They were perfectly aware that they had no money to get, but it seemed to me that they were trying to intimidate Mr Walker ... they were cursing and swearing and making great noise going back and fore in the Office fencing about with their clenched fists and refused to allow any of us to go out of the Office till they would get money.* Contrary to that statement however, the clerk, George Houston, did leave the office to dispatch a telegram to the Procurator Fiscal and to round up the blacksmith, Frederick Finlay, and another two men to go to Walker's aid.

John and Hugh Harris, Henry and William Andrew were duly arrested and imprisoned. On 17th November they appeared in court before Sheriff Substitute Major Thomas Mouat Cameron.

John Harris said that he had gone to see Mr Walker about his work because he [Walker] had broken the contract. The money he was asking for was his steamer fare to Granton. Hugh Harris also asked for enough money to take him off Shetland. He said: *I was in debt to the Company ten shillings and ten pence for a fortnight's work.*

Likewise Henry Andrew wanted to escape from the debt trap: *Mr Walker brought me to the country and I asked him to give me a ticket to take me to Granton by the steamer.* William Andrew was owing the company two pounds three shillings.

189

On 19th November the four miners were committed to prison in Lerwick to remain there until tried for the crime of breach of the peace. Unfortunately information seems to end there, so we don't know when or how the miners got home to Yorkshire, but surely this incident would have stopped Walker bragging about the merits of 'south' miners, at least for a while.

It appears that there was a system of advancement of money to the miners resulting in debt which, on their wages, was difficult to pay off. A system very similar to that which Walker had condemned in his evidence to the Truck Commission seven years earlier.

On 12th November, 1880, another fatal accident occurred at Sandlodge. With three others, Matthew Tulloch had been working during the night at sinking a shaft to a lower level. After an eight-hour shift the men had come to the pit head about 7am, and Matthew told the other men that he was going to the engine house to hang up his working coat to dry. Going towards the boiler he had to pass a pumping rod. He apparently went underneath the rod when it was on the down stroke and was fatally injured.[22] Exhausted after working underground all night, a second's deadly lapse of concentration was all that was needed. Some safety measures were introduced after that accident, making it impossible to pass under the rod, and steps were erected for the use of the engineer.[23]

Sketch Plan.

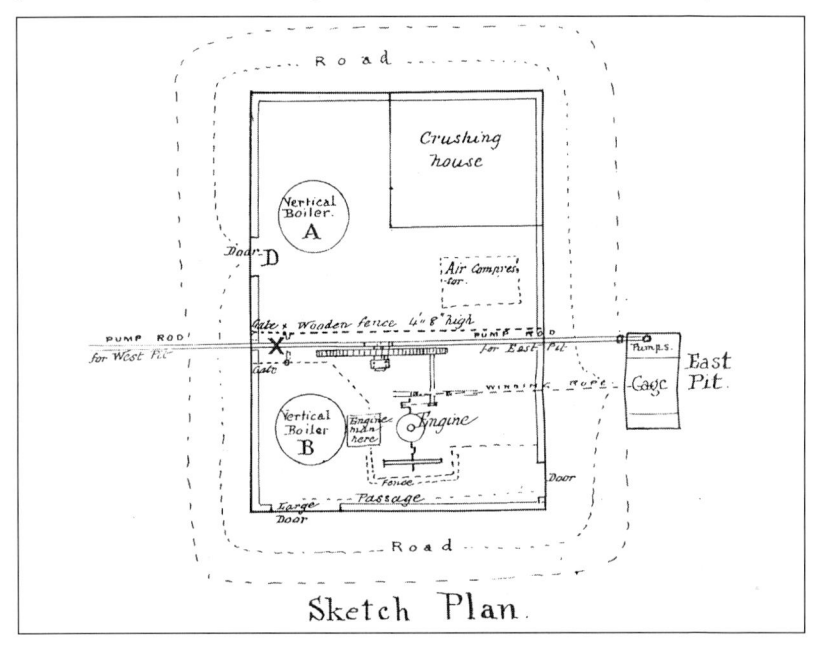

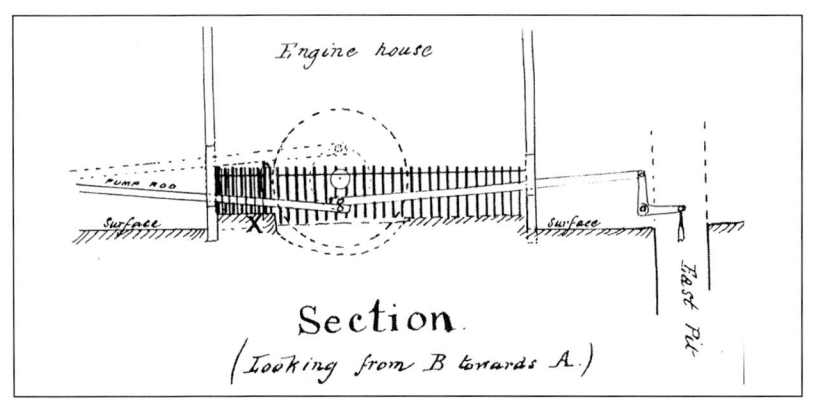

Plan (left) and section (above) of the engine house were Matthew Tulloch was killed.   *Original in Shetland Archives AD 22/2/17/60/1*

Almost exactly a year before Matthew Tulloch's accident, and perhaps not coincidentally only four days before the trouble with the Harris brothers, Walker himself had a narrow escape when descending the shaft of the mine:[24] *It appears that the gear in connection with the cage was not in working order, and that the engineer could not check its too great velocity by the brake, so that the concussion when touching the bottom of the shaft must have been severe.* Happening so close to the dispute with the Harris brothers it is tempting to ask whether this might have been a deliberate 'accident'. Was a point being made about safety? The *Shetland Times* rounds off the incident: *We understand that Mr Walker is not feeling so ill as might have been expected under the circumstances, and let us hope that he will soon be restored to his wonted vigour.*

** ** **

His 'wonted vigour' was soon to receive a severe blow however, and mainly because of heavy investment in the Sandlodge mine. Within a year John Walker was declared bankrupt.

Meanwhile, at their home in Edinburgh, Mary is unwell. Writing to Alexander Sandison in February 1879, John tells him:[25] *We are all well except Mrs Walker who is very weak – no doubt in anticipation of having another baby towards end of the month but chiefly from a cold.*

March 6th: *I got another daughter on 4th at 6am and I am very glad to say that Mrs Walker is wonderfully well – the cough she had was almost away ere her troubles came and so I sincerely trust all will go well – Baby* [Caroline] *could not be better.*

John Walker's Shetland

1 Derek Flinn, *Richard Trevithick, Arthur Woolf and the Shetland Mining Company*, The Journal of the Trevitick Society, No.17, 1990, pp.23-28
2 N.A.S. CS 3181371321
3 S.A. D 25/45
4 J.S. Flett, *Shetland,* Memoirs of the Geological Survey, Scotland. Special Reports on the Mineral resources of G. Britain Vol. XVII, p.148
5 S.A. AD 22/2/101/1875/39
6 *Newcastle Daily Journal,* copied in *Shetland Times,* 18th March, 1876
7 J.S. Flett, The Sandlodge Mine, *Shetland,* Memoirs of the Geological Survey, Scotland, Special Reports on the Mineral Resources of Gt. Britain, Vol xi, pp.217-220
8 *Shetland Times,* 22nd April, 1876
9 Shetland Wreck Register, Vol xviii, Island of Bressay, No.1
10 *Shetland Times,* 1st July, 1876
11 *Shetland Times,* 26th August, 1876
12 *Shetland Times,* 2nd September, 1876
13 *Shetland Times,* 2nd December, 1876
14 Shetland Wreck Register, Vol. xxii, Parish of Cunningsburgh
15 *Shetland Times,* 9th December, 1876
16 *Shetland Times,* 6th July, 1878
17 S.A. AD 22/2/16/4
18 S.A. D 25/45/129
19 S.A. AD 22/2/101/1879/7
20 Derek Flinn, *Richard Trevithick, Arthur Woolf and the Shetland Mining Company,* p.27
21 S.A. AD 22/2/101/1879/7
22 S.A. AD 22/2/17/60/1
23 S.A. AD 22/2/17/60/2
24 *Shetland Times,* 8th November, 1879
25 Sandison's Archive

Chapter Nineteen

BANKRUPT

On 25th August last Mr James Tytler, Aberdeen, informed me that he had been appointed by the Banks to insist upon my signing a Trust deed in his favour for behoof of all my creditors.
from statement by bankrupt, John Walker, 15th November, 1880

O<small>N</small> 24th September, 1880 John Walker wrote to Alexander Sandison:[1] *I know you will be sorry to learn that my Bankers have compelled me to sign a Trust Deed, altho if my debtors pay me I have 40/- in the £. Still what must be must be and I go home tonight to face the world anew and suspect it is not over kind to those overtaken in misfortune. Many in Shetland will rejoice but I believe there are many who will feel sympathy and I count you amongst those. I cant say what we will turn to only my wife proves all she has ever been, more than kind.* Praise indeed for Mary!
 From the statements made in Court at Edinburgh on 10th December, 1880, we learn that many of Walker's business ventures had failed, but the biggest loss of investment had been in the Sandlodge mine:[2] *When I began to work the Copper Mine I did so in Company with Henry Aitken and Robert Millar* [sic]. *My two partners retired about two years afterwards, and I continued to work the mine alone until I think June 1879. In 1877 I entered into an agreement with Mr John J. Hamilton under which he was to purchase the half of the mine for £20,000. That agreement has never been fulfilled.* Walker invested over £24,000 in the mine at Sandlodge.

193

JOHN WALKER'S SHETLAND

John James Hamilton was resident manager at the mine since 1877, and his brother, George Hamilton, Sheriff Clerk of Kirkcudbrightshire, was a director of the Mining Company.

There are reams of paper, dating from 1880 to 1892, held in Edinburgh on the legal ramblings of John Walker's bankruptcy. These include many lengthy letters (one of which runs to forty-six pages) from Robert, John's brother, in his attempts to remove James Tytler from his office of trustee in the sequestration of John Walker's estates. John seemed to accept the whole situation much more philosophically than brother Robert.

Most of his assets and losses were Shetland based and appeared in the examination of the bankrupt, 10th December, 1880. Worth £20,000 at Martinmas 1873, the inclusion of other assets and bank loans brought an overall total of income to £60,155. Losses totalled £62,160 including – *House furniture, Carriage etc, £2000,* and *House expenses for seven years (including personal expenses), £5,950.*

To compare these sums of money with present day value it might be helpful to look at wages paid to mine workers at that time. In one of his letters[3] Robert Walker quotes a total weekly wage bill at the mine for four men and four boys as £4:18:6d. Two of the men, an engineer and dresser, got £1 each, two men who brought ore to the crusher and fed it, got 15 shillings each, and the four boys got £1:8:6d among them. As the engineer's pay for the week was £1, if we multiply any of the above sums, e.g. income or losses, by a present day engineer's weekly earnings, we can have a better idea of the huge amounts of money involved.

The Sumburgh Mining Company, Limited, was constituted on 25th June, 1879 with a capital of £60,000. As we know, all the Walker brothers were financially involved. According to a report drawn up by John James Hamilton, manager, in June 1881,[4] considerable additions had been made to the mine since the formation of the company. These included the building of a large reservoir to regulate the water supply, machinery capable of crushing and dressing twenty tons of ore in twelve hours, furnaces, more housing for workmen, and sinking the main shaft to a greater depth.

In the statement of his affairs produced by Walker at the first meeting of his creditors he claimed that, when James Tytler was appointed by the banks to sequestrate his estate, Walker had asked for a week's delay. This was to enable the completion of arrangements being made by the Sumburgh Mining Company. These arrangements would possibly have enabled the company to settle Walker's claims. Tytler said the banks refused to grant the extra time and so Walker was obliged to sign the Trust Deed. Walker then went to London and had a meeting with

BANKRUPT

George Hopkins (chairman of the Richmond Mining Co.). He subsequently received a letter[5] from Hopkins saying that he and a Mr Watson (chairman of the Great Devon Consols) were willing to join the board of the Sumburgh Mining Company, provided by so doing it would ensure Walker got reasonable terms from his bankers, to enable him to work through his financial difficulties. Yet again an example of Walker's powers of persuasion.

When Tytler asked the company's law agent whether Hopkins and Watson's names on the circular would ensure the sale of the company's unissued shares, the reply was:[6] *As certain as that the sun will be in the heavens to-morrow.*

At the same time Sir Francis Knowles, chairman of the company, was to visit Sandlodge and the banks agreed to wait for his report. According to Tytler, Sir Francis' shares in the mine had been paid for by Walker.[7] The very day on which Sir Francis returned to Aberdeen from Shetland, a meeting was held in Tytler's office and Sir Francis reported:[8] *Of minerals hitherto considered valueless there could be made a profit of £70,000 p. annum for 136 years.*

Within twenty-four hours Tytler had declared that the banks considered the meeting and the minute a sham, and that if the company were put into his hands, the banks would advance the necessary funds to successfully carry it through. So Tytler assumed management of the Sumburgh Mining Company, but did nothing to further its cause. He failed to reply to, or take action on, correspondence; failed to call meetings to consult shareholders; failed to turn up at an important meeting in London of parties interested in the mine, although he had expressed a desire for such a meeting to be held.

Some of the problems caused by Tytler's procrastination are illustrated in a letter from John James Hamilton, mine manager, to him on 26th April, 1881:[9] *Your telegram of 20th inst. only arrived last night, and I have no other communication from you since I last wrote.* Hamilton went on to say that he has raised £200 to pay the men's wages and would need this refunded as soon as possible: *I cannot at all understand what is meant by this silence on your part. You tell me to look to you for everything, and forbid any writing on the Company's affairs to anyone else, and still you take no notice of anything that is written, give no advice when asked for.* He fears that for want of funds he will have to stop the works and then the mine would flood: *It will cost a good many hundred pounds to extract it* [flood water] *again, and the damage done underground will be incalculable.*

The reason for Tytler's action, or rather lack of action, is not clear, but it would seem that Robert Walker was right in his attempts to oust

195

him, as he was obviously determined to drag down the mining company. Figures for output of ore from Sandlodge for two years prior to the sequestration had shown a promising increase – in 1878, 708 tons of copper ore, worth £1,770 and 1,241 tons of haematite, worth £1,550. Two years later, 1,995 tons of copper ore, worth £5,814 and 396 tons of iron ore, worth £344:15s.[10]

To the dismay of the shareholders he had the company liquidated, and in so doing ruined the chief asset of the estate for which he was acting as trustee. He gives this explanation in a letter written in December 1881:[11] *The bare fact is, that I was asked to be a party to floating the Sumburgh Mining Company, and get parties to take shares in it, and I refused to do so because I was convinced in my own mind that the Mine was a perfect bubble.*

Sandlodge has not been worked since then. It would be interesting to know which of the many conflicting reports on the viability of the mine was closest to the truth.

**   **   **

For twenty years, from 1860 till 1880, John Walker was deeply involved in Shetland affairs, although not resident in the isles after 1872. Because of the questionable methods used in removing tenants to make way for sheep, his legacy as a factor is a bitter one, especially in Yell and Unst. Fragments of the galvanised, three-ply wire he used to enclose the sheep farms can still be found in the North Yell hills, and memories, hostile towards the man held responsible, have also survived. He was factor for Garth and Annsbrae during the ten years, 1866-76.

John Walker had little patience with those who possessed less drive than himself. To list even some of his Shetland projects illustrates his boundless energy – 1860-72, farming in Bressay, hailed by contemporary writers as exemplary, his stock regularly taking prizes at the Agricultural Shows; active in initiating the Shetland Agricultural Society in 1864 and secretary for a number of years; serving on and chairing Parochial Boards from 1862; factor for the Garth share in Unst minerals from 1869, and for a time organising export of the Unst ores for all the proprietors, ending in fraud charge, 1876; lessee of chromate ore mine in Haaf Grunie, 1872-1876; initiator, director and chairman of Shetland Steam Shipping Co. Ltd, 1868-72; shareholder and director of the Shetland Fishing Co. Ltd, 1872 until it went into voluntary liquidation in 1880; early 70s, chartered vessels to trade to and from Iceland; elected to five school boards and chairman of three, from 1873; active in exposing the Truck system in Shetland, early 70s; Commissioner of Supply 1874-76; J.P.; insurance

BANKRUPT

agent; agent for imported fertilisers; numerous court appearances; wrote well over a thousand letters on estate matters alone; involved in many smaller business ventures which are listed in the bankruptcy statement (see appendix); shareholder and managing director of Sandlodge Mine from 1872 until the company was liquidated in 1880.

What inspired him to move to the isles remains a mystery, but his bankruptcy finally severed his Shetland business connections.

1   Sandison's Archive
2   N.A.S. CS 318/37/321 Sederunt Book Vol 1, p.33
3   N.A.S. CS 318/37/321 6/12/1881, To the Official Liquidator
4   Shetland Library, Reid Tait Collection 20/17
5   N.A.S. CS 318/37/321 Sederunt Vol 1, p.13 Statement by Bankrupt
6   Ibid
7   N.A.S. CS 318/37/321 Note of Appeal for James Tytler p.3
8   N.A.S. CS 318/37/321 Sederunt Vol 1, p.14
9   N.A.S. CS 318/37/321 Sumburgh Mining Co. & Mr James Tytler pp.10 & 11
10 1921 Memoir of the Geological Survey
11 N.A.S. CS 318/37/321 Sumburgh Mining Co. & Mr James Tytler, p.19

Chapter Twenty

SOUTH AFRICA

I cannot too strongly impress upon you that it would be misleading people were they to be induced to come out here under the idea that they will get 'first class land'.
The Crown Lands Commissioner, John X. Merriman, reproving John Walker for over-zealous advertising, Dec. 1881

ON 1st April, 1881 John and Mary Walker sailed for Cape Town on the *Garth Castle* – a steam ship of 3,537 tons, built the previous year. With them went eight of their family – two sons, John and Thomas, and six of the daughters. It is not clear which of the girls travelled with them, but we do know that Catherine had died when almost fourteen. The older girls would have been in their teens or twenties and Caroline, the youngest, was two.

Shortly after arriving, John wrote to his friend Alexander Sandison, in Unst:[1] *Our passage out was not very rapid – 22 days from Dartmouth – my belongings except Caroline were all sick until we passed Madeira & neither Mary Senior or Mary Junior enjoyed the voyage at all – indeed the latter was never able to be at Table all the way ... On arriving here we could get no lodgings for such a family so after remaining on board from Saturday to Wednesday we got an empty house at Roudeborch and bundled in there – It was a perpetual Pic Nic for more than a week before we could get anything in order ... but now we have a nice snug cottage of six rooms and a kitchen and managed very well – It is in a most lovely*

SOUTH AFRICA

neighbourhood amongst splendid Trees & with the back of Table Mount overhanging – with a good income we could get on here well – a Train once every hour is within two minutes & we are only five miles from Town.

He had been appointed as a temporary special agent, to inspect vacant land in the East London district and then to recruit up to three hundred agriculturalists for a 'Scotch settlement'. His salary was £700 per annum, plus travelling expenses.[2] To gain some insight into how he acquired this position we have to look at correspondence with Alexander Sandison, before the family sailed for Cape Town:[3]

24th Feb., 1881
I'm fixed that I leave for Cape Town on 29th March ... I think my Unst friends may do me a good turn without much trouble to themselves. I'm so far arranged with the Agent here that if he gets an application from your Agricultural Society to ask me to report upon the capabilities of the Colony for Agriculture & settlement he would arrange to pay sufficient to enable me to take stock *of the Colony.*

Will the Unst Agricultural Society agree to this and what sort of recommendation will they give him? But the latter was taken care of, as the next sentence reveals: *Now would you kindly get your society together & pass some such resolution as enclosed scroll and in anticipation thank my friends for carrying it.* Wife Mary featured briefly in the first post-script, *Mrs Walker not strong, sore eyes.* The second P.S. asks for a personal reference: *In sending Extract you would add a favour by saying something yourself about J. W.*

Walker had written the 'enclosed scroll' himself, composing (as follows) a minute for a meeting that had not yet taken place: *The meeting then considered a proposition from the Secretary suggesting that the Society should request the Government of the Cape Colony to offer facilities for a representative to visit and report upon the various Districts in the Cape Colony now open for settlement and that Mr John Walker of 1 Polwarth Terrace, Edinburgh should be named as this Society's representative – The meeting unanimously resolved that the Secretary's suggestion should be carried out and that an extract of their minutes should be sent to W. C. Burnet Esq. the Colony's Agent in London with an explanation that Mr Walker is personally known to the members and has for many years been connected with the Parish and the County and being himself a practical Agriculturalist has always taken a keen interest in matters.*

The minute, as dictated, was sent from Unst. This is confirmed by a reply from Mr Burnet from the Cape of Good Hope Government Emigration Office to Alexander Sandison. Burnet's letter ends:[4] *I shall be very glad to arrange for the carrying out of this proposition and have communicated with Mr Walker on the subject.*

199

Pleased that his scheme had worked, Walker wrote to Sandison:[5] *I think I've got a good share of my spirits back altho it's a heavy look out but I shall trust and work ... Minute and letter to Burnet just the thing.*

Alexander Sandison was a religious man, often reflected in Walker's correspondence with him. Writing in March, just before leaving for Cape Town:[6] *Thank you for your good kind letter – I'm well aware that everything is wisely ordered and I am conscious that I deserve heavier chastisement than I've received and so in this spirit I am trying to bear up and to work for the <u>future.</u>* He went on to say how thankful he was that the dark cloud was breaking and that he had acquired agencies from forty leading business firms *in almost every line.*

23rd May:[7] *I've worked up the town fairly well and succeeded quite as well as I expected – having got a good many orders as a fair beginning.* Again Mary merits a mention in a P.S. *Mrs Walker rather better in fact as well as we can expect.* He also had his agricultural reports to make: *I've got <u>carte blanche</u> to travel all over the Colony and start this afternoon with a general letter to all officials to do what they can to show me their districts.*

20th September:[8] *I have now been wandering over three months on behalf of the Government about their lands and emigration schemes ... have got much information and insight ... the Government have appraised my suggestions and authorised me to carry them out ... will most likely return home on behalf of the Government to push their land matters ... I'm not sure if <u>you</u> will not be tempted to come out here when you know the inducements which will be offered ... Several Orkney people are here but few if any Shetlanders. I would like to see some settled comfortably here so if at settling time or before you know of any really energetic families that would emigrate I can arrange for them and if you will head a body of them I'll get you a whole Parish to yourself ... I was pained to read the account of the heavy losses amongst old friends in the Isles storm,[9] glad to see that some substantial aid has been forthcoming ... All are well altho Mrs W. is not so strong as I would like – she is not herself yet.*

In his efforts to attract settlers to the Cape he was placing adverts in newspapers, including the following in the *Shetland Times* of 10th February, 1883:

CAPE GOVERNMENT
AGRICULTURAL EMIGRATION
THE CAPE GOVERNMENT OFFER
A FREE PASSAGE

to approved Agriculturists, their wives and families, proceeding to the Colony to become Tenant Farmers, or to take up Crown Lands. Those selected to settle upon Crown Lands receive grants of good Agricultural Land upon easy conditions as to capital, occupation and cultivation at

SOUTH AFRICA

TEN SHILLINGS PER ACRE,
payable in ten yearly instalments of one shilling per acre.
For further information apply to **JOHN WALKER,**
Special Agricultural Emigration Agent,
Cape Government Emigration Office, 10 Blomfield Street, London E.C.

So far I haven't found out whether any Shetlanders took up the offer. Having John Walker's name attached to it might have been a deterrent, especially if any prospective 'agriculturalists' had read an article which had appeared in the *Shetland Times* three months earlier. Under the title *Mr John Walker Again* readers were told how Walker, in his role of Emigration Agent, had promised eight acres of land at George to a couple with seven children. When the family arrived at Cape Town the authorities informed them that there was no land available. Mr Valle, the father, *grew ill from anxiety of mind,* and subsequently died. It seems that our over-enthusiastic agent was exaggerating the attractions of the colony, and was admonished for this by the Crown Lands Commissioner, John X. Merriman:[10] *It would be a misnomer to call it first-rate and the govt. is, before everything anxious not to give a handle to those who may accuse it of misleading statements ... It is no Tom Tiddler's ground, where a fortune is to be picked up without working for it. In any future advertisements or circulars, I beg that the land may be described as 'fair' and not as 'first class'.*

Nevertheless, in Walker's obituary in the *Shetland News*, Merriman is credited with declaring, while discussing emigration policy in Parliament: *We want more John Walkers.* Merriman was also active in the formation of the Cape Central Railway Ltd, a private company, subsidised by the Government and set up in London in 1883, for which Walker was appointed company's agent in South Africa.

As a multi-faceted agent he made many trips between the Cape and Britain during the years the family was resident in South Africa, and he sometimes visited Shetland. It is reported in the *Shetland News* of 28th January, 1893: *Mr Walker, formerly of Bressay, is at present on a visit to Shetland.* We know he took Mary with him on at least one of these trips. Writing to Alexander Sandison[11] from Aberdeen in March 1895, he tells how they have spent three nights in Shetland at the Whalsay manse, *not a long but a very pleasant visit.* Their daughter Isobel was married to Rev. Charles Stobie who had been ordained in Whalsay in 1876.

In D. M. Rhind's book *A Chronicle of the Cape Central Railway* we find out how Walker fared in his involvement with railway contracts at the Cape. First he was appointed agent for the company, then in 1883 also became contractor for the building of forty-two miles of railway from Worcester, via Robertson, to Roodewal. Work started in April 1884.

In March he had made one of his frequent trips to Britain and met John Bruce jun. of Sumburgh who wrote to his father: *I saw John Walker yesterday. He is over in this country about some new Government Railways at the Cape. He seems to be flourishing and desires to be remembered to everybody.*[12]

But by early 1885 the project had acquired the nickname 'Walker's Folly'. July saw only seven miles of earthwork completed and the company was struggling financially. A new company was formed in England, in the hope that it would be more competent. By April 1886 more than two hundred men were working on the line. There was considerable unemployment in the colony at the time and competition for jobs was high. It is not clear when or why Walker relinquished the contract, but by October 1886 the contractor was a John Munro and relations were strained between him and Walker who was still the company's agent.

Dave Rhind tells a story which illustrates the trust, or lack of it, held by the workmen towards Walker and is reminiscent of the trouble with the Harris brothers at the Sandlodge mine: *The general monotony of life in Worcester was enlivened on 5th October 1886 by the presence of a large number of workmen from the railway construction who were waiting patiently for their pay. They discovered that Mr Walker was in town and moved to the front of the Masonic Hotel to see what would happen when Mr Walker met Mr John Munro, the contractor. During the day promises of pay were made hourly to the men, but as the day passed they became tired and, as many of them had nowhere to go to rest, dull threats of tarring and feathering began to be heard. At 6pm Mr Munro told them they would be paid as soon as the bank opened in the morning, but feelings were still running high when Mr Walker went to the station at 7am to catch the train to Cape Town. He was met by Mr Munro, accompanied by two of his foremen, Bohn and Gray, and about a hundred of his men, and prevented from entering the station. An attempt was made to seize his luggage.*

In the general uproar, Charles Bohn was said to have struck Walker in the chest and called him a damned scamp. Walker and Munro then moved into the station office, where Walker handed over a cheque for £250, while protesting that it was not due until the 15th of the month. Even so, Walker was not allowed to go onto the platform until a messenger had been to the Bank and returned with the cash.

A week later, in Worcester Magistrates Court, Walker charged Munro and Bohn with robbery and assault. Conducting his own case, Walker described himself as manager of the Cape Central Railway and claimed to know a great deal about the construction of railways. Where had he learned that? Certainly not in Shetland! He explained that the company had no banking account in the colony and that all payments were made in his name. As given in his evidence, the details of the financial position between himself as agent and Munro as contractor were somewhat confusing.[13]

Trains were running on the Robertson Line, as it was known, early in 1887 but the editorial of the local newspaper was critical of the charges and the timetable. A letter signed 'An Indignant Merchant' suggested that Walker should make a statement of the cost of his construction because it had been done at a time when labour was cheap and plentiful. The writer pointed out that the company had also been able to obtain materials cheaply at a time of depression in Britain, and implied that it should have been possible to build the entire line within the amount of the subsidy alone – £75,000.

As the railway was also being discussed in Parliament, Walker decided that it was time for a public relations exercise. On 7th July, 1888, about one hundred invited guests, including M.P.s, made an excursion to inspect the line. At journey's end they sat down to a luncheon in the goods station, catered for by a local hotel. Walker was in the chair, and in his lengthy speech he stressed that they were there on his invitation, not that of the railway company. He also made the point that the railway had been financed by his personal friends. This sounds ominously like the set-up in the Sandlodge mine where John's brothers were the principal shareholders. Robert Walker invested, and lost, a large sum of money in John's third railway venture, the Grand Junction Railway in the Eastern Cape.[14]

A year later the company went into liquidation. Walker then ceased to be manager, but remained a shareholder. In the Supreme Court in Cape Town he established his claim to shares in the company to a total of £4,117:14s:5d. At the same time it was ruled that he owed the company £291:7s:10d.

This is how Dave Rhind ends that chapter of his chronicle: *There can be no doubt that Mr Walker's personality was in large measure the cause of the Company's trouble. His overlapping role of Agent, Manager and sometimes contractor, was an anomalous one which was not eased by the fact that all financial transactions passed through his personal banking account.*

At the time of the liquidation, the local paper, writing of Walker and his dealings with the railway, commented that *there might be much about Mr Walker's conduct which was disliked, and perhaps not understood, but he had, at any rate, taken the initiative and his merits should not be totally overlooked by the general public.*[15] Difficult to overlook the man, wherever he went!

JOHN WALKER'S SHETLAND

But our plausible railway constructor was not finished yet. He again became agent, manager and contractor for an eight-kilometre line from Cape Town to Sea Point. John junior was traffic manager and, for a while, son Thomas was secretary. Until then, Sea Point, a flourishing suburb, had been served by horse-drawn trams.

We can now turn to *Early Railways at the Cape* written by Jose Burman: *The moving spirit of the* [railway] *project was a hard-headed and cantankerous Scot, John Walker, who was prepared to invest money with the idea of a good return. Walker's overbearing attitude soon had the public up in arms, and in 1890 another indignation meeting was called, this time aimed at Mr Walker who was digging up Green Point Common for ballast, and had built a cottage near Three Anchor Bay for a gatekeeper. Even more offensive was the fence he was building along the line, cutting off residents from the sea. The blowing up of some favourite rocks on the beach front was the last straw.*

In spite of that the Sea Point railway opened in September 1892, and, in the short term was a great success. However, because the coaches and engines which the Cape Government provided, at a high rental, were

Published in *The Lantern* in 1891 this cartoon shows John Walker ruthlessly driving a steam engine through the people who raised objections to the Sea Point Railway Scheme.

worn out, the line was dogged by frequent break-downs. Jose Burman again: *In order to try and cure the latter evil, Walker imported two locomotives in 1896 from John Fowler & Co. of Leeds, which he named 'Sea Point' and 'Green Point'. The engines were fine, but the curves in the track were too sharp for their long wheelbases and they derailed themselves regularly. All Walker could do was store them, until the Mashonaland railway eventually bought the engines during the Anglo-Boer War.*

Horses could not compete with steam and the tramway company had seriously lost custom. But in 1896 they pulled out a trump card and converted to electricity – so now the trams travelled faster than the trains. This was the beginning of the end for the railway company. A crash between two trains in June 1897 was the final blow. One person was seriously injured. He sued, and was awarded £3,000 damages. The company couldn't pay and the following year went into liquidation. On John Walker's losses of some £37,000 in debentures, shares and interest, D. M. Rhind comments:[16] *He got nothing for his 19,292 shares, but it is probable that many of them had been issued to him free of charge as part and parcel of the many financial arrangements he had come to with the Company throughout its hand-to-mouth existence. These arrangements were always obscure and the subject of comment by the other shareholders. He recovered the £25,000 owing to him in respect of the debentures as well as the interest and, as he must have done quite well out of his contract and related activities, his overall losses are likely to have been considerably less than was apparent.*

A year before the Sea Point Railway opened, the *Shetland News* reported on a 'Fashionable Marriage in Africa'. In September 1891, Janie Parke Walker married Rev. J. S. Maver, pastor of the Woodstock church where the marriage took place. The bride was described as *daughter of Mr J. Walker of Welgelegen, Rosebank.* (No mention of Mary). Her sisters Janet and Caroline were bridesmaids.[17]

Meantime Walker had acquired yet another contract, trading as John Walker & Sons, for the construction of a section of the Grand Junction Railway in the Eastern Cape. Perhaps undercapitalised because of his losses on Sea Point he was unable to complete it in time, and had to forfeit the contract in 1899. However, while his contract lasted, the labourers were obliged to patronize the trading stores he had established for this purpose, close to their work, and it is thought he made a worthwhile income this way.[18] Again we are reminded of Walker's condemnation of the Truck system used by the merchants in Shetland. His own use of similar methods of trading seems to confirm the suspicion that it was the Shetland merchants he was opposed to, rather than their mode of operation.

John Walker's Shetland

In November 1896, on one of his business trips to London, Walker received a letter from the Cape. In it he learned that the terms of his last contract in regard to the mileage and subsidy could not be extended without parliamentary sanction. Penning his reply to Mr Elliott, general manager of Railways at the Cape, he spattered it with double underlining and uncharacteristic errors. The letter ends:[19] *We insist that we are entitled to improve the road and works free from interference – We think it impossible to construct a worse line that what has been planed [sic] by the Department but if and when we attempt to do so we shall be thankful for your officers to interfere but we cannot accept such childish interference as has lately taken place and feel sure that you will put an end to this annoyance.*

The general manager passed a copy of Walker's letter to the engineer in chief who ended his acknowledgement with: *I shall reserve to myself the privilege of replying to Mr Walker's strictures and animadversions at a future date.*

The person responsible for pointing out that the Walkers' railway mileage and subsidy could not be extended without parliamentary sanction was Sir James Sivewright, who had control over the railways. He had been appointed by Rhodes as Minister of Crown Lands and Public Works.[20]

It is ironic that Walker came up against another Sivewright or Sievwright when he moved to South Africa. James Sivewright was born in Fochabers, Moray, and had graduated from Aberdeen University.[21] William Sievwright, the Lerwick lawyer, was educated at Edinburgh University and his grandfather was a baker in Lerwick.[22] It seems unlikely that there was any connection between the two, but probable that the name Sievwright was not Walker's favourite. Whether deliberate or accidental, when referring to Sir James in his irate letter to Elliott, he spelt the surname *Sievwright*.

The Grand Junction Railway was John Walker's final venture in railway construction. It appears that he tried to get away with too much, was taken to court, and lost. The case rumbled on for years, and by 1911, not surprisingly, the liquidator was anxious to have the matter settled.[23] Brother Robert brought an unsuccessful action against the liquidator, an appeal was made to the Privy Council, but that was also unsuccessful (see appendix).

Other schemes which John toyed with while at the Cape included plans for improving Table Bay harbour, a pier at Sea Point and a funicular railway up the face of Table Mountain. But none of these came to anything.[24]

SOUTH AFRICA

John and Mary Walker were back in Britain and Mary was dead long before the final outcome of the Grand Junction Railway case. They left the Cape in 1899, just before the outbreak of the second Anglo-Boer war. By then they had been resident in South Africa for eighteen years, six years longer than they were resident in Shetland. Yet it is a Shetland connection that appears on a tombstone at St Peter's Cemetry, Mowbray. Two of the Walker daughters who were born in Bressay, died while the family was at the Cape. Janie, whose wedding was mentioned earlier, died in 1895 aged 30. She is buried beside her eight-month-old daughter, May, who had died in 1893. Jane Smith Walker died in 1888, aged 25, and it is inscribed on her tombstone that she was sixth daughter of John Walker, J.P., Shetland.[25]

Again, no mention of Mary, her mother.

1   Sandison's Archive
2   Marjory Harper, *Adventurers and Exiles*, London 2003, p.140
3   Unst Heritage Centre
4   Sandison's Archive
5   Ibid
6   Ibid
7   Ibid
8   Ibid
9   20/7/1881 Haaf fishing disaster. 58 men & 10 boats lost from North Isles of Shetland.
10 Marjory Harper, *Adventurers and Exiles*, London 2003, p.141
11 Sandison's Archive
12 S.A. Sumburgh Papers 134
13 D.M. Rhind, *A Chronicle of the Cape Central Railway*, Cape Town 1995, p.8
14 *The Cape Argus*, 24th August, 1911
15 D.M. Rhind, *A Chronicle of the Cape Central Railway*, Cape Town 1995, p.26
16 Ibid p.37
17 *Shetland News*, 24th October, 1891
18 D.M. Rhind, *A Chronicle of the Cape Central Railway*, Cape Town 1995, p.38
19 Photo-copy of letters, courtesy D.M. Rhind
20 S.E.S.A. p.650
21 Ibid
22 Margaret Robertson, *Sons and Daughters of Shetland*, Lerwick 1991, p.175
23 *The Cape Argus*, 24th August, 1911
24 D.M. Rhind, *A Chronicle of the Cape Central Railway*, Cape Town 1995, p.38
25 Information from a photograph taken by D.M. Rhind

Chapter Twenty-one

HOME AGAIN

> *My only connection with Shetland now is that I still am as I have been for over forty years a J.P. of the County and that the Minister of this Parish is my son-in-law.*
> John Walker writing from Whalsay, Shetland, to the
> Congested Districts Board, Edinburgh 8/4/1908

BACK in Britain, the Walkers set up house at 19 St. John's Avenue, Putney, and in 1902 Walker was elected to the Wandsworth council at a by-election for the Putney Ward in April 1902. It created so little interest that the local paper didn't even report the occasion.[1]

In July of the following year Mary died, having suffered from diabetes for some time. She was buried in Putney Vale Cemetery. Eight of her children were still alive, two sons and six daughters. In common with most of the women of her day, little is known about Mary. The fact that she lived to the ripe old age for the time, of sixty-eight, in spite of bearing fifteen children, is probably because she would have led a comparatively easy life. I wonder if she worried about her husband's business ventures and failures, or whether she even knew much about them.

She was artistic. A great-granddaughter in South Africa has some of her art work, including a sampler embroidered by twelve-year-old Mary, with the text:-[2]

> *O guide me through the various maze*
> *My doubtful feet are doomed to tread,*

And spread thy shield's protecting blaze
Where dangers press around my head.

John Walker's gold pocket watch is in safe keeping beside his great-grandson in Germany. Inside the back cover it is inscribed: *To John Walker, with his wife's love, 1873.* On the back, in Latin, *cura et industria* [care and industry] and a picture of Cornucopia [the sign of plenty].[3]

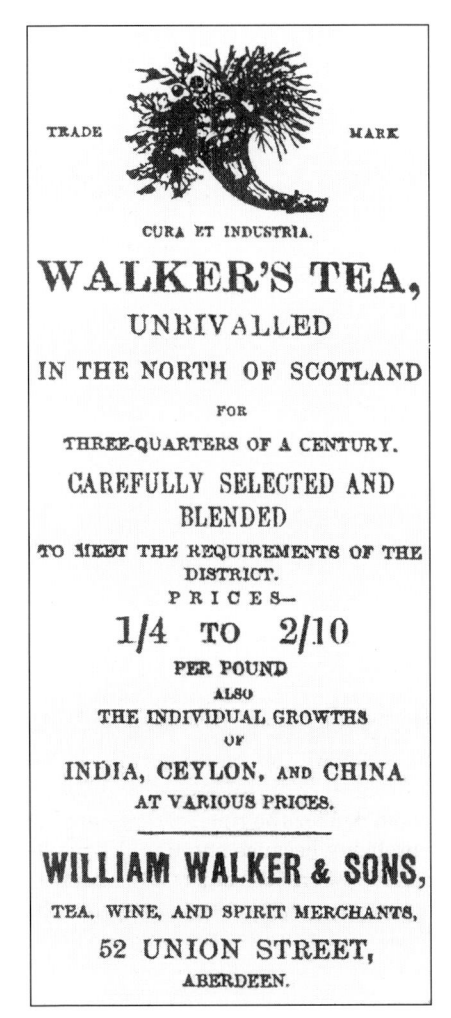

TRADE MARK

CURA ET INDUSTRIA.

WALKER'S TEA,
UNRIVALLED
IN THE NORTH OF SCOTLAND
FOR
THREE-QUARTERS OF A CENTURY.
CAREFULLY SELECTED AND BLENDED
TO MEET THE REQUIREMENTS OF THE DISTRICT.
PRICES—
1/4 TO 2/10
PER POUND
ALSO
THE INDIVIDUAL GROWTHS
OF
INDIA, CEYLON, AND CHINA
AT VARIOUS PRICES.

WILLIAM WALKER & SONS,
TEA, WINE, AND SPIRIT MERCHANTS,
52 UNION STREET,
ABERDEEN.

Cornucopia and *Cura et Industria* appear in this advert as the trade mark for Walker's tea. *Aberdeen Journal* of 3rd February 1903.

The 1881 bankruptcy must have adversely affected Mary with the loss of their home at 1 Polwarth Terrace, Edinburgh. Their furnishings were superior, as we can see from the auction list:[4]

Dining-Room – Suite of mahogany, in handsome pedestal sideboard, with mirror plate, 68x35in.; set of expanding screw tables, fourteen feet long, with cabinet bookcase, plate glass front and recess for table leaves; twelve stuffed back and easy chairs, in marone morocco; mantelpiece mirror to correspond with sideboard, plate 68x60in.; marble clock, Brussels carpet, &c.

Drawing-Room – *Coverings of crimson repp and silk, with sateen slips.* – Couch, two easy, five ecarté, and six small chairs of walnut, magnificent console and mantelpiece mirrors, in corresponding frames, richly gilt, *plates* 124x64 and 92x58; very choice inlaid ebonized cabinet; writing, centre, card and fancy tables of exquisite designs; walnut whatnot and ornamental items; green ground Brussels carpet.

Library – *Dark Oak* – In handsome bookcase, with plate-glass doors; small bookcase, very fine cylinder writing table, oval table, sofa, reading and small chairs in green morocco, cottage pianoforte, painting of Old Aberdeen University Chapel, by George Reid; column barometer, fire screen, fine Brussels carpet &c. Parlour furniture of small set of telescope tables, chairs in haircloth, &c.

The Bedrooms – *(walnut, mahogany, ash and birch)* are fully supplied with winged, French, and other wardrobes, having mirror doors; pedestal toilets and basinstands, with marble tops and ware; brass and iron beds, with spring hair mattress and other superior bedding; and all other usual requisites for bedrooms and nursery.

Furniture for servants' rooms. Hall furniture, kitchen and laundry tables, lawn mower, garden tools, and miscellaneous effects.

House for sale, with immediate entry after sale. Grates, gasfittings and blinds at valuation.

When the evicted crofters had to move, a list of their practical and essential belongings would not have made such refined reading.

No doubt the house in Putney would have been comfortably furnished too, as it is thought that Walker did quite well out of his South African deals, in spite of the failed railway contracts.[5] Nor was he deterred from taking part in public life, as in 1906 he was returned without opposition to the Wandsworth Council – as always, a Conservative. Since joining the council in 1902 he was said to have *fearlessly expressed his opinions at all times ... succeeded in securing a substantial profit on the working of the Burials Committee, and has recently persuaded the Council to issue a clear and concise epitome of its accounts, which may be readily understood by the ratepayers.*[6] He definitely believed in the maxim, 'Don't do as I do, do as I tell you'.

HOME AGAIN

This set of photos of the six sons of William Walker was framed in 1903, the year both Mary and Alexander died. William and James had died in 1893 and 1895. It is typically Victorian in that it represents only the men of the family with no mention of their mother, Amelia, or sisters Catherine, Isobel, Helen and Amelia. Aberdeen City coat of arms completes the picture. *Courtesy Elizabeth West.*

211

However he did not serve much longer on the Wandsworth Council as the last meeting he attended was in June 1907, and was still sending apologies for non-attendance in September 1908.[7] Correspondence which we will look at later indicates that he spent at least part of the year 1908 in Whalsay beside daughter Isobel and the Rev. Charles Stobie.

In August 1904, the year after Mary's death, John attended a dinner in the Grand Hotel, Lerwick, held to celebrate forty years of the Shetland Agricultural Society.[8] Because he had been so active in the formation of the society, he was asked to take the chair. In his toast to the society he spoke of the many changes in Shetland since the days of the first shows – the great increase in numbers of sheep and cattle and carts, the building of new roads and the improved steamer service. He reminded the thirty gentlemen present, no ladies of course, that at the first show they even had an ox with a wooden leg. He professed to have been the means of getting a steamer run to Shetland in the winter, because, he said, when he built the house at Maryfield he had an agreement with the contractors that they should carry all the material by steam. When winter approached they refused to do so, but, being an Aberdonian like themselves, he compelled them to do it and so they put on the old *Sovereign*. Many a time he was the only passenger on that vessel, and he recalled one instance of how they left Lerwick on Monday, and only got to Aberdeen on Friday.

It seems that he was a guest of the Bruces of Sumburgh on that occasion, as he is recorded in their visitors book on 9th August. The Bruces' visitors' books kept in the late 19th and early 20th centuries are somewhat unusual in that they record the weight, and sometimes the height, of their guests. John Walker was weighed there, three times! On 18/9/1874, weight 14st. 3lb., and then thirty years later 9/8/1904, weight 14st. 1lb. 7oz. Apparently proud to have maintained a stable weight he adds a note:- *see 18/9/74*. Three years later he's back in Sumburgh again, weight 14st. 2lb., with a reminder of the two previous records.[9] His height was not recorded, so we are not much wiser as to his build.

Around that time he may have been involved in travelling back to South Africa in connection with the Grand Junction Railways liquidation. In August 1911 it was reported in the *Cape Argus* that: *Mr John Walker had been repeatedly before the Court in connection with this matter, and there had been a repeated course of obstruction to proceeding with the settlement, while as far as Mr Robert Walker was concerned, proceedings had been going on since 1907.*

By 1913 he had been resident in Aberdeen again for a time, and in November of that year campaigned for, and was elected to, Aberdeen Council, St. Machar Ward. He laid great stress on the subject of city finance during the run-up to the election, as ever being outspoken in his criticism of how financial affairs were being managed.

On the subject of city finance he was challenged to a debate by a Mr Reilley, and it was arranged that they would meet at the Arcadia Picture Palace in Sunnybank Road. A large crowd gathered at the appointed time, but Mr Reilley failed to appear, so Walker had the stage to himself and made the most of it. In his, no doubt lengthy, speech he declared that he had never seen Mr Reilley, but was told that he was about six feet six. He himself was a much smaller man but he was not afraid of the heckling of Mr Reilley or any other man. This declaration was met with applause and then he mounted his usual hobby-horse of criticising other people's bookkeeping. This time, the target of his disapproval was Aberdeen city and harbour accounts.[10]

After the election results were declared, he was received with the singing of 'For he's a jolly good fellow' and a hearty ovation. Undoubtedly flushed with success, he promised that the first thing he would tackle in the Council would be decency in proceedings. He said that, unlike the Lord Provost, he would not refuse the courtesy of answering a letter addressed to him. He would square accounts and stop the games that were going on.[11] Considering the number of financial 'games' that Walker himself had played over the years, he was likely well qualified to nose out corruption.

A Harbour Commissioner from the time of the election, he served on various committees – Docks and Pilotage; Landings and Fishings; Locomotive Haulage; Ferry Service; but significantly, not finance!

It is doubtful how successful he was as a councillor in Aberdeen. Reports of meetings are full of Mr Walker putting forward motions which found no seconder, and the Lord Provost declaring, 'It falls to the ground'. He had got off to a bad start with the Lord Provost, and by 1915 had likely offended many others. On at least one occasion he advised Aberdeen Council to take an example from the way business was conducted at Wandsworth![12]

In Walker's obituary in the *Shetland News* we read: *In the Council and at the Harbour Board he was 'agin the government'* [Liberal Government, Prime Minister Asquith]. *He was a Burgess of Guild of the city, and latterly took a keen interest in the financial affairs of the Guildry.* There was an amusing incident in connection with his return to Aberdeen, as he had been listed in the Guildry as a deceased member. Putting in an appearance at a meeting *he at once proceeded to show that he was very much alive.*

John Walker died, age 81, on 31st December, 1916, at 33 High Street, Old Aberdeen where he had been resident for some years. It seems that he died intestate. Described on the death certificate as a retired railway contractor, it states he had suffered from paraplegia for six months. Brother Robert, who lived in Tillydrone House, Old Aberdeen, was the informant. Granted leave of absence from meetings during his last illness, John retained his seat on the council to the end. Buried in Banchory churchyard, the funeral was attended by the Lord Provost and representatives of the Council, Harbour Board and University.[13]

The obituary which appeared in the *Shetland Times* was, like that of the *Shetland News,* copied from the *Aberdeen Daily Journal,* but with an extra paragraph on his activities in Shetland:[14] *There are few people of a past generation in Shetland who will not recall the name of John Walker of Maryfield, Bressay. In the early seventies his name was on every lip in these islands. What others had failed to do by persistent effort, extending over a long period, he accomplished in a very short time by sheer force of character. Crofters were evicted by the score, and many acres which had furnished the means of livelihood to numerous families were converted into sheep runs and the people turned out to sink or swim. His views upon the land question were extreme even for his day, and in his desire to promote what he considered the right he allowed nothing to stand in his way. He was always a leading power whether in the goldfields of Australia or in the sheep rearing in Shetland. At the shows of the first Shetland Agricultural Society, he was not only an active official but a very successful competitor. He seemed to harbour the idea that despite climatic conditions and poverty of soil he could raise the standard of agriculture and stock quite as high in Shetland as it was in Aberdeenshire. He failed in this as he was bound to do, but before he left the islands many a smiling township was represented by the falling remnants of houses and office-houses, with the inhabitants scattered to the four winds.* Unusually honest for a Victorian obituary!

As this story has been pieced together mainly by reading hundreds of letters, it seems appropriate to end on one of Walker's, written as late as 1908. It's a long letter, the first one of his I've found that had been typed, with many pen and ink corrections, addressed to the Congested Districts Board, Edinburgh.[15] He was staying in Whalsay beside the Stobies, and had been studying the Crofters Act (1886) and the Congested Districts Act (1897) and wished to pass on his views and suggestions. As these Acts were intended to encourage the return of population to the country districts, it seems ironic to have a man who was responsible for many tenants leaving those areas, now writing with advice to the C.D. Board.

On the depopulation question he asserted that the Acts had failed in their aim to improve conditions for crofters and fishermen: *So far as these Islands are concerned ... The population has decreased in all the Rural Parishes with the exception of this Island.* [Whalsay]

Home Again

He started with agriculture, listing his own experience and making recommendations, then moved on to roads: *Five small carts have been brought to this Isle but their use restricted to a radius of about a mile. One owner of a cart taking his wife along the road, had at every gate to take the wheels off and carry the cart through ... This winter the roads here were <u>impassable</u> until I complained to the Road Committee.*

Then on to the fishing: *When I knew this Isle first there were only nineteen 'sixearn' boats employed, now there are some thirty 'Big' boats but no safe boat-harbour exists – one boat was driven from her moorings in September last from what is the best anchorage, and totally lost. Some twenty of the boats have to be laid up at Lerwick at an average expense of £10 per boat.*

He then elaborated on two proposed schemes for a harbour, giving his suggestions and ideas for financing this development. He offered his assistance in drawing up plans and estimates of cost – perhaps he was feeling a bit bored at the Manse! Work, he said, should be done by local labour wherever possible: *If nothing is done to conserve the present Capital in the Boats and the enthusiasm of the Fishermen, Whalsay must be denuded of its population as Fetlar has been.*

Walker, no doubt proud of his epistle, let his son-in-law the Rev. Stobie read it. He couldn't have foreseen Stobie's reaction, penned the very same day to the Congested Districts Board:

8th April, 1908

My Wife's father, John Walker, who is here now, has shewn me a letter which he intends forwarding to the C.D. Board on Whalsay matters. As I do not approve of the letter, please do not connect me with it in any way.

There is no indication of a reaction by the board to Stobie's letter, but there are notes from board members on Walker's. Their comments are varied:

I have for many years been familiar with the name of this <u>Walker</u>. Apparently he belongs to a class of Sheep Managers – on large clearances in the Highlands. Those men generally succeeded in sinking their masters and then swell out to be large sheep farmers themselves – in their turn to disappear and leave very little healthy traces behind them of good done in the localities where they operated. Personally I am unable to feel goodwill towards or believe in men who helped to destroy the rural population.

Another: *You must really excuse me but I attach no importance to this man or his letter.*

And: *As to the agricultural suggestions in fact this gentleman suggests that we should perform every function of the landlord except collect the rent.*

JOHN WALKER'S SHETLAND

Yet another introduces a note of sarcasm: *I suppose the C. D. Board will always be the better of being told what their duties are.*
Lastly, a crumb of approval, *Mr Walker writes intelligently.*

A polite, but non-committal reply was sent to Walker, pointing out difficulties the Board were facing and thanking him for perusal of the pamphlet which they were returning as requested.

So which pamphlet was that? We find out from a handwritten P.S. at the end of his laboriously typed letter to the Board. He had sent them a copy of the 'Articles, Regulations and Conditions of Lease' – the rules imposed on the tenants when he became factor for Garth and Annsbrae in 1866, forty-two years earlier. There's a certain pathos here, but he still comes across as an arrogant old man:

P.S. As it may interest the members of your Board I enclose a copy of what was known in the sixties as "Walker's Catechism" but regret I must ask you to return it sometime as it is my last copy.   J.W.

THE END

1	Local History Librarian, Battersea Library
2	Courtesy of Elizabeth West
3	Courtesy of Hamish Walker
4	S.A. D 6/292/24
5	D.M. Rhind, *A Chronicle of the Cape Central Railway,* Cape Town 1995, p.38
6	*Wandsworth Borough News,* 6th October, 1906
7	Local History Librarian, Battersea Library
8	*Shetland News,* 13th August, 1904
9	Courtesy of Mr & Mrs George Bell, Sandlodge
10	*Aberdeen Daily Journal,* 4th January, 1913
11	*Aberdeen Daily Journal,* 5th November, 1913
12	*Aberdeen Daily Journal,* 21st September, 1915
13	Obituary, *Shetland News,* 11th January, 1917
14	Obituary, *Shetland Times,* 20th January, 1917
15	N.A.S. AF 42/4916 B20443 (see appendix)

APPENDICES

Chapter Two
William and Amelia Walker's Family

OLDER than John were Catherine, Alexander, Isobel, James, William and Helen. Younger siblings were Amelia, and Robert and George, the twins.

John and his five brothers all attended Aberdeen Grammar School and at least three of them went on to university. Two little boys, William and Adam, died aged one and two. John left the Grammar School at fifteen declaring that he had got more than enough of Latin and Greek and wanted to be a merchant. The other brothers all went on to become prominent in their chosen professions.[1]

Alexander, the eldest, joined his father in the family business, perhaps somewhat unwillingly. We read in his obituary: *But while in his youth his ideas were fixed otherwise than on commerce, at the request of his father, backed up by the entreaties of his mother, he entered the business in which he was to spend his life.* We are not told on what his youthful ideas were fixed, but it may have been writing, as, among other historical works he published a book in defence of Mary, Queen of Scots. Alexander was Dean of Guild 1873-80 and his photograph still hangs in Trinity Hall, Aberdeen. The honorary degree of LL.D was conferred on him by Aberdeen University.

Some of the Walker family – left to right – standing: James Sutherland, Alexander, Catherine. On bench: James, Helen, William (Snr.). Front: twins, Robert and George.   *Courtesy Dorothy Duncan*

The next brother, James, became a junior partner in the family business and was well known in musical circles.

William, M.D. was Deputy Surgeon-General in the Bengal Service.

One of the twins, the Rev. George, was minister at Castle Douglas for forty-two years and Robert, M.A. Aberdeen (with honourable distinction) and B.A. Cambridge, was prominent at Aberdeen University as – Assistant Professor, Librarian, Registrar, Secretary of University Court and Clerk of General Council.

While John was in Australia he would have missed the wedding in 1855 of sister Catherine to the Rev. James Rose Sutherland who had been minister in the parish of Northmavine, Shetland, since 1848. Catherine was to live in the manse there until her death in 1888.

Of the other three sisters we know little. Helen married William Dunn, an advocate. Amelia died in Aberdeen in 1856, age 18, of kidney failure. Isobel didn't marry.

William Walker's shop (grocer, tea, wine & spirit) was in George Street 1827-55 and thereafter at 52 Union Street, Aberdeen. It was described as *unique and attractive in the rarity of its windows, with Eastern vases and figures of heathen deities, an unfailing source of attraction to those who pass.* (From *Shetland News* 11/1/1917, *Aberdeen Daily Journal* 11/2/1903 & Aberdeen Directories.)

APPENDICES

First entry in John Walker's diary of a voyage to Australia

Tuesday 30th November, 1852 – This day crossed the Bar of Aberdeen Harbour the Good Ship Lord Metcaffe, under command of William Cargill, at 3o'clock P.M. bound for Melbourne, Australia, with passengers, 12 in the Cabin & about 80 'tweendecks, those in the Cabin consisted of – Mr & Mrs Maxwell; Miss Jack; Miss McKenzie; Mr John Anderson; Mr James Anderson; Mr Hepburn; Mr R. Taylor; Mr Shirres; Mr A. Farquhar; Mr Cobben (Doctor); Mr John Walker.

After getting clear of strangers we set sail with a smart breeze from S.S.W. but to all appearance coming on to blow a <u>gale</u>.

Chapter Three

The Garth Estate

LANDS acquired by one branch of the Mouat family in Shetland, taking the name from the original holding at Garth, Sullom Voe. By the 1800s the estate had consolidated mostly in Yell and in Unst where the Mouats of Garth had lived since the mid 17th century. During the 19th century the estate came near to bankruptcy, principally due to the irresponsibility of William Mouat of Garth who died in 1836. This could explain the desperation of his nephew, Major Thomas Mouat Cameron to establish economic farming units under the factorship of John Walker.

The Cameron Mouat family owned the estates of Garth and Annsbrae. The double surname came from the decision in 1839 of Captain and Mrs Cameron (she was Margaret Mouat, heiress of Garth in her own right) to assume the name Mouat, a move followed by their three daughters but, confusingly, not by their son. Thus, although their surnames differ, Major Thomas Mouat Cameron is the full brother of Anne Cameron Mouat – the redoubtable "Miss Mouat".

Thomas Cameron's grandson was Captain N.O.M. Cameron of Garth and Annsbrae who died in 1967.[2]

Maryfield, Bressay

The house of Maryfield was built at estate expense for John Walker when he took over the tenancy of Keldabister Farm, renaming it Maryfield for his wife, Mary. It is a solid Victorian building with its own pier and store and adjacent gardens. It is now a hotel.

Chapter Four
Alexander Sandison

IN AUGUST 1861 brothers Alexander and Peter Mouat Sandison renewed their seven year lease from Major Cameron of properties in North Yell – the farm at the Booth of Cullivoe, with the dwelling house, shop etc and the right to cure fish on the beaches of Crooksair & Kellister, also Booth of Whallery, Gloup, yearly rent £20.[3] Alexander was also tacksman for the Garth and Annsbrae property in North Yell. By 1866 Alexander Sandison had been living in Gardiesfauld, Unst for about eight years. He and his wife and family moved there from Beach House, Cullivoe, leaving Peter in charge of the Cullivoe business of fish curing and general merchandise.

Alexander was one of the partners of Spence & Co (1867-74). He later purchased and leased several sheep farms in Unst.[4]

Chapter Seven
Heads of households in Delting who signed acceptance of eviction in September 1866 with various conditions for renting or leasing dwelling houses only.[5]

ELIZABETH Pole, William Robertson, Laurence Copeland, Arthur Gifford, Janet Hay, William Hay and Laurence Cogle - all from Garth; Joseph Gunn from Millburn; Donald Anderson from Upper Scatsta; Catherine Cupper and Peter Mouat from Laxobigging; John Murray and Robert Robertson from Urka; Magnus Blance, Thomas Laurenson, Thomas Blance, John Blance, Laurence Smith, William Blance, Robert Blance, Peter Gray, Bruce Blance – all from Calback; Charles Nicolson, James Irvine and Magnus Irvine from Swinister; and George Irvine from Bordigarth.

Chapter Eleven
Commissioners Of Supply

ORIGINALLY appointed to allocate the 'cess' or land tax among their fellow landowners. Qualification was ownership of land at the level of

£100 per annum. Duties included assisting in educational provision, helping in supervision of roads and bridges, collecting 'rogue money' for the upkeep of prisons.

The Valuation of Land Act of 1854 which introduced the rating system which existed in Scotland until 1989, greatly reduced the role of the Commissioners of Supply. With the establishment of county councils in 1889 they virtually became redundant.[6]

Lampooners

(Below is a spoof sale notice which appeared presumably about the time the Walker family left Bressay)

FOR SALE,
BY AUCTION OR OTHERWISE, AS MAY BE HEREAFTER RESOLVED.

I. – The whole Lands, Tenements, Houses, Heritages, and Moveables of whatever description or tenure, and by whatever name known or called, the property, or lately so, or in the lawful or unlawful possession of T-o-as Mo-at C-m-r-n, late Captain of H. M. Bengal Army.

The lands are almost all fenced with iron, the people are all under iron rule, and chromate of iron is found on part of the Estate. The territorial exchequer has recently been thoroughly drained, the lands partially so, but still remain slightly marshy; and, although a large sum has been already expended opportunities for future outlay have been carefully reserved for men of enterprise who may be at a loss to dispose of their own or other men's surplus cash.

II. – Two large and commodious erections of stone, slated and otherwise finished in the most improved style, intended originally for Sheep Sheds; but Shepherds having departed hurriedly, and Sheep now following their example leisurely, these erections would answer admirably for Meeting Houses. They demand the attention of all religious bodies of a dissenting persuasion. Men, "young, active and energetic" would find here a wide sphere of Christian usefulness, as 224 natives will be sold along with the premises, and can be relied upon as a "ready people". The foregoing is specially recommended to persons of a philanthropic disposition – the creatures offered being in every varied stage of starvation and general wretchedness, and will be sold without reserve. – *Vide* Catalogue for Sex and Ages.

III. – Major's half-pay, with chance of reversion of Island of Bressay, with all Rents, Payments, Charges, Feu-Duties, Ground-Annuals, or other real burdens or incumbrances, and various other accompanying advantages, for which *vide* Catalogue.

IV. – The whole Crop, Stock (farm and domestic), at Maryfield, comprehending – Horses, Oxen, Asses, Man Servants, Maid Servants, and Strangers, that may be within the gate. The Maidens – reared on pigs' livers and other nutritious diet – will be warranted free from vice by me, and bear certificates to the same effect, by Presbytery of Olnafirth, and Kirk Session of Bressay.

V. – Life Interest in Presbytery of Olnafirth, with right to powers of Ruling Elder in Parish of Delting; also, Dispensation granted unto me, my heirs, and assignees, for doing all manner of work on the First Day of the Week, together with Special Dispensation, when abroad, to attend Theatres and all places of Amusement and recreation on same day, both of which dispensations are given under Sign and Seal of the reverend Courts before referred to.

VI. – Right to sit-at, on, above, or upon eight Parochial Boards, with full control over the Consciences of four native, and one Scotch, Inspectors of Poor, together with unlimited powers to bully and browbeat all members who may attempt to express their own opinions; also, the gratification of withholding from a pauperised populace the necessaries of life. The attention of persons of an anti-philanthropic character is demanded to this!

VII. – Right to act as correspondent to the *North British Agriculturist* and *Daily Review* newspapers. The latter carries with it the right to relief from the Free Church Sustentation Fund, does not require that the truth should be given by its correspondent, and will allow no statement of his to be controverted.

VIII. – Supreme right to control all Lunatics or Idiots, Fatuous or Furious Persons, male and female, within the Shetland Islands generally, and especially the Presbytery of Olnafirth, either in its fatuous or furious state; said Presbytery consisting of Six Divines, with bodies and souls, or with such part of each or either, or both or neither, as may still remain.

IX. – Copyright of some volumes of Historical Reference, to be hereafter published, viz. :- "Australia in Relation to the North of Scotland"; "Garth, Viewed in Connection with Botany Bay". This latter work, the author confidently asserts, will be one of surpassing interest, and will at once edify and amuse a discriminating public. Copyright of Song and Music –

When ye gang awa' Johnnie, | When ye gang to the far countrie,
Far across the sea, laddie, | What will ye leave to me, Johnnie?

will be sung by a certain gallant soldier, at a select concert. A second to this song is about to be composed, and will be specially adapted for Sheriff Mure's voice.

X. – A revolver: has never been used, except to shoot a dog, although purchased with a view to operate upon higher game – if the native population may be justly considered as such.

CONDITIONS OF SALE

The Exposer will demand a purchase price, according to the value he may himself consider the afore-mentioned subjects worth. Any person or persons who may object to give the value so fixed and determined by the said Exposer, he, the Exposer, will publish in the *Times, Daily Review, Dundee Advertiser,* and *People's Journal* Newspapers. He will stigmatize them by the use of every opprobrious epithet in the English language, will make every possible insinuation against their moral and social status, and every such opprobrious epithet and insinuation shall be published anonymously in one or other, or all of the above-named newspapers, and shall be so worded that no legal proceedings can successfully be taken.

In conclusion, the public are warned not to treat this manifesto with "overbearing negligence", but to repair to, and attend at Maryfield House, Bressay, on Sunday next, between the hours of Two and Three afternoon, to hear the various Bills of Sale read over; and after having listened quietly and respectfully thereunto, thereafter to proclaim aloud with one accord —

"GOD SAVE JOHN WALKER"

** ** **

The following verses were written by "An Observer" after John Walker gave evidence to the Truck Commission.

LINES TO JOHN WALKER

For who make the paupers? Who does it? – O, who?
Full well you know, Walker; 'Tis you, sir; yes, you.

Those by you now ejected – A destitute horde –
In towns must take refuge, and fall on the "Board".

And if still you continue your merciless plan,
Poor-rates will be doubled, prevent it who can.

If you had been careful to give each his due,
And the right, with the wrong, to bring forth into view,

You might have had thanks, for we do wish to see
From truculent dealing this country set free.

Let the culprit be found out and punished instanter;
Not the whole class of merchants lie under your banter.

In the cause of the poor as a champion you'll never
Get credit, I'm sure, for honest endeavour.

It has even been said your attack on "King Truck"
Is the wish to succeed him with *spirit* and *pluck*.

"May the day be far distant," I hear the poor cry;
"If he ever attempt it, let him just mind his eye."

And the proverb remember, with penitent groans,
"Those who live in glass houses should never throw stones."

Chapter Seventeen
Walker and the School Boards

THE letter[7] below, recipient unknown, suggests that Major Cameron had trusted his Factor completely even with financial affairs, to his cost. By the time it was written Walker was in South Africa. It also gives some idea how school matters were handled before the Education Act.

Ferncliff
Gutcher
Shetland
1881

My Dear Sir

I duly received your letter dated 9th May with Mr Webster's letter which I now return – I may say that I was very happy to receive your letter And shall herein explain to the best of my knowledge the way matters stand relative to the school house at North Yell It seems that in the year 1869 It was purposed to repair and enlarge the school house And that a meeting of Heritors was called. At that meeting Mr Irvine Mr Pole and Captn Henderson met – Leveled the assessment and appointed John Walker (then Factor for Major Cameron) Collector with power to pay the school contractor out of Major Cameron's Bank Ac and collect from the Heritors and repay the Major. This he did – viz pay the Contractor out of the Major's cash And collected the Amount of Assessment required for said repair But

APPENDICES

failed to pay it back to the Major. Of course the Major now wants to get his money back And must call on the heritors to pay it Since Mr Walker who was appointed by them has failed to do so.

I may mention here that the Major was not aware that Mr Walker had not repaid him till last year After Mr Walker's failure and Sequestration When he received his (the Major's) books which had been in Mr Walker's possession. The assessment now required to pay the Major will be about 1/7 per Merk – It is rather hard to pay twice over but I suppose it must be done Or at least I am inclined to pay it rather than take it to a court of law Altho I think a good case could be made against those who constituted the meeting in 1869 and who appointed J Walker to act for the Heritors if it can be proved that you and others did not receive due intimation of such meeting In that case the meeting was not a legal one And only those who constituted it are responsible for the results.

At last meeting of Heritors of which you received intimation from Mr Webster many of the Heritors then present declared that they never got intimation of the meeting of 1869.

I may also mention that the meeting of Heritors of which you received intimation from Mr Webster met and adjourned to meet again some day in July when the matter will be fully investigated. Should you be inclined to give me a Mandate to vote for you at this or other meeting I shall be most happy to do so.

Hoping you are all well, Yours faithfully,
James Hoseason

Chapter Nineteen

John Walker's assets & losses listed at examination of bankrupt 10th Dec. 1880[8]

Walker declared himself worth £20,000 at Martinmas 1873, as follows:-

430 Iceland ponies	£4,300
Due by the Marquis of Londonderry	3,000
240 Benhar Coal Shares	4,300
Value of sheep stock	3,600
Value of fish in hand	1,000
3 Shares of Shetland Fishing Co.	750
25 Lochore Coal Shares	275
50 Emma Shares	300
Leith & Clyde & Hull Shares	120
Unst Road Bonds	750
Shetland Properties	650
Shipping	500

225

John Walker's Shetland

Sundry Debtors	50
Total	£20,045

To this James Tytler added £40,110 which included several bank loans; £2,000 from brother Robert; £1,400 - John's share of his father's estate, and various other sums making an overall total of £60,155 income.

His list of losses and cost of investments amounted to £62,160 viz:-

Lost by death, keep and sale of Iceland Ponies	£3,000
" on Benhar Shares	500
" on Emma Shares	300
" on Lochore Shares	610
" on Farm Stocking	800
" on Charter of Wicklow to Iceland	750
" on Norwegian Fish	3,000
" on Fish Speculation with R. Miller Son & Co	600
" on Whale Speculation	1,000
" p: Action Earl of Zetland & others - R.Miller & Co. should pay half	2,000
" on Canadian Horses & meat Co	400
Cost of Iceland Mineral Lease	500
" " Dryad	1,000
" " Farmer	900
" " Lilly & Contest Shares	280
" " Shetland Fishing Co	750
" " House Furniture, Carriage etc	2,000
" " House (£3,800. Bonds £3,000)	800
" " Lands in Shetland	990
" " Insurance Premiums	1,000
" " Cottage Furniture & outlays a/c Mining Co	600
" " Calls on 455 preference Shares in Mining Co	1,000
Paid John Bruce Jr. on a/c Mine Grassum	300
" Bath & Sons a/c Norwegian Ore Action	430
" A/c Chrome Ore Groner [Grunie?] workings etc	600
" Union Bank	750
Difference on Unst Roads Bonds	150
Paid Law expenses	1,000
Interest (of which £1,200 due by Mining Co.)	5,500
House expenses for seven years (including personal expenses)	5,950
Sundry other losses	500
Expended in Sandlodge p. Books exclusive of many items not included	24,000
Total	£62,160

APPENDICES

Chapter Twenty
Robert Walker d.1920

HIS later life was harassed by financial troubles involving a suit before the South African courts, which unfortunately decided against him. This meant the loss of about £28,000, and many a man's spirit would have succumbed under such disaster: but never his. As it happened, he considered his honour was involved, and this was more precious to him than his money. In the face of every conceivable discouragement, he still kept fighting – appealing against the judgement, imploring M.P.s to ask questions in the House, protesting against the venality of the South African administration – all with his characteristic vehemence and energy. It was to no effect, but nothing would induce him to cease his pursuit of justice, and his fine belief that it must ultimately stand forth vindicated, buoyed him up to the day of his death.[9]

Chapter Twenty-one
Congested Districts Board

ESTABLISHED in 1897 to administer a fund of government money which would be used for the benefit of certain parishes deemed 'congested'.[10]

John and Mary Walker's family

I have only a sketchy knowledge of what became of John and Mary's family. For some I know nothing except their dates of birth and death.
Amelia Mary, born Victoria, Australia 8/11/1855, died 9/3/1920.
Mary, born Victoria, Australia 29/4/1857, died 3/2/1938.
Isobel Anne, born Westerton, Cults 26/9/1858, married, 6/1/1881, Rev. Charles M. Stobie who was minister in Whalsay, Shetland until 1910. They had three children, Mary, Charles and John. Charles jun. also entered the ministry, as did his nephew, John's son, another Charles. The latter Charles was ordained to Uyeasound, Unst, where he ministered from 1942 until 1947, then for a short time in his grandfather's parish of Whalsay. Isobel died in Aberdeen, 21/5/1923.
Catherine Sutherland, born Westerton, Cults 15/4/1860, died at Banchory-Devenick 12/3/1874.
Helen Dunn, born Bressay, Shetland, 14/7/1861.

JOHN WALKER'S SHETLAND

Jane Smith, born Bressay 9/2/1864, died at Cape Town, 5/1/1888.
Jean Park, born Bressay 27/7/1865, married Rev. J. S. Maver in September 1891. They had one daughter, May, born July 1892, and died April 1893. Jean died at Woodstock, Cape Town 31/10/1895.
Janet Smith Gray Emily Lawrence Lee Octavia, born Bressay 30/11/1866, married Rev. Philip L. Phelps in July 1904. Janet died of cancer at St Mithian, Cornwall in September 1944. She was nursed during her last months by her sister Caroline.
William, born Bressay 17/9/1868, died 13/1/1869.
John, born Bressay 30/10/1870, married Bessie Collard at Cape Town 10/10/1893. They had two sons, John, born 9/9/1894, and Cameron Gordon, born 21/5/1898. John Sr. died at Croydon in July 1914.
Thomas Mouat Cameron, born Marine Terrace, Aberdeen, married Kate Cleghorn at Cape Town 18/6/1901. They had two sons and a daughter, Keith, Derek and Kathleen Mavis. Thomas was fatally injured in a car accident at Bloemfontein 19/11/1949. His daughter was driving the car but neither she nor her two young daughters, also passengers in the car, were seriously hurt.
Caroline Ball Agnes Elizabeth Jessie, born 4/3/1879 at 1 Polwarth Terrace, Edinburgh, married Bertram James Ambrose 5/1/1917. Their son, Dermot, married Betty 1/1/1944.

Besides these twelve, Mary had three still born babies.

1   *Shetland News* 11/1/1917, *Aberdeen Daily Journal* 11/2/1903 & Aberdeen Directories
2   Information from Wendy and John Scott
3   Gardie Papers 1861/11
4   Brian Smith, *Toons and Tenants,* Lerwick 2000
5   Gardie Papers 1866/78-83
6   Donnachie & Hewitt, *A Companion to Scottish History*
7   S.A. 390/51/6
8   N.A.S. CS 318/37/321 Sederunt Book Vol. 1, pp.44-46
9   *Aberdeen University Review* Vol. 8
10   Ewen A. Cameron, *Land for the People*

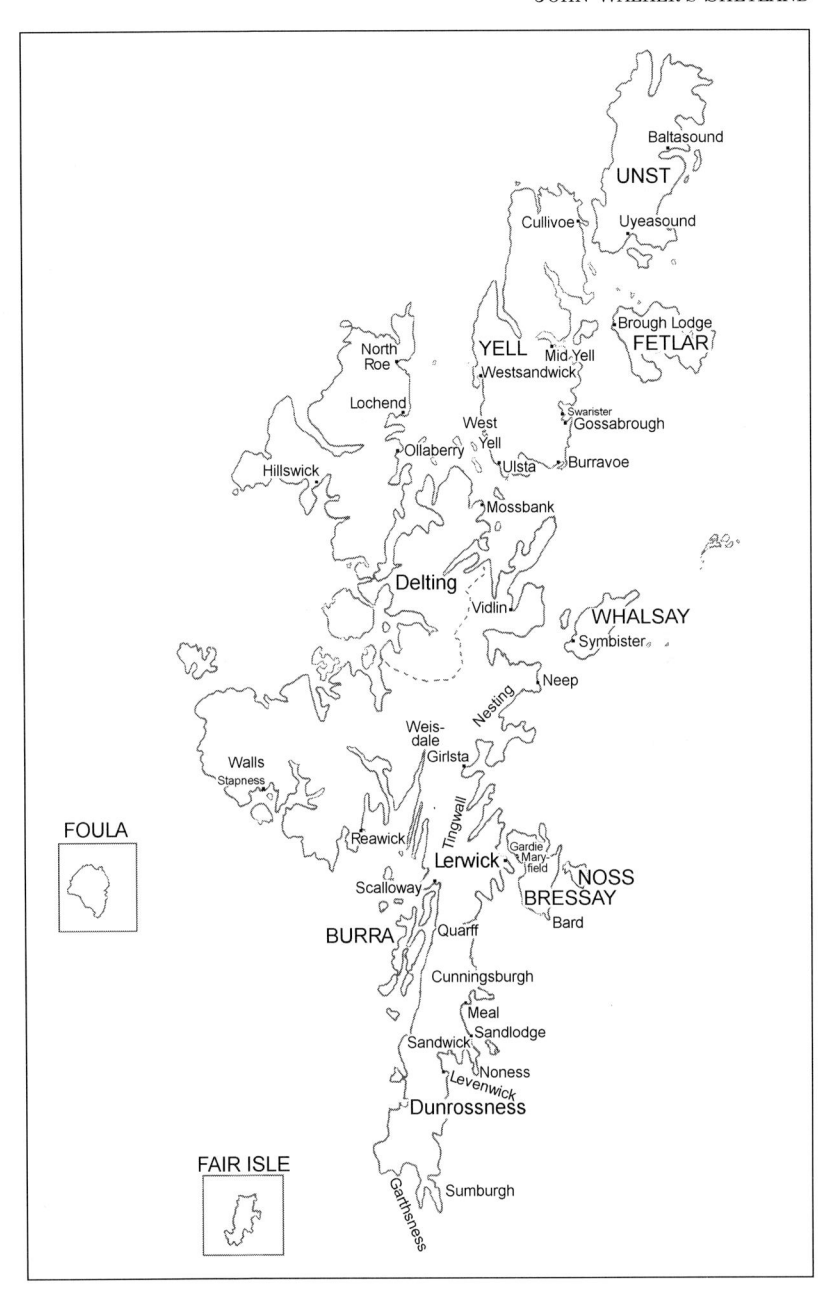

John Walker's Shetland

Map of Shetland showing locations: Baltasound, UNST, Cullivoe, Uyeasound, Brough Lodge, North Roe, YELL, Mid Yell, FETLAR, Westsandwick, Lochend, Swarister, Gossabrough, West Yell, Hillswick, Ollaberry, Ulsta, Burravoe, Mossbank, Delting, Vidlin, WHALSAY, Symbister, Nesting, Neep, Weisdale, Girlsta, Walls, Stapness, Tingwall, FOULA, Reawick, Gardie, Maryfield, Lerwick, NOSS, Scalloway, BRESSAY, BURRA, Quarff, Bard, Cunningsburgh, Meal, Sandlodge, Sandwick, Noness, Levenwick, Dunrossness, FAIR ISLE, Garthsness, Sumburgh.

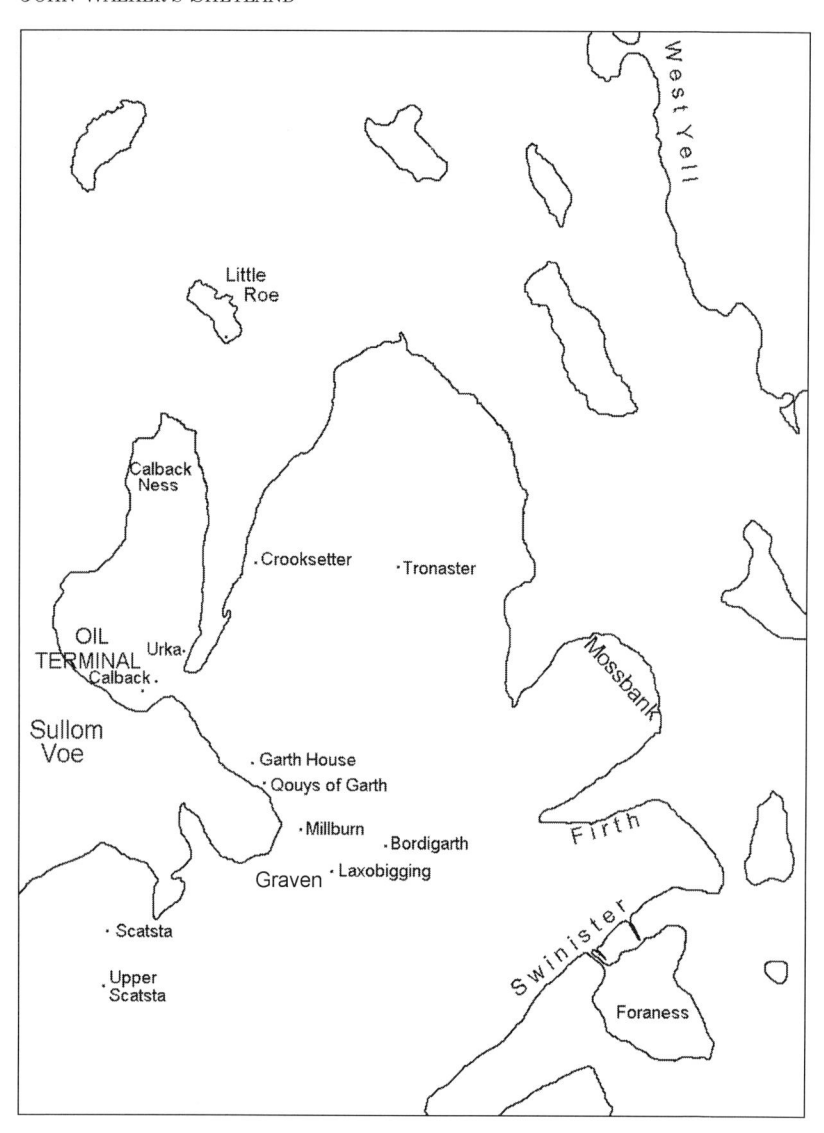

Map showing locations including Sullom Voe, Oil Terminal, Calback Ness, Little Roe, Crooksetter, Tronaster, Urka, Calback, Garth House, Qouys of Garth, Millburn, Bordigarth, Graven, Laxobigging, Mossbank, Scatsta, Upper Scatsta, Swinister, Foraness, Firth, and West Yell.

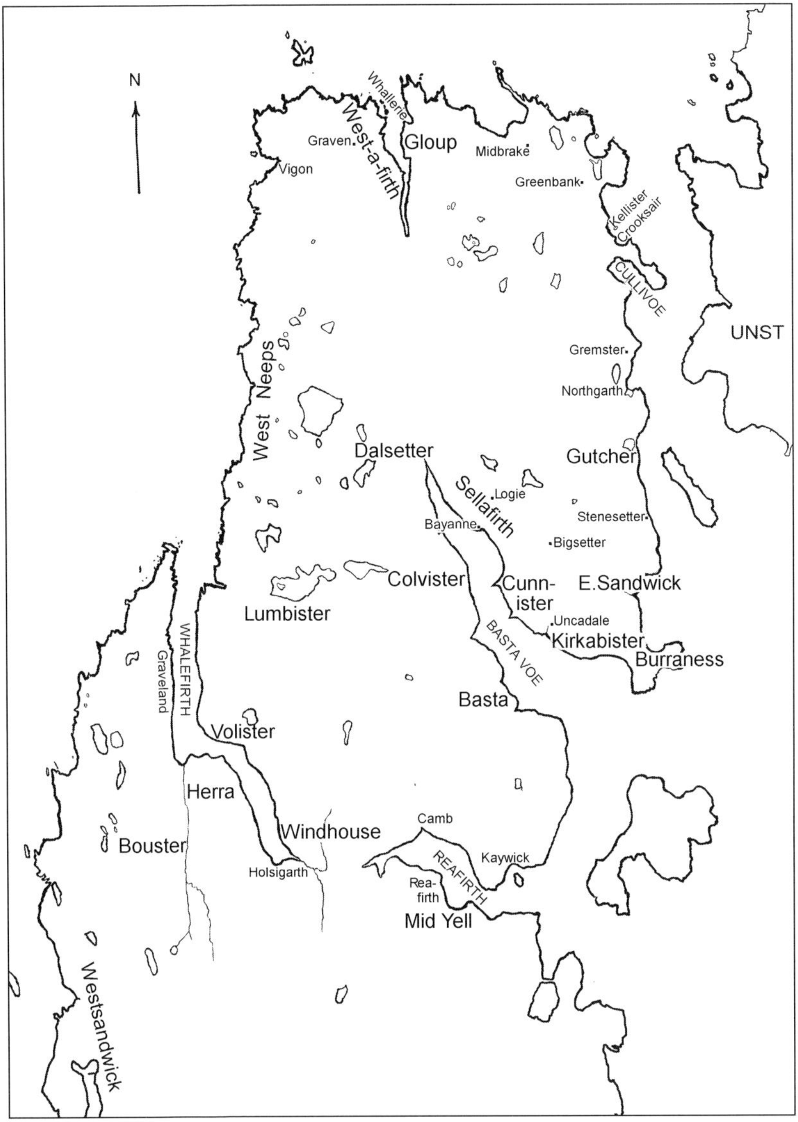
N
Whallerie
West-a-firth
Graven
Gloup
Midbrake
Greenbank
Vigon
Kellister
Crooksair
CULLIVOE
UNST
Gremster
Northgarth
West Neeps
Dalsetter
Gutcher
Sellafirth
Logie
Stenesetter
Bayanne
Bigsetter
Colvister
Cunn-
ister
E.Sandwick
Lumbister
Uncadale
Kirkabister
Burraness
WHALEFIRTH
Graveland
BASTA VOE
Basta
Volister
Herra
Windhouse
Camb
Bouster
Holsigarth
REAFIRTH
Kaywick
Rea-
firth
Mid Yell
Westsandwick

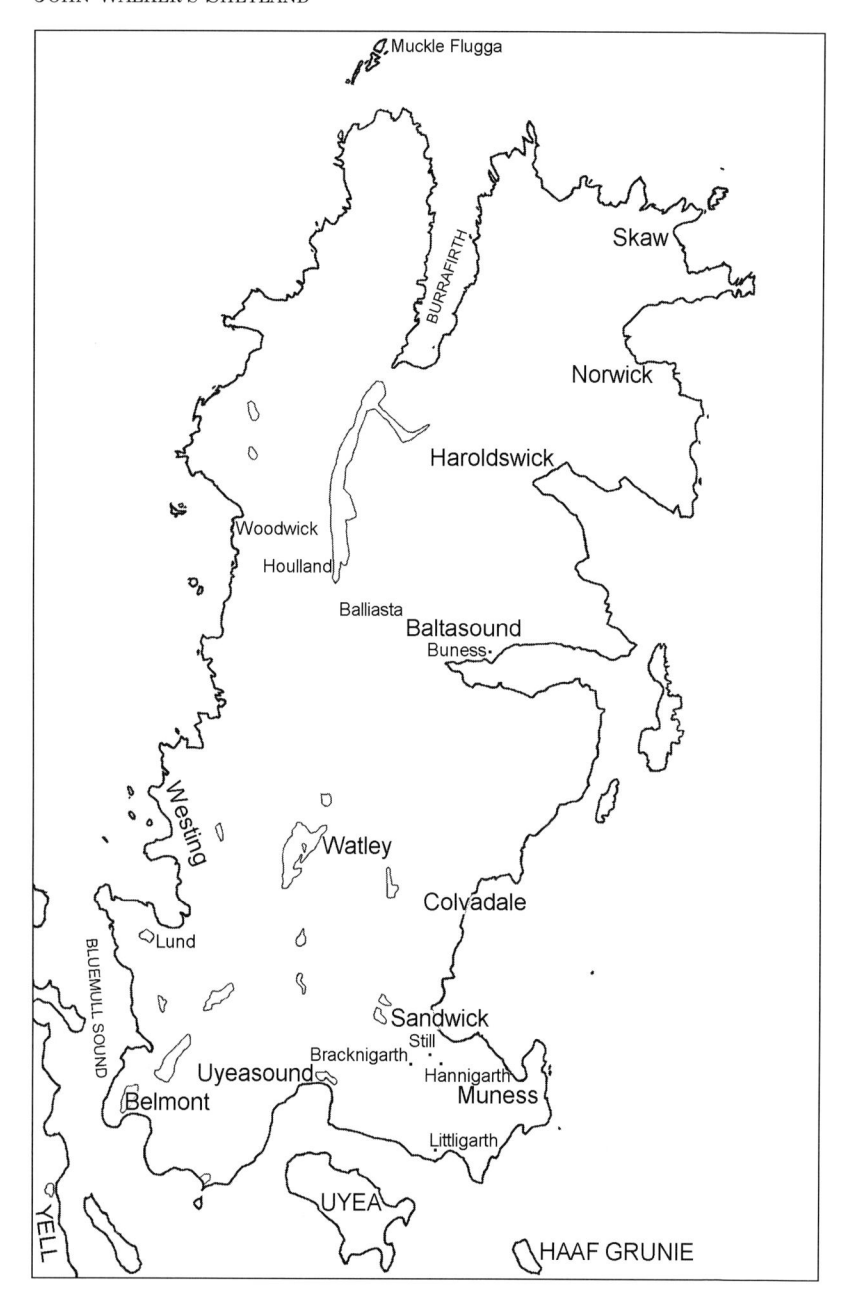

JOHN WALKER'S SHETLAND

INDEX

— A —

Aberdeen 2, 35, 102, 116, 142, 153, 172,
173, 181, 195, 212, 213, 217-219
Aberdeen, Leith & Clyde Shipping Co 115, 116
Adelphi Court, Aberdeen 5, 10, 150
Airth, John 111
Aitken, Henry 180, 193
Alice 41
Ambrose, Bertram 228
Anderson
    Andrew (*Chieftain's Bride*) 112
    Andrew A. (Kirkabister) 36, 55, 63, 64
    Andrew (Unst Quarry) 169
    Ann 40
    Arthur 15, 120
    David 67
    Donald 220
    Edward 65-67
    Gilbert 105
    James (Logie, Sellafirth) 65, 66
    James (*Lord Metcalfe*) 6, 8, 219
    Jerome 40
    John (Kirkabister) 54-57
    John (*Lord Metcalfe*) 219
    Robert 68

Andrew
  Henry 189, 190
  William 189, 190
Ardmillan, Lord 143, 161

— B —

Ball, Mary 14
Balliasta/Ballista, Unst 133, 151, 157, 163, 165, 178, 232
Ballarat, Australia 11, 12
Baltasound, Unst 113, 131, 133, 229, 232
Banchory-Devenick 214
Barclay, Mr 176
Bard o Bressay 182, 229
Basta, Yell 39, 67, 70, 95, 101, 231
Basta Voe 1, 37, 68, 113, 231
Bayanne/Bayan, Yell 67, 231
Beatty/Beith, R. 181, 184, 185
Belmont, Unst 61, 102, 104, 232
Bigsetter, Yell 1, 37, 68, 69, 129, 231
Black, David Dakers 21, 124, 125
Blance
  Bruce 220
  Jimmy 79, 80
  John 220
  Magnus 220
  Peter Simpson 31
  Robert 220
  Thomas 220
  William 220
Blue Bell 159
Bluemull Sound 132, 232
Bo'ness 182
Bohn, Charles 202
Bolt, James 112
Bordigarth, Delting 220, 230
Bouster, Yell 42, 46, 231
Bowen, Charles 126, 129
Boyndlie, nr. Fraserburgh 67, 146, 149
Bracknigarth, Unst 106, 232

234

INDEX

Bressay 2, 4, 18, 23, 24, 26-28, 83, 121, 135,
                       137, 144-154, 182, 196, 201, 207, 229
Brixton 14
Brough Lodge, Fetlar 113, 117, 229
Brown
    Ann 64
    James 69, 70
    Peggy 64
    William John 69
Bruce
    Alex 13
    F. C. 89
    George 117
    James William 133
Bruces of Sumburgh 112, 117, 180, 185, 188, 202, 212, 226
Budge, Lady 131, 134
Buness, Baltasound 48, 232
Burgess, Doctor 187
Burman, Jose 204, 205
Burnet, W. C. 199
Burra 18, 26, 172, 229
Burrafirth, Unst 175, 232
Burraness, Yell 35-38, 52-56, 69, 71, 90, 93, 152, 231
Burravoe, Yell 67, 113, 123, 229

— C —

Cabel, Christian 150
Caithness 79, 80, 150
Calback/ Coldback, Delting 52, 77-79, 93, 220, 230
Cameron
    Captain N.O.M. 219
    Major T. M. 23, 24, 26, 28, 31, 33-39, 41, 44, 48, 52-56,
                                  58-60, 63, 66-68, 70, 72, 77, 78, 80, 83-86,
                                  89, 90, 92, 93, 96, 101, 103, 104, 107, 108,
                                  111, 112, 118, 122, 124, 125, 132-135, 144-154,
                                  163, 166, 168, 188, 189, 219-221, 224, 225
    of Locheil 135
Cape Central Railway Ltd. 201, 202
Cape Town 4, 198, 199, 200, 201, 203, 204
Cargill, Captain 4-7, 10, 219

235

JOHN WALKER'S SHETLAND

Caverhill, John 81
Charleson, Nina 63, 76
Chieftain's Bride 94, 112-118, 123, 160
Clark
    James 37, 38, 58
    John 108
Cleghorn, Kate 228
Cluness, Andrew 105
Cobben, Doctor 9, 219
Cogle,
    Laurence 220
    Robert 177
Collard, Bessie 228
Colvadale, Unst 106, 232
Colvister, Yell 39, 95, 231
Commissioners of Supply 124, 196, 220
Copeland, Laurence 220
Coutts, Magnus 169
Cowie, Doctor 111
Craigie, Mrs 152
Crooksair, North Yell 220, 231
Crooksetter, Delting 80, 93, 230
Cullivoe, Yell 36, 49, 52, 70, 71, 93, 101, 113, 117, 220, 229, 231
Cunningsburgh 177, 185, 229
Cunnister/Cunningster, Yell 68-70, 101, 231
Cupper, Catherine 220

— D —

Dalsetter, Yell 95, 231
Deas, Lord 161
Dixon, Sarah 13
Donaldson, Meran 68
Douglas, James of Cavers 100
Dryad 185, 226
Duncan & Galloway 140
Duncan
    Charles Gilbert 24, 28, 63, 65, 125, 188
    William 35, 76, 81, 83
    Malcolm 186-189
    of Hoswick 184, 185

Dundas, Frederick M.P 103, 120-124
Dunn, William 218

— E —

Earl of Zetland 118, 185
East London, South Africa 199
Edinburgh 2, 11, 163, 172, 174, 175, 186, 193
Edmondston, Thomas 48, 54, 93, 104, 112, 127, 164, 175
Elliot, Mr 206

— F —

Fair Isle 178, 229
Farmer 185, 226
Faroe 20, 137, 138
Farquhar, Mr 7, 8, 219
Fetlar 37, 46, 53, 113, 215, 229
Finlay, Frederick 189
Flying Meteor 123
Fochabers 206
Foraness, Delting 93, 230
Forbes, Mary 24
Fort Charlotte, Lerwick 67, 122
Foula 131, 132, 229
Fowler, John & Co., Leeds 205
Frankfort 181
Fraser
    George 71
    J. D. 36

— G —

Galloway, James Kirkland 160
Garden, Unst 132, 133
Gardie House, Bressay 3, 24, 144, 229
Gardiesfauld, Uyeasound, Unst 220
Gardner, George 161, 169
Garriock & Co. 88

237

Garriock, Peter 142
Garth Castle 198
Garth House, Delting 77, 230
Garth, Delting 76, 80, 81, 85, 90, 93, 94, 219, 220, 230
Garthsness 180, 229
Georgeson, Magnus 19, 20
Gifford
    Arthur 220
    Lord 160, 161
Girlsta 113, 229
Glasgow 139, 165, 166
Gloup, Yell 44, 65-67, 231
Gossabrough, Yell 113, 229
Gossamer 123
Goudie, Gilbert 130
Grand Hotel, Lerwick 212
Grand Junction Railway 203, 205-207, 212
Grant
    Sir Alexander 173
    William 124
Graveland, Yell 71, 231
Graven, Delting 95, 230
Graven, Yell 40, 231
Gray
    Andrew 54-57
    Peter 220
Great Britain 42, 46
Greenbank, Yell 37, 91, 231
Gremster, Yell 52, 57, 231
Grierson, Andrew 19, 20
Gunn, Joseph 220
Gutcher, Yell 44, 52, 77, 101, 224, 231
Guthrie, (Truck Commissioner) 129, 130

— H —

Haaf Grunie, Unst 156-161, 164, 196, 226, 232
Hamilton
    Doctor 23, 24, 149
    George 194
    John James 186, 189, 193-195

INDEX

Hannigarth, Unst 106, 232
Haroldswick, Unst 108, 151, 163, 165, 178, 232
Harris
    Hugh 188-190
    John 188-190
Harrison, John 111, 112
Hay & Co. 130, 142
Hay
    Arthur James 125, 127
    Capt. C. Leith 90
    George H.B. 112, 151, 163-167, 178
    Janet 220
    William (Lerwick) 20
    William (Delting) 220
Henderson
    Brucie 79
    David 52-57
    George 35
Henry 137
Hepburn, Mr 6, 219
Herra, Yell 46, 231
Hibbert, Samuel 18, 156
Hillswick 21, 100, 131, 229
Holsigarth, Yell 46, 231
Hopkins, George 195
Hoseason
    James & Co. of Mossbank 55, 68, 76, 77, 81, 83
    James (Gutcher) 225
Houlland, Unst 94, 95, 232
Houston, George 189
Hughson, Thomas 77

— I —

Iceland 137, 140, 154, 196, 226
Imogene 113, 123
Inclosure Commissioners 88-90, 92, 93, 95, 96
Ingram, Rev. John 175

239

Irvine
  George 220
  James (Bath) 72, 73
  James (Delting) 220
  Magnus 220
  Osla Barbara 64
  Robert 111
  Thomas of Midbrake 58, 63, 72, 73, 100, 102, 152, 172
  William (Kirkabister, Yell) 36, 64
  William (*Chieftain's Bride*) 112

— J —

Jack, Miss 10, 219
Jaffray/Jeffray
  Elizabeth 61, 72
  James 102, 104, 175
James Stevenson 137, 139
Jamieson
  George 106
  Jacobina 106
  James 105, 106
  Ogilvy 140
  William 181
Jeromson, Robert 86
Johnson
  Laurence 112
  Samuel 40
  Thomas 60, 61, 70
John Walker 137, 138
Jones, Thomas 182

— K —

Kaywick, Yell 131, 231
Keldabister, Bressay 22, 23, 27, 219
Kellister, Yell 220, 231
Kirkabister, Yell 36, 37, 53-56, 63-65, 68, 69, 90, 93-95, 152, 231
Kirkwall 124
Knowles, Sir Francis 195

INDEX

— L —

Lady Ambrosine 118
Langdales Chemical Manure Co. 142
Laurenson
    Morgan 76
    Nicol 187
    Thomas 220
Laurie, Simon 175, 176
Laxobigging, Delting 86, 93, 220, 230
Leask, Joseph 125
Leisk,
    George 156, 157, 160
    Joseph 25
Lerwick 23-25, 37, 48, 81, 111, 113, 117, 122, 123, 125,
                130, 131, 138, 140-142, 145, 172, 206, 212, 215, 229
Levenwick 174, 229
Little Roe, Delting 76, 77, 83, 84, 93, 230
Lively HMS 131
Lochend 113, 229
Loch, James 8, 9
Loeterbagh, Dr. P. D. 111, 116
Logie, Yell 65, 231
London 122, 150, 171, 181, 194, 195, 199, 208
Londonderry, Marquis of 154, 225
Longhope, Orkney 5, 7
Lord Metcalfe 4, 5, 10, 219
Lumbister, Yell 40, 41, 60, 61, 71, 93, 94, 231
Lund, Unst 60, 102, 232

— M —

MacKenzie, Sir Kenneth 135
MacMillan, Doctor 187
MacLeod, Donald 8
MacPherson, Francis 187
Makin, Rev. George 175
Mann, John & Grace 40-42
Manson, Alexandria 150
Manson, Jean 160
Mars 143

241

Maryfield, Bressay 2, 24, 28, 115, 150, 153,
154, 212, 214, 219, 223, 229
Mathewson
    Andrew Dishington 176
    Arthur 176
    Mathew 105
Matilda 113
Maver, Rev. J. 205, 228
Maxwell, Rev. & Mrs 6, 7, 9, 219
McBeth, Donald 80, 81, 84, 85
McGregor, Mr 138
McGuffy, Mr 181
McIntosh, Robert 80
McKay
    Anne 150
    Hugh 91
    Peter 157, 169
McKenzie, Miss 9, 10, 219
McLean, Capt. Hugh 112, 118
Melbourne 11, 13, 14, 219
Menzies, Rev. John 18
Merriman, John X. 201
Merrylees, C. 111, 116
Mid Yell 1, 63, 113, 131, 132, 229, 231
Midbrake, Yell 45, 231
Mill, Mr 60
Millburn, Delting 220, 230
Miller, Messrs James & Robert 151, 157-161, 164-168, 180, 193, 226
Milne, John 115
Moar
    Arthur 39
    Daniel (Colvister) 39, 64
    Daniel (Cullivoe) 133
    Jeremiah 36
    Nicol 71
    Thomas 68
Moncrieff, Lawrence 157
Mossbank 71, 81, 83, 113, 229, 230
Mouat
    Anne Cameron 23, 52, 104, 105, 152, 219
    Board of Trade Inspector 117
    John of Annsbrae 40, 41

INDEX

Margaret of Garth 144, 145, 163, 168, 219
Peter 220
Robert 69, 71
William G. 104, 175
William of Garth 219
Mowbray, South Africa 207
Muckle Flugga, Unst 117, 232
Muness, Unst 106, 232
Munro, John 202, 203
Murdoch, John 48, 51
Mure, Andrew 160, 172
Mure, Lord 143, 161
Murray
    Alexander 187
    Gilbert 80
    George 72
    John (miner) 187
    John (Delting) 220
    Rev. C. S. 172
    Robert 76

— N —

Naiad 123
Napier Commission 131-136
Napier, Lord Francis 21, 131, 135
Neep, Nesting 113, 229
Newcastle 142, 143, 181
Nichol, Archibald 97
Nicolson
    Sir Arthur 21, 37
    Arthur 77
    Charles 220
    Capt. William 118
    Lady 117
Nisbet
    Ann 105
    Magnus 37
    Marion 1
    Robert 36, 57, 68
    Thomas 36, 70

William (Cunnister) 69
William Gilbert 55-57
North Garth, Yell 95, 231
North Roe 113, 229
North Star 131, 132
Norwick, Unst 175, 232
Noss, Bressay 23, 154, 182, 229

— O —

Ogilvy, Charles 20
Ollaberry 113, 229
Omand, James 46, 47
Omand, John 40, 44, 46, 47, 71, 131-133
Orr, Dan 81

— P —

Parocial Board 25, 26, 89, 103, 154, 196, 222
Peel, Sir Robert 88
Pennie
    Margaret 24
    William 41, 42, 60-72, 102
    Thomas 23
Pera 140
Peterhead 141-143, 166
Petrel 140-142
Phelps, Rev. Philip 228
Phin, John 23, 124
Plummer, Charles 14
Pole
    Elizabeth 220
    Thomas M.C. 37
    William 91, 172
Prince Consort 15, 70
Prince of Wales 182, 183

INDEX

— Q —

Quarf 18, 26, 172, 229
Queen 140
Queens Hotel, Lerwick 129, 138
Quoys of Garth, Delting 80, 81, 85, 230

— R —

Ramsay
    Robert 39
    Professor 170, 172, 177
Ratter, Jonathan 21
Reawick 28, 90, 229
Reid, John T. 100
Reilley, Mr 213
Rhind, David 201-203, 205
Riddell, Henry P.A. 122-124
Ritchie
    Bell 7
    Charles 88, 89, 91, 93
Robertson, South Africa 201
Robertson
    Charles 111, 112, 116
    Elizabeth 63
    John 111, 125
    Magnus 112
    Mathew 134, 135
    Robert 220
    Robina 66, 67
    William 220
Robert Kirkwood 137, 139, 140
Robert Miller 137, 139
Rockall 137, 138
Ronnan, Uyeasound, Unst 94
Roodewal, South Africa 201
Roudeborch, South Africa 198
Russell, John 64

245

— S —

Sandison
    Alexander 35, 98, 99, 102, 104, 107,113-116, 156,
                              159-161, 169, 175, 178, 191, 193, 198-201, 220
    Peter Mouat 36, 39, 58, 75, 76, 99, 172, 220
Sandlodge 161, 177, 178, 180-191, 193,
                                     195-197, 202, 203, 226, 229
Sandwick, North Yell 68, 95, 231
Sandwick, South Mainland 180, 182, 184, 229
Sandwick, Unst 105, 106, 232
Saunders, Rev. 121
Scalloway 157, 172, 173, 229
Scatsta, Delting 31, 86, 95, 220, 230
Scollay
    Charlotte 44, 66, 67
    Thomas 36
Scottish Drainage & Improvement Co. 88, 89
Scott
    J.D. of Brechin 62, 68
    Robert 116, 117, 138-140
Scott-Skirving, R. 28, 70, 77, 137, 154
Scrabster 122
Seaham 154
Sea Point, South Africa 204-206
Sellafirth, Yell 37, 68, 101, 175, 231
Sellar, Alexander 126, 127-130
Shand, Lord 142
Shetland Agricultural Society 48, 196, 212, 214
Shetland Bank 20
Shetland Fishing Co. Ltd. 130, 137-140, 196, 226
Shetland Mining Co. 180, 226
Shetland Steam Shipping Co. 111-118, 121, 196
Shirres, Mr 219
Sievwright, William 26, 39, 83-86, 105, 106, 121, 157, 160, 167, 206
Sinclair
    Douglas 108
    Laurence 181
Sivewright, Sir James 206
Skaw, Unst 95, 108, 232
Slater, Peter 160

INDEX

Smith
    Alexander 181, 187, 188
    Andrew 40
    Archibald 133
    Elizabeth 66
    George (clerk) 124, 127
    George (miner) 187
    Hance 140
    Laurence (Bressay) 149
    Laurence (Delting) 220
    Mary 66
    Willa 66
    Rev. William 170, 175, 176, 178
Sovereign 212
Spence
    Andrew 133, 134
    Ann 157
    Doctor Basil 48, 54
    Jane Mary 1, 2, 37
    John of Spence & Co. 104, 105, 107, 108, 175
    John Wm. of Windhouse 60, 63, 70, 121
    R. Niven 152
    William & Margaret 1-3, 37, 68, 128
    William (Ballista) 133
Spence & Co. 58, 98, 104-108, 220
St. Clair 142
St. Machar Ward, Aberdeen 212
Stapness, Walls 80, 229
Stevenson of Glasgow 157, 159
Stewart, George 174, 176
Still, Unst 106, 232
Stobie, Rev. Charles 201, 212, 214, 215, 227
Stonesetter/Stenesetter, Yell 70, 95, 231
Stowe, Harriet Beecher 8, 9
Stromness 122, 124
Sullom Voe Oil Terminal 77, 230
Sumburgh Mining Co. 181, 194-196
Sutherland
    Duchess of 8, 9
    Hanna 105, 106
    Rev. James Rose 21, 218
Swarister, Yell 76, 229

Swinister, Delting 76, 81, 93-95, 113, 220, 230
Symbister, Whalsay 113, 229

— T —

Tait
    George Reid 111,112, 117
    John 112
Taylor
    Col. 121
    R. 6, 10, 219
Thermopylae 11
Thoms, George 125
Thomson, John 104
Tingwall 178, 229
Tronaster, Delting 77, 80, 93, 230
Truck System 4, 33, 59, 75, 76, 126-130, 135,
                                                      137, 150, 157, 190, 196, 205, 223
Tulloch
    Basil 52
    David 77
    Helen 52
    John (Graven, Yell) 40
    John (Little Roe) 77
    Laurence 40
    Matthew 190
    Tom 44, 45
    William 52, 53
Twatt
    Thomas 140
    William 140
Tytler, James 194-196, 226

— U —

Ulsta, Yell 71, 113, 229
Umphray, Andrew 28, 71, 90-96
Uncadale, Yell 36, 37, 68, 69, 231
Union Bank of Scotland, Lerwick 89
Unst Agricultural Society 199
Unst Shipping Co. 113, 114

INDEX

Urka, Delting 220, 230
Uyea, Unst 72, 102, 156, 160, 232
Uyeasound, Unst 35, 94, 113, 140, 141, 229, 232

— V —

Valle, Mr 201
Victoria, Australia 11, 12, 15, 133, 227
Vidlin 113, 229
Vigon, Yell 44-47, 67, 101, 132, 231
Volister, Yell 40-42, 60, 61, 94, 231

— W —

Walker
    Adam 217
    Alexander 111, 181, 217
    Amelia (mother of John) 5, 6, 10, 217
    Amelia Mary (daughter of John) 14, 150, 227
    Amelia (sister of John) 217, 218
    Caroline 191, 198, 205, 228
    Catherine (daughter of John) 15, 150, 198, 227
    Catherine (sister of John) 21, 217, 218
    George 10, 217, 218
    Helen (daughter of John) 26, 150, 227
    Helen (sister of John) 6, 217, 218
    Isobel (daughter of John) 15, 150, 201, 212, 227
    Isobel (sister of John) 217, 218
    James 111, 150, 217, 218
    Jane Smith 96, 150, 207, 228
    Janet 96, 150, 205, 228
    Jean/Janie Park 96, 150, 205, 207, 228
    John (son of John) 150, 198, 204, 228
    Mary (wife of John) 2, 13, 14, 24, 27, 72, 112, 145, 150,
        154, 191, 193, 198-200, 207-210, 227
    Mary (daughter of John) 14, 150, 198, 227
    Robert 10, 111, 194, 195, 203, 206,
        212, 213, 217, 218, 226, 227
    Thomas Mouat Cameron 154, 198, 204, 228
    William (father of John) 5, 112, 217, 218
    William (brother of John) 217, 218

William (son of John) 2, 112, 115, 228
Walter Hood & Co. 11
Wandsworth 208, 210, 212
Watson, Mr 195
Webster, Rev. David 46
Weisdale 124, 229
West Neep, North Yell 95, 231
West Yell 77, 113, 229
West-a-Firth, Yell 35, 44, 45, 58, 71, 90, 93, 94, 231
Westing, Unst 133, 232
Westsandwick, Yell 71, 113, 229, 231
Whalefirth, Yell 40, 42, 46, 71, 231
Whallerie, Gloup 44, 220, 231
Whalsay 113, 201, 212, 214, 215, 229
White, Messrs 157, 164
Wicklow 140, 226
Williams
    John 182
    Robert 182
Williamson
    Agnes 21
    Alexander 40
    Andrew 41
    Barbara 36
    C. C. 40
    G. W. 132
    Hay 80-85
    Helen 80, 84, 85
    Janet 76
    John 84-86
    Laurence 36
    William 36, 37
Windhouse, Yell 58, 60, 61, 63, 68, 70-72, 90, 94, 231
Woodwick, Unst 93, 94, 232
Worcester, South Africa 201, 202

— XYZ —

Yorston, Christina 24
Yorston, Magnus 146
Zetland, Earl of 163, 168, 226